The Press as Public Educator

The Press as Public Educator
Cultures of Understanding
Cultures of Ignorance

Colin Lacey and David Longman

UNIVERSITY *of*

LUTON PRESS

British Library Cataloguing in Publication Data

A catalogue record for this book is available from the British Library

ISBN: 1 86020 536 4

Published by
John Libbey Media
Faculty of Humanities
University of Luton
75 Castle Street
Luton
Bedfordshire LU1 3AJ
United Kingdom
Tel: +44 (0)1582 743297; Fax: +44 (0)1582 743298
e-mail: ulp@luton.ac.uk

Cover Design by Morgan Gravatt Design Consultants, Luton
Typeset in Berthold Baskerville and Univers
Printed in Great Britain by Redwood Books, Trowbridge, Wilts

Contents

Preface

The national press is a major public institution. It is recognised as having functions that are essential to the workings of democracy. Yet it remains in private hands, controlled by a few powerful men and regulated by a body that is largely regarded as weak and ineffective. The national daily newspapers are the central defining organisations within the press. They have been much researched and yet there is still deep disagreement about their power in influencing public opinion and hence the need for further regulation. Within this book we have attempted to resolve some of these issues. No doubt there will be much criticism of our methods and conclusions. Nevertheless we have produced an argument, supported by empirical research which calls for a radical overhaul of the press.

Within the next millenium our society will be tested by global problems that have emerged during the last decades of the present century and will develop in intensity and complexity. We take the view that a broadly based public understanding of these problems will be essential if the reorganisation of many aspects of our material life is to be accomplished in time and without the kind of massive disruption that has affected parts of the former USSR, parts of Central Africa and other societies which have approached difficult problems with inadequate and at times positively harmful solutions.

We argue for substantial reforms in which the national press (and other media) become a major educational asset, a forum for open debate and a means to improve the quality of that debate and the intelligence of our cultures of understanding. These may seen extravagant and utopian ideas. However, the book is based on arguments that stay very close to the ground and are tested wherever possible by research. We invite you to contribute to this debate and hope that you enjoy the challenges that you find as much as we have enjoyed forming our arguments.

This book has been nearly six years in the making. Six years in which we have devoted all our research time and much of our spare time. Even so we could not have accomplished the many arduous research tasks without help. We are grateful to the ESRC for a small grant[1] which enabled us to carry out most of the analyses on the Sussex University Data Archive responses. We give our thanks to the WWF and Peter Martin for a small grant that enabled

1   Award number R000221272

us to keep our office support going when other funds had been used up. We are grateful to Dorothy Sheridan of the Data Archive who supported our request for an enquiry into the press coverage of the Rio Earth Summit in June 1992. Without her assistance one central strand of the research would not have been possible. We give our thanks to Robert Worcestor and Roger Mortimore of MORI who have facilitated our use of the MORI Omnibus Poll and gave advice and support in finding and organising the datafiles. We owe thanks to our colleagues in the Sussex University Institute of Education who supported our research effort in times of financial stringency and increasing stress from expanding work loads. We owe particular thanks to Mary Hoar who undertook many research activities well outside her original brief as office secretary and who kept the voluminous data archives in order when we seemed to be doing our best to cause chaos.

This book has been a truly co-operative effort. We have both contributed our best effort and enjoyed working in a field that has led us into so many new areas of enquiry. The completed research spans political science, media studies, studies of the environment, sociology and less obviously education. Clearly we are not experts in all of these fields and without doubt there will be some important works and approaches that have been omitted. Nevertheless we feel that we have produced a coherent and important study. We have worked in a field which is technically demanding, despite this we have attempted to convey our research findings in a straightforward, non-technical way so that the book is open to all.

We owe thanks to many individuals who have read and commented on our early research, in particular: Dr John Abraham, Mr Ian Bride, Professor Martin Hammersley, Dr Barry Cooper, Dr Peter Dickens, Dr Terry Hinton, Dr Margaret MacLure, Mr Peter Martin, Mr John Parry, Dr John Pryor, Professor Roger Silverstone, Dr Harry Torrance.

We also owe thanks to others who have assisted in typing and preparing the book for publication, Beryl Clough, Hayley Kirby, Julia Martin-Woodbridge and Lorna Pidgeon.

Colin Lacey
David Longman
May, 1997

Introduction

There is a commonly held view that education is for children, young people and the relatively few adults who wish to follow interests, retrain or upgrade their qualifications. It is carried out within institutions where the 'qualified' instruct or teach the 'unqualified'. Progress is measured at various stages by tests and examinations and when they have been 'passed' a certificate or qualification is awarded to mark the successful or not so successful passage to the job market.

We reject this as a partial view of education. Instead we view education as a process in which individuals acquire information, skills and values which they process into knowledge and understanding and which they relate to all aspects of the social and physical world. Information, skills and values are usually received in complex packages. Some of these packages are clearly matters that are traditionally dealt with in the curricula of schools and specialist institutions while others are acquired from the family, the community or the wider society. A list, which might contain items such as how to ride a bicycle, how to solve quadratic equations, how to use a computer, how to dance and to understand how plants produce carbohydrates, would provide no problems for most people in allocating the tasks to an institution or area of social life.

The institutionalisation of education seems to depend on how important or developed a given area of knowledge is within any society. However, there are some important exceptions. For example, how to make a judgement about the competence of government policy regarding the homeless or mentally ill, how to make a judgement about the extent to which our society is polluting the atmosphere or perhaps, more crucially, the relative importance of issues like these and many others like them. Issues of this kind are highly controversial but they are often marginalised or excluded from the curriculum of formal education and are left to individuals in their role as the public to make up their own minds in the context of a public arena.

The process by which the public achieves information and develops understandings about these kinds of issues within a public debate is clearly an important matter. Should it be regarded as a form of education or is it distinctly different? We take the view that there are compelling similarities to institutionalised education.

First of all, almost all the information, skills and values are received via the large institutions that constitute the media. The large majority of the public are dependent on these sources for their information on matters beyond their immediate experience. Hence to some extent it affects almost all the knowledge and understanding that individuals develop about a wide range of issues.

Secondly, these configurations of information and values are passed on to those who 'don't know' by specialists 'who do know'. The presentation is authoritative; it is published or it is broadcast in a polished, professional manner by charismatic presenters, experts and talented journalists.

Thirdly the presentation of information and values in the form of the news is routinised and ritualised. It is presented in a trusted format which does not encourage questions or disbelief, to an audience which is not in the main going to give the information too much attention or devote too much energy to critical appraisal.

We therefore argue that the media have embedded within them a system of public education that should be recognised as such. This is not to imply that these 'packages' of information and values handed on by powerful élites constitute an agreed 'truth'. Quite the opposite. These packages are often not in agreement on the most fundamental aspects of the event or issue which is being described, explained or reported. Nevertheless, the struggle to inform, influence and hence to educate the public is a potent element in most media activity, particularly, in our view, in the dissemination of 'news'.

We recognise that this view of the media has been hotly disputed and until recently there has been no convincing research to settle the question. This is no longer the case. Within this book we review recent major studies and present our own data to demonstrate that, at least one branch of the media – newspapers – exercises a powerful influence not only on the way that their readers understand what is going on in the world but also what should be an appropriate response.

However, we take our arguments beyond this demonstration. Using computer-based methodologies it is possible to explore large amounts of newspaper text and compare the way individual newspapers cover similar topics. When this is done it becomes possible to make judgements about the adequacy and bias imparted to the presentation of accounts. For example, the withholding of important information can be interpreted as a device for keeping readers in ignorance of the full facts. It can be expected that this ignorance will affect the understandings reached by their readers. Beyond this, we discuss devices by which a newspaper can celebrate the inadequacy of its coverage by trivialising, poking fun and making no attempt to present the issues relating to an important event. We label this a device for perpetrating 'idiocy'. We consider this to be an unacceptable way for national newspapers to carry out their function, which we will demonstrate also includes the function of public educator.

1 The Myth of Public Opinion and the Manufacture of Consent

Democracy and the myth of public opinion

In 1922 Walter Lippman wrote a classic study of the formation of public opinion in the USA. He was deeply worried by his experience of the manipulation of public opinion during the first World War. His study revealed that the allied publics (French and American) were often grossly misled by war communiqués from which they could only be expected to glean a carefully manufactured impression of the conduct and outcomes of battles and campaigns. In one case study he revealed that the French High Command invented a bloody, non existent battle over Fort de Douaumout. In fact the French generals had no knowledge that the fort had been captured by the Germans until several days after the event when it was reported via the German war communiqués in the international press. In order to fill the credibility gap the French High Command issued a report on the battle to capture the fort in which they stressed the enormous losses suffered by the Germans. At a later date a study of French documents revealed that the Germans had simply crawled through an open door into the fort unopposed because the French garrison which was supposed to have been relieved had left the fort but no relief force had been assigned to take up the position. The few French soldiers who remained in the fort had been captured without a battle.

In the American case presented by Lippman the effort to create public opinion was organised on a massive scale. They succeeded in manufacturing what Lippman calls 'one public opinion'. In order to accomplish this they

> ... had to assemble a machinery which included a Division of News that issued..., more than six thousand releases, had to enlist seventy five thousand Four Minute Men who delivered at least seven hundred and fifty five thousand, one hundred and ninety speeches to an aggregate of over three hundred million people. Boy scouts delivered annotated copies of President Wilson's addresses to the homeholders of America. Fortnightly periodicals were sent to six hundred thousand teachers. Two hundred thousand lantern slides were furnished ... (46)

The description continues for another half page. It illustrates both the power of the state to influence and educate the public and the vast energy and resource required to do so at the time that Lippman was writing. The latter is one aspect of social life that has changed markedly in the period since he wrote. The advent of television and other forms of electronic communication has transformed the media, the means by which 'the news' reaches individual members of society.

Lippman's study of public opinion will act as a starting point for our study of the press as public educator because his analysis outlines the connection between democratic theory and public opinion. He establishes the centrality of the process of building an informed, responsible and active public opinion to the establishment of viable democracy and the good society.

Lippman points out that modern democracy rests upon a flawed concept of public opinion. He shows that even in the 1920's when there were few other means of obtaining news about events outside of the individual citizens immediate environment most Americans spent only about fifteen minutes reading newspapers each day. In addition he points out that only a proportion of this time would be spent on major political events and issues because most people preferred other sections of the paper dealing with topics from sport and gardening to the lives of actresses or local issues.

Even when the average citizen is conscientious in the pursuit of news about national or world events there are many obstacles to overcome. The sheer scale, variety and complexity of major events means that even when a problem or issue is selected 'A few words must often stand for a whole succession of acts, thoughts, feeling and consequences'. These key words must encapsulate so much, like the phrase 'frightful and barbarous' which was frequently used to describe the activities of the Japanese in Korea.

The problems of communication do not end there. It depends on the interests, values and culture of the audience. For as Lippman points out, while a sophisticated anarchist might differentiate sharply between the followers of Bakunin, Tolstoi and Kropotkin a member of the Union League Club might not differentiate at all between democrat, socialist, anarchist and burglar. In summary he brings together a long list of factors that stand between the ordinary citizen and their attempt to understand the world outside their everyday experience.

> Thus the environment with which our public opinions deal is refracted in many ways, by censorship and privacy at the source, by physical and social barriers at the other end, by scanty attention, by poverty of language, by distraction, by unconscious constellations of feeling, by wear and tear, violence, monotony. These limitations upon our access to that environment combine with obscurity and complexity of the facts themselves to thwart clearness and justice of perception, to substitute misleading fictions for workable ideas, and to deprive us of adequate checks upon those who consciously strive to mislead. (76)

The question of adequate checks on those who strive to mislead becomes the central issue in Lippman's analysis and is, of course, a central concern of our empirical chapters later in the book. However, before proceeding in this direction he revisits a set of unconscious constellations of feeling; values prejudices and culture Lippman points out.

> In the great, blooming, buzzing confusion of the outer world we pick out what our culture has already defined for us. (81)

But as his analysis makes clear, cultures are not necessarily tolerant, open and based on judgements made from the best evidence. They are frequently narrowly conceived, based on prejudice, stereotypes and not disturbed by the consideration of evidence.

> The stereotypes are ... highly charged with feelings that are attached to them. They are the fortress of our tradition, and behind its defences we can continue to feel ourselves safe in the position we occupy. (96)

This element of security and dependency is an important insight. Newspapers are not just conveyors of news. The reader develops a relationship with their daily paper, in which he/she subconsciously perhaps, gains a feeling of security and belonging.

So in Lippman's model the great difficulties of bringing news that is sufficiently accurate to ensure the formation of a well informed public opinion is compounded by a public that is ill prepared to receive it. The public is prejudiced, lazy, easily diverted, rushed for time and also lacking independence. The theory of a democracy based on public opinion is therefore flawed. Historically democracy in the USA and elsewhere was based on small communities in which events could be known about first hand and in which local occupational and cultural knowledge was relevant to local problems. As soon as large complex units of the scale of the nation state are involved then in Lippman's view government is in practice either authoritarian or based on the myth of an informed, interested electorate.

In these large democracies, the notion that each private citizen has an 'interest' that will ensure that they inform themselves about events and issues that will in some way affect them is not borne out in practice. Individual citizens do not have the time, the information or the inclination to put in the work to be 'omnicompetent'. They can be misled or led by their prejudices. So who is to blame? Lippman does not lay the blame on capitalism or the press although he acknowledges that:

> The verdict is made to depend on who has the loudest or most entrancing voice, the most skilful or the most brazen publicity man, the best access to the most space in the newspapers. (401)

He dismisses what he calls Upton Sinclair's 'brass check theory' of capitalist fault by pointing out that the quality of news we require is no more likely to emerge in non-capitalist newspapers. He deflects criticism of the press by pointing out that the press is simply unable to do the job. Its resources are too small and it really depends on other social institutions for news. In addition, in a competitive market the press is bound by the prejudices and stereotypes of its readers. As we have seen if their prejudiced and distorted views are threatened then they will react in anger and the newspaper will suffer a loss of readers and cease to exist. 'The trouble lies deeper than the press, and so does the remedy'.

Lippman sees the solution residing in a kind of social audit. This audit will be carried out within government institutions and to some extent within private companies by a new kind of statistician/accountant/social scientist professional who will provide information about the performance of the institution and its social role.

...on the whole, the quality of the news about modern society is an index of its social organisation. The better the institutions, the more all interests concerned are formally represented, the more issues are disentangled, the more objective criteria are introduced, the more perfectly an affair can be presented as news. (363)

Lippman's hypothesis has in some ways been tested by the building of better institutions in the government and private sectors in the last seventy years. In addition many of the kinds of indicators that he argued would be required for the purpose of informing a reluctant public have been built by social scientists and statisticians. We have various measures of the standard of living, cost of living, unemployment, homelessness, hospital waiting lists and wage rates. There would appear to be substantial transparency in areas where Lippman found only obscurity. In addition to the development of better information there are new powerful NGOs and charities which speak for the underrepresented sections of the public, the poor, the homeless, refugees, the poor in third world countries, many sick or otherwise disadvantaged groups and even animals and the natural environment. Also the universities and various research organisations, sometimes in partnership with charities and sometimes in collaboration with government, publish numerous research reports on the state of almost every social institution. Finally there are new regulatory bodies which monitor and publish reports on the new privatised industries and many public services from OfWAT to OfSTED. There would appear to be a surfeit rather than a dearth of information.

One of Lippman's major criticisms of democratic government can no longer be held to be true. In addition to these developments in the collation and presentation of data and research by professionals we have experienced the development of direct communication by electronic media which has revolutionised information flows. World-wide audiences can observe battles in progress, can view the remains of massacre victims, can see the reporter speaking during the battle, wince as shells land near by and can see the effects of famine and other disasters at first hand. The world-wide electronic flow of information can record for the public in great detail the fluctuations on the Bombay stock market, the progress of the first massive civil rights demonstration in Tiananmen Square and or the first hand experience of US bombing raids in Baghdad. More recently the Internet has ensured that the ordinary citizen can access information ranging from how to make a bomb, through to the most advanced protocols for the treatment of cancer to secret memos which describe how major tobacco companies lied about the links between nicotine and addiction, and smoking and lung cancer. Both links having been established by their own internal research. The intelligence system that he advocated has in many respects come into being and been surpassed but has the intelligence of the electorate increased as a result or is it still controlled and limited by its prejudices and in addition, by powerful groups that Lippman failed to recognise?

The centrality to Lippman's argument of the need for reliable information gleaned by the major social institutions is illustrated in the following quotation.

> It is because they are compelled to act without a reliable picture of the world that governments, schools, newspapers and churches make such small headway against the more obvious failings of democracy, against violent prejudice, apathy, preference for the curious trivial as against the dull important, and the hunger for sideshows and three legged calves. This is the primary defect of popular government, a defect inherent in its traditions, and all its other defects can, I believe, be traced to this one. (365)

Lippman's analysis was, for its day, formidable. It is possible to discern in his writings almost all the preoccupation's of academic discourse on this topic for the next seventy years. He had described in great detail the importance of existing cultures, the effects of the competitive market place in which the press (media) operates, the technical difficulties of selecting and reporting news and the power of the proprietors and unscrupulous politicians. But he felt that these difficulties could be overcome; swept away by a flow of excellent analyses, and top quality intelligence produced by a new professional elite. Since we have now attained in many respects the state of excellent intelligence that he described we can test his theory, isolate and make clear his errors and move on to produce a more contemporary understanding which can in its turn be tested and refined.

The manufacture of consent

Lippman was greatly concerned about the 'manufacture of consent' practised by those that made unscrupulous use of the ignorance of the mass of the population. In 1988 Edward Herman and Noam Chomsky published a book *Manufacturing Consent* in which they revisited this theme in great detail.

Herman and Chomsky investigated a wide range of contrasting cases of news coverage of similar kinds of events. In the chapter 'Worthy and Unworthy Victims' they contrast the press treatment of Jerzy Popieluszko, a Polish priest murdered by the Polish police with the numerous murders of religious personnel including the Archbishop Oscar Romero and four US religious women murdered in El Salvador. They show that despite the fact that the murders of Popieluszko were brought to trial and sentenced and the perpetrators of the religious murders in El Salvador were not, the outpouring of indignation and the amount of media space for the Popieluszko murder was much greater. Romero was almost certainly murdered by government murder squads for his criticism of the government's record of violent killings and their refusal to bring the murderers to justice. Herman and Chomsky see this as a substantial exercise in news manipulation. Its aim was to bring the Polish (Communist) regime into disrepute with the American public while minimising the effects of a large number of brutal murders on the reputation of the Central American (friendly) regimes.

> ... the press did not comment upon or explore the significance of the fact that there was a relatively serious trial in 'totalitarian' Poland, while state murders were being carried out on a daily basis without any investigations or trials of the murderers in a number of countries within the US sphere of influence called "fledgling democracies". (42)

The investigation into the press coverage of these events is extremely detailed. There is little doubt that the case study fits what Herman and Chomsky describe as the Propaganda Model.

> As we have stressed throughout this book, the US media do not function in the manner of the propaganda system of a totalitarian state. Rather they permit – indeed encourage – spirited debate, criticism and dissent, as long as these remain faithfully within the system of presuppositions and principles that constitute an elite consensus, a system so powerful as to be internalized largely without awareness. (302)

This analytical description is very close to Lippman's model of a weak press bound in by cultures of understanding to powerful élites. Our description of Herman and Chomsky's work does not do justice to the wide range of detailed comparisons that they made for example between the treatment of the struggles in Cambodia and in East Timor and between the two sides in the Vietnam conflict. Nevertheless this first example is reproduced in sufficient detail to show that Lippman's theory that more information produced by a more critical professional body has produced very little indication of change from Lippman's analysis in 1922. It would appear that on the evidence produced by Herman and Chomsky, Lippman's hypothesis fails.

The British Case

The examples that we have discussed this far have been taken from the North American (USA) press. Perhaps the British press is different. It has a reputation for independence and to judge from the recent quarrels with the government over 'sleaze' and with the Royal family (because the press has pried too deeply into their private lives) the press has an independence that they defend and practice robustly. The British press is differently structured from the US press with large circulation national dailies which are read by the great majority of the British public. In the USA the network of local papers have smaller circulations and are more reliant on the wire services for their national and international news. Perhaps this difference in structure gives the British press the greater strength and independence that Lippman saw as essential to an informed and intelligent electorate which is in turn essential to a healthy democracy. The two examples that we describe below are selected for their contemporary relevance. We will be looking at others in greater details in later chapters. The examples that we have chosen are from the work of a journalist, Maggie O'Kane and a political scientist Martin Shaw.

In December 1995 Maggie O'Kane published her record of the *Guardian*/Channel 4 investigation into the reporting of the Gulf War. Early in her report she writes:

> This is a tale of how to tell lies and win wars, and how we, the media were harnessed like two thousand beach donkeys and led through the sand to see what the British and US military wanted us to see in this nice clean war. And the story of how, five years later, they're still telling lies about what happened to thousands of sick allied soldiers who were exposed to chemical weapons.

Maggie O'Kane demonstrates that two of the major pieces of evidence put forward by the Western democracies for going to war were 'lies'. They were invented to gain public support for a war that George Bush and Margaret Thatcher had already decided must go ahead, despite the apparent willingness of the Iraqis to withdraw from Kuwait.

The first propaganda lie involved the threat that Iraqi troops were massing on the Saudi border and were preparing to take over the Saudi oil fields. The second involved some of the atrocities said to have been committed by Iraqi troops after they took Kuwait.

The threat of more than a quarter of a million Iraqi troops waiting to invade Saudi Arabia was discovered, it was said, using satellite photographs, which were and are classified for security reasons. However, military satellites were not the only satellites photographing the Middle East and a Florida paper (the St Petersburg Times) was able to obtain photographs from a commercial source. Maggie O'Kane records that these commercial photographs showed an empty deserted space where thousands of troops should have been billeted.

> There was no massive build-up. But by then, the war was fought and won and it didn't matter that the 'proof' of Saddam's bloodthirsty intentions was a fraud.

The second fraud was designed by an American public relations firm hired by Kuwaitis at more than $1,000,000 per month. The story told of Iraqi soldiers entering the al Adan hospital and tearing babies from incubators and leaving them to die. A nurse who had worked in the hospital appeared before Congress in November 1990 and told the moving and horrific story of the brutal event. President Bush made use of the story in five speeches as did many senators. It was widely reported on British television and in UK newspapers. In fact the story was completely fraudulent. The young girl who misled the US Congress, the UN and the world's press was the daughter of the Kuwaiti ambassador to the US. She had not worked in the hospital and with six others had been coached by a public relations firm to provide the false story. Maggie O'Kane reports that two nurses who really did work at the hospital at the time of the invasion were amazed to see her testimony on television. They had not experienced the events that she described.

The pool system for informing and controlling the press was developed during the Falklands war by the Ministry of Defence and used to great effect during the Gulf War. It ensured that relatively few reporters ever got to the battle areas. When they did they returned with trivial stories about the heat and sand and lack of mail from home. The news and film footage about the war was released by the military who like the French generals during the First World War carefully concocted a story (see also Knightley, 1975)

The system ensured that the media picture that emerged from the war to be conveyed by the British media, was of a clean surgical attack which minimised civilian and alliance casualties. In fact the picture that emerges in retrospect is of enormous damage to civilian property and many casualties. In addition many alliance troops were damaged by exposure to chemical weapons. The attack was unparalleled in its ferocity, using napalm cluster bombs and killing many Iraqi conscripts drawn from the Kurdish and Shia communities who had more reasons to detest Saddam and his regime than most Kuwaitis.

It would appear that Maggie O'Kane's experience of the Gulf War accurately reflect Herman and Chomsky's *post factum* analyses and accounts of the wars in Guatemala, El Salvador, Vietnam and Cambodia. It also recapitulates the experiences of Walter Lippman in his research into the press reporting of the First World War. Despite the huge increase in media resources (there were 2,500 media personnel trying to cover the Gulf War story), despite the amazing improvements in communication and the speed of delivery of any new development and despite the fact that the public could see rockets being fired, buildings exploding, tanks racing into battle, the story that emerges from foreign wars is still as strictly controlled and regulated as it was for Walter Lippman. Perhaps the major difference is that today the story is more immediate and has more impact. The public is misled more convincingly.

The issue of whether or not to go to war is one of the most important decisions a nation can take. In a democracy the public support for war is essential if it is to be waged successfully. It would appear that this decision can still be taken by a very small elite group who can then impose that decision, as a just war, on the majority by persuading them with the aid of fabricated evidence and an 'independent' press.

There is a second and perhaps more encouraging difference between Lippman's situation in the 1920's and our present predicament. We now possess far more knowledge about how public opinion is formed and manipulated. Since Lippman's day there had been a long and tortuous debate about the role of the media in the formation of public opinion. Many early studies failed to show decisive effects (Lazarsfeld, 1944, Katz and Lazarsfeld, 1955) and the methodological problems of simultaneously monitoring the vast flow of press or media messages within a sufficiently large and rigorous design were outside the competence and resources of social science. In the absence of authoritative studies which demonstrate the powerful shaping influence of the press and other media, their influence could always be denied. There were and are powerful individuals and groups who have an interest in denying the influence of the press, in particular newspaper proprietors and politicians who enjoy that power and want to see it maintained.

Denying its existence through the powerful channels that they control was and is one way of protecting that power. Maintaining the myth of public opinion as something independent of the media helped to support their argument that the press under their ownership or influence was essential to ensure and maintain a healthy democracy – not undermine it. Lippman attempted to expose the myth of public opinion and although his study has remained an inspiration to journalists and academics over the years, the means to finally succeed in demonstrating influence and to understand the educative function of the press has only emerged in the last decade. Herman and Chomsky and Maggie O'Kane demonstrate that the news is shaped by powerful interests but they do not show that the public is convinced by it. The myth of an independent, self informed and free to choose public could still be maintained.

Maggie O'Kane's analysis is from the standpoint of a participating journalist. It is a well researched contribution which demonstrates the power of
central institutions of the state (the army and government) to mislead the press
and other media in times of crisis and war. This happened despite the presence
of large teams of reporters and the possibility of the immediate transmission
of information from the war zone to millions of television sets. However,
O'Kane gives the impression that all the media carried the same stories and
the same interpretation of events. This was not the case, there were also some
important divergences in news carried by television and newspapers.

Her account was also limited to assessing the deceptions within the message, it could not extend to assessing the impact of the message on the UK
public. Very recently, Martin Shaw's account (Shaw, 1966) of the representation of distant violence by the media does extend to measuring its effect on
public opinion and part of his case study of the Iraq/UN conflict is able to
focus down to the detailed effects of differential accounts

Shaw is able to show a wide range of issues on which newspapers varied
widely in their reporting of the war. They differed in their support of the war,
their interpretation of events and the degree to which they trivialised it and
used it to foster narrow patriotism and jingoism. Shaw describes the general
differences in treatment of the war as follows:

> While television coverage tended to homogeneity and was not
> informed by highly distinctive editorial stances, newspaper editorialisa-
> tion and their coverage – despite homogenizing tendencies produced
> by media management and a common support for the war – was dif-
> ferentiated by the contrasting positions, styles and ethos of the papers.
> (97)

The response to these different presentations of the war was measured using
opinion poll data. Shaw concludes,

> These differences in perceptions of and attitudes to the war between
> readers of newspapers were more extreme and significant than any of
> the other variations that we measured in our study. (144)

The differences remained important after all other factors, for example, age,
social class, gender, political affiliation, that were available to the study, were
taken into account. This finding is very important because it can be interpreted
as an indicator of newspaper influence. It is also open to the interpretation that
people with specific values and ways of looking at the world buy a newspaper
that reflects those perceptions. Within this range of issues there were two
which were very specific and unlikely to be explained simply by the particular characteristics of the different newspaper audiences or even their predis-
positions. One concerns the perceptions of the different readership groups of
the bombing of the Amiriya shelter, the other concerns the possibility of using
limited nuclear weapons on the Iraqi troops in the desert.

The aftermath of the bombing of the Amiriya shelter was covered by UK
television because the Iraqi authorities immediately opened up the site to
international television cameras and horrifying pictures of the slaughter were
transmitted around the world. UK television reports overwhelmingly confirmed that there was no evidence of military activity. The shelter was what it

seemed to be, a civilian shelter. Large sections of the UK press, however, insisted otherwise. The *Sun* reported it as a Saddam Hussein 'trick'. The *Star* reported that the victims had been herded into a military bunker that Saddam Hussein knew would be targeted. The *Daily Mirror* was alone among the tabloids in asking 'Whose Fault?' and corroborating television coverage. The Express and *Daily Mail* echoed the military bunker line, In addition the *Daily Mail* attacked the television accounts as pro-Saddam. The *Daily Telegraph* gave prominence to the military bunker explanation and the *Times* did the same but also published eye witness accounts disclaiming its military use. The Independent was similar in giving prominence to the military purposes slant within a more balanced presentation. Only the *Guardian* came out against the war. Both these papers gave prominence to the Iraqi death toll.

The perceptions of the bombing held by groups reading specific newspapers were revealed to be more closely aligned with newspaper accounts than the television coverage.

Table 1.1: Perceptions of the bombing of the Amiriya shelter by newspaper readership(%) (Shaw, 1996, 139)

	Military centre	Civilian shelter	Saddam propaganda	Casualties of war	N
Sun and *Star*	21	9	58	12	33
Daily Mirror	30	6	32	32	47
Other tabloid	28	7	39	26	34
Broadsheet	19	45	13	23	19
All respondents	26	14	36	24	168

Chi squared = 39.2, DoF = 9, p = 0.0000

Despite the small numbers involved in this tabulation it must rank as an important piece of evidence supporting the view that the firmly shaped interpretation of events proffered by newspapers hold the power to influence their readers.

The second example is much more limited in its scope but much sharper in its focus. Shaw points out that of all British media sources which reported the Gulf War only the *Sun* advocated the use of limited nuclear weapons to attack the 'elite Iraqi Republican Guard'. He found that among *Sun* readers, 21 per cent favoured using nuclear weapons against Iraq. No other reader group reached double figures. Shaw summarises his results as follows:

> Where particular events were strongly ideologically represented in the press, as with the Amiriya bombing, newspaper interpretations may overcome television images in forming perceptions and attitudes. (146)

This evidence therefore suggests that Lippman, Herman and Chomsky, and O'Kane are not wrong in supposing that the power to build a bias into news reports is, in effect, the power to influence public opinion. However, despite Shaw's evidence this position is strongly contested and we will be examining more evidence very closely in the later chapters of this book.

The examples of the manipulation of news described by Lippman, Herman and Chomsky and O'Kane are not, it would appear, narrow conspiracies by press proprietors and reporters. All the examples focus on foreign wars or conflicts in which powerful élites (civil servants, politicians, armed forces élites and powerful industrialists) have the job of interpreting events, forming policies and then gaining a mandate for these policies in open public debate. These élites finally act for the nations as a whole. There are times when public debate of these policies is seen as divisive and weakening and in the extreme case damaging to the national interest. In these cases, particularly in war time (or in a cold war), these élites develop cultures of secrecy. They become used to the power of taking decisions and to their lack of accountability. They may also develop ways of subverting democratic principles, accountability procedures and open debate. The press sometimes goes along with this process in what they see as the national interest, sometimes they do so because they do not see how far the manipulation has changed their consciousness (the propaganda model) and sometimes because they are lied to but lack the resources, the skills or a sufficiently developed professional culture to see through the lies and obtain a truer picture of the events.

It would appear that the struggle to inform the public within a democracy is a never resolved conflict. The state of the struggle at any time reflects the strengths of opposing forces; those for closure and those for openness. There will always be examples of secret deceptions not uncovered by the press or academic research and never revealed by whistle-blowers. However, the struggle will be to ensure that more and more individuals do come forward and are supported and perhaps rewarded for coming forward. Recent examples of this trend are the Arms to Iraq/Scott enquiry within the UK in 1996 and the role of President Nixon in prolonging the Vietnam War in 1968. In the latter case it has recently been revealed that Nixon actively encouraged Saigon to withdraw from talks with the North Vietnamese because he feared that the chance of peace would ensure a victory for the democrat Hubert Humphry in the Presidential election. Nixon's role has only recently been revealed by the testimony of William Bundy, Johnson's Assistant Secretary of State (Observer, 4/2/96). However, the messages recorded by bugs which were placed by Lyndon Johnson were available at the time but kept secret. Nixon went on to win the election by a narrow margin and the war continued at an enormous cost in lives.

The 'arms-to-Iraq' affair promised a unique insight into the secret workings of government ministers and top civil servants and their redefinition of guidelines constraining arms exports to Iraq – despite denials to Parliament. Two businessmen caught exporting arms in contravention of these guidelines by another department not privy to these changes were sent for trial. The government then sought to withhold information that would have verified the evidence produced by the businessmen that they had informed government and had been given permission. The Scott enquiry was set up to investigate whether guidelines had been changed and why two innocent men, serving this government, had almost been sent to prison.

Its contemporary nature means that the demonstration of deception will carry implications for a sitting government and ministers who still hold office. The battle over the interpretation of the findings will then be fought with great vigour and all the powers of the government, the Conservative Party and the section of the press that is sympathetic to them will be brought to bear in a defensive debate designed to limit damage.

Both of these examples will lay bare the workings of government in ways that the public have never seen before. The cycle of deception laid bare by an authoritative demonstration of that deception (the Scott Report) could constitute a new learning experience and generate new understandings; a step in the process of establishing a more intelligent public which expects more, not less, open government. On the other hand this debate might be stifled by government manipulation and lack of media interest. To date there has not been a single ministerial resignation over these issues.

This book is an attempt to reinforce the culture of openness. It will attempt to do this using three methods. We will redefine a series of concepts and attempt to clarify the issue of public debate. We will bring to bear the results of research which attempt to make clear the role of the media in the formation of public opinion. Finally we will focus on a narrow sector of press publishing and analyse it and the public's response in great detail in order to test the theory that the media (in this case the press) educates the public. We will discuss the corollary of these findings and suggest reforms that could produce a more intelligent electorate, better government and a more promising future.

In order to demonstrate these educational effects we will exploit the fact that the press is not a homogeneous body. It is differentiated in a number of ways. At one extreme within the tabloid press it is difficult to find news about contemporary issues among a welter of fantastic stories of unlikely sexual adventures and advertisements while at the other end of the range, within the broadsheet press it is almost impossible to read and assimilate the full content of domestic and foreign issues debated and explained. In addition to the amount of coverage the national dailies differ very markedly in their political allegiance and hence the selection and presentation of news. While there is undoubtedly a concern about what constitutes the main news items at any one time, the choice about which item gets the most coverage and the type of coverage it gets varies considerably from paper to paper. Not surprisingly this variation is in keeping with the newspapers' political biases or affiliations and reflects the interests of those affiliations to a greater or lesser extent. However, while these broad facts have been apparent to even a casual observer of the British press, the ability to quantify those differences and to do so with speed and accuracy has only become possible over the last decade. This has opened the door to researching the educational effects of the press (and eventually television) in ways which should shed new light on the workings of democracy and inform the need to reform its major institutions.

In order to debate the role of the press it will be necessary to provide some context for the debate. The orthodox model of traditional liberal democracy has in the past underpinned many of these debates and it will also be examined here. However, it is part of the thesis presented here that the certainties of traditional society are no longer available to us. These models may never have been true in the past but they provided a central consensus that gave them a working validity. This consensus is now shattered. The examples described in this chapter are only one small measure of that destruction. In the uncertainty that follows, lies the possibility of improvement or regression. Both require quite dramatic breaks with the past. We will examine the work of

Giddens (1994) for these contextual frameworks and will interpret our results within the understandings that emerge.

Manufactured uncertainty

Giddens characterises contemporary society by describing a number of changes and processes that have effectively broken down the old order and left uncertainty and change as major characteristics of society. The radical movements of the nineteenth century, in particular socialism was based on the belief that,

> The more we, as collective humanity, get to know about social and material reality, the more we shall be able to control them in our own interests. In the case of social life in particular, human beings can become not just the authors but the masters of their own destiny. (3)

Giddens argues that this has not proved to be the case, on the contrary, it is a world of 'dislocation and uncertainty, a runaway world'. As an illustration he draws on the uncertainties of global warming: Is it happening? What are its consequences? When will they occur? He describes this as manufactured uncertainty; when human intervention and knowledge increases rather than decreases the uncertainties about the future.

He proceeds to point to three developments that have contributed to this problem over the last four or five decades, globalization, the emergence of a post-traditional social order and social reflexivity.

Globalization is not simply an economic phenomenon nor according to Giddens should it be regarded as the emergence of a 'world system'. He sees it as a transformation of space and time and defines it as 'action at a distance'. It is a complex mixture of processes with contradictory outcomes. Trade and its global ecological outcomes are one example but the emergence of new nationalisms are also outcomes, which seem to contradict the move towards integration.

The post traditional social order does not mark the end of tradition. According to Giddens it describes a change in the status of tradition. Traditions now have to 'explain themselves, to become open to interrogation or discourse'. Fundamentalism is seen as a reaction to these trends, a defence of tradition using traditional methods. As such it is seen by Giddens as doubly dangerous because it is a refusal of dialogue.

> ....it is a rejection of a model of truth linked to the dialogic engagement of ideas in a public space. It is dangerous because edged with a potential for violence. Fundamentalisms can arise in all domains of social life where tradition becomes something which has to be decided about rather than just taken for granted. There arise not only fundamentalisms of religion but of ethnicity, the family and gender among other forms. (6)

The role of the press (and the media) in a post traditional society is clearly of utmost importance in the creation of a public space for dialogue. However, it is in the third development, social reflexivity that the educational function of the media becomes critical.

Social reflexivity is an individual adaptation to a de-traditionalizing society.

It involves taking decisions where there are no longer traditional modes which relieve uncertainty. Giddens describes it as filtering all sorts of information relevant to life situations and routinely acting on the basis of that filtering process. The example he gives is marriage where the traditional sexual division of labour has almost disappeared, where couples may marry or not at any stage in having a family and where behaviour within marriage is based on new principles. However in a global society, social reflexivity will also relate to and affect, work, patterns of consumption and the political reconstruction of national and international institutions.

We have adopted Giddens definition of these processes as a starting point. As the analysis proceeds it will become clear where we differ and why. However at this stage it is important to point to one major difference of view and definition. In doing so we will be linking Gidden's analysis to the work of Lippman, Herman and Chomsky and O'Kane. In his discussion of social reflexivity Gidden's writes:

> A world of intensified reflexivity is a world of *clever people*. I don't mean by this that people are more intelligent than they used to be. In a post-traditional order, individuals more or less have to engage with the wider world if they are to survive in it. (7)

This description is very close to what Lippman described as the 'omnicompetent person'. Of course Lippman was writing from within a much more traditional society (Giddens starts his clock ticking at four to five decades ago and Lippman was writing in 1920 – seven decades ago) and he baulked at even imagining the possibility of the common person becoming omnicompetent. Instead Lippman envisaged the emergence of a class of elite social commentators and analysts who would feed pre-digested truths to the majority. Giddens on the other hand sees no difficulty in spreading even scientific knowledge in ways that would be 'routinely interpreted and acted on by lay individuals in the course of their everyday lives'.

We do not share Giddens' optimism nor do we share Lippman's pessimism. To start with we disagree that cleverness is an appropriate description of the outcome of the process of social reflexivity. Intelligence has three main meanings. It is the faculty of understanding, intellect; it is understanding or the action of understanding and it is the obtaining of information (Little *et al*, 1983). What Giddens' describes is a new way of understanding, the understanding of uncertainty and the obtaining of information to facilitate understanding. If he means anything by the paragraph quoted above he does mean that people will need to become differently and more intelligent in order to survive. By labelling this cleverness Giddens glosses over the enormous difficulties involved. We therefore differ from Giddens by stressing the need to focus on the issue of public education and intelligence. The quality of news, information and public debate to which the public can relate become crucial issues. And the effects on the public of receiving or choosing to receive various versions of this news needs to be studied and understood. It is by understanding the interface between news, information and the quality of debate that we can test Lippman's pessimistic prediction that the average individual could never become omnicompetent or Gidden's more optimistic prediction.

Lippman wrote at a time when a strong traditional society militated against omnicompetence. There was less uncertainty and less call for social reflexivity. Just as there was less call for autonomy – one of Giddens indicators of social reflexivity.

The examples described from the work of Herman and Chomsky and O'Kane demonstrate the danger of assuming that the openness and questioning that Giddens sees as almost ubiquitous in a global society can emerge without a struggle. The class on which this duty rests is not an elite. It must arise from the class of middle professionals and from among those whose skills and purpose mean more to them than their careers or service to an elite of managers and controllers. Without this effort it is doubtful that a real debate could emerge. Where people with this open and questioning orientation become a majority and develop autonomy they can begin to flourish and produce the kind of critique that Herman and Chomsky value. Where they exist in isolation their only option is that of the whistle-blower or leaker of documents with all the accompanying risks and difficulties (Abraham *et al*, 1990).

We therefore portray social reflexivity in a post traditional society as the result of a struggle between the forces for openness and closure. No one political party or organisation or social group will always be on the side of openness or on the side of closure. Individuals, groups and organisations will always want to choose what is open and what is secret and because there are areas of legitimate privacy the argument will always rage about what is appropriate for the public sphere and what is not, similarly with what is to be questioned and what is not.

Giddens sees the progress of social reflexivity as closely associated with the emergence of globalism and post traditional society. He also sees the growth of social reflexivity as a major factor introducing a dislocation between knowledge and control, a prime source of manufactured uncertainty.

A question that emerges from this discussion is, if society exists to provide structures and reliable frameworks for social life how long can public debate that questions and critiques existing structures be encouraged before the process causes more pain and suffering than it solves? At what point do fundamentalisms produce the kind of stability for which people crave. Clearly in some sections of some societies this point has already been reached. In the United States small sections of the impoverished rural hinterland have produced semi-autonomous communities of fundamentalist Christian militia; in Iran Islamic fundamentalism dominates the state; and in N. Ireland two fundamentalist groups vie to control the six counties.

The answer is that the descent into fundamentalism is not caused by being included in a debate that is critical of malfunctioning state institutions or self interested private organisations. Quite the opposite. The descent into fundamentalism is more likely to be caused by being excluded from participation in society and from not being represented in these debates (Pateman, 1970). The exclusion can take many forms but one of the most debilitating forms of exclusion in recent years in the UK has been economic exclusion. However, this has in most cases been heightened by the decay of other social forms from local communities to political parties. In particular, Giddens analysis makes clear that one potent form of exclusion is and will be the exclusion from intelligence; the ability to filter and act upon relevant information derived from a global society. It is the part played by the media, in our case the press, in this central process that we will examine in detail. Does the press function to include its readers in the debates of centrally important issues and construct positive cultures of understanding or does it exclude its readers and seek to develop cultures of ignorance or even idiocy? The construction of these latter cultures would indicate a descent into fundamentalism in those areas where selective exclusion was strongest. The question still remains to be answered in the context of Giddens' analytical framework.

> There is a very real and difficult issue to be faced, however: the problematic relations between knowledge and control exemplified by the spread of manufactured risk. Political radicalism can no longer insert itself, as socialism did, in the space between a discarded past and a humanly made future. (10)

The answer for Giddens is a series of six shoulds: we should repair 'damaged solidarities', recognise the centrality of 'life politics'; improve the conditions for 'generative politics'; stress the importance of 'dialogic democracy' and rethink the 'welfare state'. With the exception of dialogic democracy we do not intend to pursue any of these solutions. They appear to us in general to be good advice but almost totally lacking in any clear discussion of 'agency'.

Despite a chapter dedicated to a 'Question of Agency and Values' Giddens leaves us with a huge area of uncertainty over the question of how to proceed. We will take up the concept of dialogic democracy because it is central to all of the processes that Giddens describes and central to the issues that this book will attempt to clarify. Dialogic democracy differs from liberal democracy in an important respect.

> ...it is a way of creating a public arena in which controversial issues – in principle – can be resolved, or at least handled through dialogue rather than through pre-established forms of power. (16)

It is surprising that the media and the press in particular receive no mention in this discussion. Giddens restricts his discussion to personal relationships, self help groups and the break up of large bureaucracy all of which are important. It is our view that the major institutions for informing/educating/influencing the public also need to be brought into consideration. In the first instance we need to know more precisely what influence the press has in forming as opposed to informing public opinion. We need careful studies in order to make it accountable in ways that the present structure based on the liberal democratic tradition fails to recognise as relevant or important. Giddens' analysis provides us with a framework for recognising these functions but then falls short of pressing the analysis home.

We will argue that the new intelligence we described earlier is a major element in finding a way forward and in coming to terms with this problem. The process of filtering and acting upon relevant information described by Giddens must be coupled with the ability to live with uncertainty and experimentation. The effectiveness of actions, in the new circumstances in which we find ourselves, can often only be assessed in experimental or trial situations in which trials or experiments are not camouflage for rail-roading an innovation into the central system for the benefit of a sectional interest. The trust that is necessary in this situation involves the questions. Can we trust institutions to report and evaluate accurately and honestly? Can we trust the institutions that constitute the forum for public debate to conduct that debate openly, informing all sections of the population on a right to know basis? Once again the centrality of the media and the press is exemplified. The kind of dialogic democracy envisaged by Giddens therefore involves a new kind of trust and new forms of certainty. It requires trust in the institutions that conduct the experiments and trust in the institutions that are central to public debate.

We now look at the history of the press to ascertain how far in the past the press has developed to perform this role and how far it can be seen to be relevant to the emergent society described by Giddens.

2 The Free Press in Britain
Rhetoric and reality

The liberal myth

The development of a free press in contemporary Britain may be portrayed as a struggle between authoritarian forces of control in which the State or government bestows the right to publish and censors the content of publications, and liberal forces of control in which the individual's right to publish an opinion is independent of and protected from State control. There are two broad ways in which to characterise this struggle. The 'Whig' interpretation, criticised by Curran and Seaton (1991), portrays the emergence of press freedom as the victory of the liberal ideal over the oppressive interference of State and government in the free discussion of political issues. On this view, the contemporary press is more or less completely free and authoritarian controls have largely disappeared in democratic societies.

Then there is the view, exemplified by Curran and Seaton although not in these terms, that liberalism offers only a spurious kind of press freedom to the individual or to the public at large. In the historical development of the press, liberalism emerges not as a response to authoritarian oppression but as a means for the dominant élites within democratic states to sustain and consolidate control over the press. Liberalism has its own devices for controlling dissident or politically threatening opinion, devices such as the 'market-place' in which political influence is intimately tied to economic power. As we shall see, criticism of the power of the press and its function in society has often focused on the contradiction between the liberal idea of press freedom and the monopolistic nature of the market in which only a small and selected range of 'voices' are in fact represented in the press and limited to a dominant, normative discourse from which radical views are excluded. This latter view is similar to Herman and Chomsky's 'propaganda model'.

Liberal theory assumes that the individual is rational and capable of exercising reason to make informed judgements. The general idea is that civilisation prospers through the exercise of reason and the role of the State is to create the conditions under which the individual's capability for taking part in such debate can flourish. Thus the press is not an instrument of government but a means for presenting evidence and arguments which can be used by people to make judgements about the handling of events and social and economic policy and also to provide a check against abuses of power. Liberalism further advocates a free market of opinions and ideas in which those that are seen to be the best, or true, will emerge and come to be generally accepted, the so-called 'self-righting' process. However, this process is often a very hit and miss affair in which the 'news' remains a biassed selection of events and viewpoints. Perhaps at best we can expect that the free exchange of ideas and opinions will raise the level of debate without necessarily producing the best version of events (Siebert *et al*, 1956, 102).

There has long been a tension between the traditional view that every individual has the right to express an opinion in a public forum without interference, and the idea that the free expression of opinions carries with it obligations and responsibilities, perhaps enforced by regulation. At the same time the realisation has also developed that such a right itself requires protection. Press regulation is an area contested by authoritarian approaches in which tighter state regulation is seen as the answer to the perceived excesses of the press, and liberal approaches which continue to advance the concept of voluntary self-regulation. The question of media ownership and the fact that the free market works to exclude voices and opinions, thereby contradicting the rhetoric of liberalism, is not on the whole a highly visible aspect of this agenda. Indeed, the rights and responsibilities of proprietors have been the concern of several Royal Commissions since the war, but such is their power that there has never been a fundamental challenge to their domination of the free trade in opinion, ideas, and knowledge:

> The press is a frail vessel for the hopes it is meant to bear. The best that it can do can never be quite good enough to illuminate ... the forces and agencies we cannot monitor for ourselves, but which affect all our lives. A free, cultivated, diverse, resourceful and honest press can only try, and if we ever get one it will be interesting to see what it achieves. In the meantime, the nature of the two distant areas of restraint is central to our understanding. The first is external: the accumulation of laws and conventions which limit and punish free enquiry... . The second is internal: the vulnerability of an editor to a proprietor, the resources available for serious journalism and the unity and purpose of the staff, including the print unions ... and a proprietor willing to support editorial judgement... . Without internal freedom there is little hope of producing a newspaper of quality and none at all of challenging the external restraints. (Evans, 1994, 460)

Later we shall investigate some of the more detailed criticisms of the press that demonstrate the degree to which bias or misrepresentation occurs in the production of news about important social policy issues such as the environment. In an extreme form these criticisms, usually emanating from academic research, or sometimes party political sources, completely reject the liberal theory of the press as a basis for describing its activity, seeing it only as an arm of the State, or at least politically powerful vested interests, delivering an official, self-serving version of political facts. In Chomsky's 'propaganda model' (Herman and Chomsky 1988, Chomsky 1989) it is 'money and power that filter out the news fit to print, marginalize dissent, and allow the government and dominant private interests to get their messages across to the public.' (p2)

All academic critiques of the press, however, accept as a basic postulate that processes of news production are situated activities embedded in complex social, political and economic relationships. All news is therefore weighted or biassed to some particular way of viewing the world (Fowler 1991). The fact of bias is of course quite consistent with liberal theory which only demands that any opinions, or version of events, can be published. If false or unacceptable such opinions will be contradicted by more reputable, well-argued opinions, or simply ignored by all but a small, minority, following.

The liberal view continues to hold commentators. Emery and Emery (1984) for example see the history of journalism as '...the story of humanity's long struggle to communicate with each other – to dig out and interpret news and to offer intelligent opinion and entertaining ideas in the market place of ideas.' (v). For them, the growth of the global village is a progressive phenom- enon which is facilitating new heights in this democratic evolution, '... a series of developments in printing and writing, beginning in the Middle East and Asia, slowly spreading to Europe and finally to America, led to today's mar- vellous linkage of reporting talent, computers, high-speed color presses, and satellites.' (1)

Criticisms of the newspaper industry which have emerged since the Second World War in several Commissions of enquiry in the United States and the United Kingdom show that all is not well with liberal theory. Writing forty years ago at the beginning of this official change of view, Siebert *et al* (1956) in *Four Theories of the Press* provides a view of the emergence of press freedom in terms of the progressive advance of the liberal theory against authoritarianism. Since the 1600s there have been two or four general theories of the press, according to how they are counted: the Authoritarian Theory and its deriva- tive the Soviet Communist Theory, and the Libertarian Theory and its deriv- ative the Social Responsibility Theory. According to Siebert it is during this period that liberal theory evolves from its classical Enlightenment form into its modern variant, Social Responsibility Theory.

The authoritarian theory and the controlled press

In the period from the invention of printing to the end of the 18th Century, controls over printing and publication, literally the press, were palpably authoritarian. During this time coercive laws and regulations enshrined the right of the Royal and then the Parliamentary State to complete control over the publication of opinion and ideas. Licensing systems in use since Tudor times ensured the control of presses and the powers to punish unlicensed uses. Throughout Europe censors first appeared as paid officials of the state whose job was to police the output of printing presses, or to ensure that licenses were given only to favourably disposed individuals. The law of treason was defined so as to include opinions which, if published, could be punished, and in England the law of seditious libel was used to prosecute any kind of opinion or criticism of government, although with diminishing effectiveness until it was revoked in 1843 (Siebert *et al,* 1956).

In practice authoritarian systems allow for some degree of tolerance but usually only to élite social groups. For the mass of ordinary people, or those groups not deemed to be politically acceptable, the press and the media generally are tightly controlled. The purpose of the press in authoritarian systems is to inform the people of the decisions and policies of the rulers, not to engage in debate or deliberation about the issues. There is no such thing as the free exchange of ideas – the first duty of the press is to avoid interference with the objectives of the government and to promote them as worthwhile goals.

Authoritarian controls over the press continue to be exerted throughout the world with varying degrees of malignancy. In 1992, 61 journalists worldwide are known to have been murdered as the result of something they had written, and at least 123 were in jail, one having been held without trial for 20 years (Reporters Sans Frontières, 1993). This picture remains unchanged since *Four Theories of the Press* was published: 'One can hazard the guess that the authoritarian doctrine has determined the mass communication patterns for more people over a longer time than any other theory of press control.'(Siebert *et al*, 1956, 10). A United Nations report of the time found that although all nations in the survey claimed a free press, the right to freedom of opinion and expression had become a 'casualty' not only in overtly authoritarian states but in liberal democracies too, where

> ... this right is constantly menaced by the tendency to sacrifice freedom in the ostensible interest of defending freedom. The result is a complex social and political problem, marked by continuous interplay between abuse and efforts to correct abuses, between attempts to restrict freedom and attempts to widen it. (Lopez, 1953, cited in Siebert *et al*, 1956, 30)

Threats to a free and effective press in liberal democracies arise from several sources not least the historical tension between the authority of government and the right of the people to criticise and debate its actions. Many UK laws and regulations exist to limit the right of the press to report on certain matters, or to prevent individuals revealing information to the press. Civil servants, for example, are subject to over 100 separate Acts prohibiting such revelations; legislation such as the 1981 Contempt of Court Act severely limits press coverage of trials; the 1983 Water Act specifically excludes the press from attendance at meetings of new water authorities; and considerable animosity developed between the press and the Ministry of Defence during the Falklands crisis because of the strict controls placed on journalists' movements, the extent of censorship, and the use of deliberate misinformation (Robertson G, 1983).

In recent times there have been examples in the UK of authoritarian responses to press activity. In 1977 the Official Secrets Act was used to prosecute two journalists, Duncan Campbell and Crispin Aubrey, who had interviewed a former soldier. The spoken words of members of the IRA and Sinn Fein were banned in 1988 leading to the absurd situation where all televised interviews were dubbed with actors voices. As recently as 1992 Channel Four was prosecuted under the 1974 Prevention of Terrorism Act in an attempt to force the journalists to reveal their sources (Reporters Sans Frontières, 1993).

The liberal theory, the free press and its problems

Liberal theory, while recognising the need for some degree of regulation, has never provided a rigorous basis for deciding boundaries between free expression and the abuse of that freedom (Siebert *et al*, 1956) and this leaves the press vulnerable to the accusation that in attempting to report on and scrutinise public affairs it is also abusing its privileges, perhaps by an invasion of privacy, or some other unwarranted infringement of individual liberty. The debate on press freedom, or rather press regulation, continues in the UK in heated terms even, ironically, by those whose activities are otherwise unlikely to be exposed. A recent speech in the Commons by Neil Hamilton MP who resigned as the result of corruption allegations against him in the press deplored its 'cavalier disregard for accuracy and balance in pursuit of profits from circulation', he continued:

> The press sometimes appears to go to any length to undermine the institutions of this country. A free press is essential to a modern democracy, but a licentious press is a threat to it. (*Guardian*, 22/11/94)

Yet without this freedom the development of the 'cash for questions' morality among lobbyists and MPs would have gone unreported and would undoubtedly have spread unchecked. Even so despite further revelations about Government Whip interference with Parliamentary enquiry procedures into the issue (eg the 'Willett's memo) there are many unanswered questions about the way lobbyists acting for powerful interests are able to influence Parliamentary procedures. Without a free press there would be little pressure to continue the Nolan enquiries and little hope of an outcome that clarified the issues.

However, although traditional liberal theory merely advanced the right of individuals to freedom of expression through the freedom to open a printing press and publish, contemporary criticisms of the press have emphasised the limitations on opportunities for individuals to gain access to the means for doing so. Post-war critiques of the press have recognised the privileged position of newspaper ownership and the monopoly conditions that prevail to limit the possibilities of expression, '... protection against government is not now enough to guarantee that a man who has something to say shall have a chance to say it. The owners and managers of the press determine which persons, which facts, which versions of these facts, shall reach the public.' (Hutchins Commission, 1947, cited in Siebert *et al*, 1956, 5).

Traditional liberalism was preoccupied with ensuring the individual's freedom from interference by the State by ending government controls. Post-war liberalism has come to recognise the concept of social responsibility, expressed in such aphorisms as 'the public's right to know' and ' the public responsibility of the press'. The role of the state is seen to be to provide the individual with the means to realise freedom; those with power do not have the right to withhold what they know about issues that affect that freedom. If the press's duty is to report on these matters, and if at the same time the press must be coerced into behaving well with respect to this duty to the citizen, then some regulation is acceptable. Thus proprietors cannot publish to please themselves but should publish what needs to be published in order to represent all significant views (Siebert *et al*, 1956).

The contemporary liberal theory of the press infused with the concept of social responsibility thus envisages several tasks for the press (Siebert *et al* 1956, Curran and Seaton, 1991):

1   to provide information, and a forum for discussion and critical debate on public/political affairs, goals and values, independent of state interference;

2   to represent a diversity of opinions and constituent groups in society;

3   to educate the public to their democratic responsibilities and to make government accountable;

4   to safeguard the rights of the individual against the state, particularly the right of free expression;

5   to service the economic system through activities such as advertising;

6   to entertain;

7   to ensure 'full access to the day's intelligence', i.e. the press should be widely available and the press itself should be able to collect the information it needs; and

8   to maintain financial self-sufficiency in a free market so as to ensure independence.

Critics of the press argue that it is deficient in 1–4; untrustworthy in 5; lacking in quality in 6; and in 7–8 market forces are increasingly seen to limit the fulfilment of any of the other goals. Fundamentally press freedom is a property right (Curran and Seaton, 1991). Thus the press has been criticised for using its own power to serve its own ends; acting subserviently to business and political interests and controlled by the same socio-economic class. It has been criticised for conservatism, as well as invading individual privacy, applying low standards of reporting and entertainment, and endangering public morals (Siebert et al, 1956).

These criticisms have emerged in the UK through a series of official investigations into the press by three Royal Commissions. In general, as Curran and Seaton argue (1991), the outcomes of this process have been unsatisfactory and few of the substantive criticisms have had any substantial effect, particularly on the issue of ownership.

The first Royal Commission was set up in 1947 following a series of parliamentary debates which raised many criticisms of the press, noting the decline in the number of newspapers, concentration of ownership in the provincial press, a decline in quality, and the suppression and distortion of news for politically partisan or commercial reasons. The Commission was established 'with the object of furthering free expression of opinion through the Press and the greatest practicable accuracy in the presentation of the news'. (quoted in Robertson, 1983, 9)

Reporting in 1949 the Commission noted the lack of public responsibility and decline in standards and proposed the establishment of a press council to act as a professional governing body regulating all aspects of the profession, from recruitment and training, to monitoring and research, and the power to adjudicate on professional conduct. The Council was finally established in 1953 (becoming the Press Complaints Commission in 1990) but more as a response to the choice between self-regulation or legislation than a deep desire to improve standards of conduct (Robertson, 1983).

Generally however the Commission took the view that proprietors and private ownership of the press safeguarded the freedom of the press because it was free from outside influence from vested interests. Although it tentatively suggested that press ownership should be monitored for the growth of monopolies, the report endorsed the operation of the free market and competition as the means for making the press accountable (Curran and Seaton, 1991)

The second Royal Commission reported in 1962 and was critical of the attitude taken in 1949 which failed to reverse the concentration of ownership; chain ownership of provincial newspapers had substantially increased. Both the 1962 and the later 1977 Commissions found that conglomerates acquired a double advantage over weaker rivals in the form of lower unit costs and higher revenues so that nearly all new start-ups came from within these conglomerates. The process of competition appeared to reduce competition. A question mark was raised over the operation of the free market, a fundamental principle of classical liberal theory (Curran and Seaton, 1991).

New legislation was proposed to provide a means to ensure controls on the size of conglomerates, and to ensure that such decisions were free from Government interference. The watered-down legislation introduced in 1965 by a Labour Government proved ineffectual and the conglomeration of press ownership continued. In 1966 Lord Thomson was allowed to acquire *The Times* in spite of his already extensive properties, and in 1981 Rupert Murdoch was allowed to acquire Times newspapers, the Government refusing to refer this acquisition to the Monopolies Commission. Murdoch's properties then gave him 30 per cent of the daily newspaper readership, and 37 per cent of *Sun*day newspapers (Robertson, 1983).

The third Royal Commission reported in 1977, though with little effect (Robertson, 1983, 15). Concern was expressed at the massive concentration of titles into the hands of a few owners and the erosion of the effects of competition in the market. Although anyone is free to start a newspaper few can afford it. The greatest acceleration of chain ownership had occurred in the local weekly press with the emergence of sub-regional monopolies in which competing papers are all owned by the same group. A greater concentration in ownership of national dailies and *Sun*days had also occurred and proprietorship was no longer seen to guarantee diversity. The Commission also recognised at this time the need to protect editors and journalists from proprietorial control of content, and drew attention to the public responsibility that lay on the whole industry:

> We define the freedom of the press as that freedom from restraint which is essential to enable proprietors, editors and journalists to advance the public interest by publishing the facts and opinions without which a democratic electorate cannot make responsible judgements. (cited in Curran and Seaton, 1991, 289)

This Commission provides an example of the tension in liberal theory between the right of individuals to own and control a newspaper, and the limitations of the free market for ensuring that the goals of a modern press are achieved, namely to inform, to educate, to debate, to represent, and to protect the public. This redefinition of the property rights of proprietors to exclude their right to manipulate or control the content of their publications was reflected in draft professional charter proposed by the Commission which stated that journalists and editors are entitled to freedom of conscience 'notwithstanding the views of his proprietor' (cited in Curran and Seaton, 1991, 289). However, this principle was contradicted by other parts of the report which appeared to re-affirm the traditional view, for example by its acceptance of the principle that editorial and managerial control cannot be separated. '[The Commission] was thus endorsing a view which it had previously contested.' (Curran and Seaton, 1991, 290). Few of the recommendations regarding restrictions on ownership were enacted and press conglomerates, who were accused of being generally right wing and too unrepresentative began to expand further into television and broadcasting (Curran and Seaton, 1991).

The contradiction between liberal theory and its practice is thus quite deep. The operation of the free market, enshrined at an early stage in the formation of liberalism, has an illiberal effect, not to say authoritarian. Freedom of expression based on the ownership of the means to produce a newspaper (or television programme, or film, etc.) does not guarantee that every significant idea or opinion is represented. Large minorities, or depressed and economically weak sections of the population lack the capital, cultural skills or organisation to enter the market place and sustain their effort in the face of competition. If *ownership* is the criterion of freedom of expression, then few opinions indeed are represented. This concentration of newspaper ownership is not limited to the UK. In 1970 there were 125 significant newspaper-owning families world-wide controlling the 'great national and metropolitan titles of their countries.' Today there are fewer than 30 (Coleridge, 1993, 2).

An historical perspective – the British case

This contradiction only arises of course if the initial argument is accepted, that the freedom to own printing presses is the same thing as freedom of expression. Curran and Seaton (1991) show that the evidence for the emergence of press freedom in the late nineteenth century as the result of a sustained campaign motivated by liberalising ideals is very slim. They argue that the debate about whether to control the official press by means of legislation and taxation, or to free it from such controls to compete in the market place was essentially a debate about how best to control and/or suppress the radical press. The real motivation in freeing the British press from state regulation in the 19th Century was not the altruistic notion of an open market in ideas but a belief that the 'right' ideas, backed by capital, would triumph if the taxes that afflicted the legally registered press were removed. 'Market forces succeeded where legal repression had failed in conscripting the press to the social order.' (Curran and Seaton, 1991, 9)

During the late eighteenth century and early nineteenth, although the press was controlled by a punitive legal framework (the law of seditious libel) and a heavy and escalating tax regime (stamp duty), the system was not effective. It was subject to political corruption (eg Walpole used secret service funds to threaten and bribe newspapers owners and editors) and the use of libel laws had lost credibility, sometimes having the opposite effect by boosting the circulation of newspapers which had been prosecuted.

Although stamp duty and other taxes ensured that press readership and press ownership were restricted to the well-off and the property owning classes, the radical press continued to flourish underground in the early 19th Century. In a period of great change the fear of political revolution was strong, with good reason, and the power of the press to inform and sustain the ideas that drove such agitation was well understood. Press controls at this time were fundamentally authoritarian and continued to be so until the mid-19th Century when reformist arguments succeeded in removing most of the old controls. By 1836 the government had acknowledged that the circulation of the unstamped press exceeded that of the stamped press. Thus reform grew out of the realisation that taxation controls were failing to control the radical press (Curran and Seaton, 1991).

The arguments in the 1848 campaign for the repeal of stamp duty , the infamous 'taxes on knowledge', recognised its contradictory effect, that the radical press flourished in spite of it. By repeal of stamp duty reformers hoped to encourage men of capital to invest in an expanding market, and through this to educate the working classes correctly. A common concern was to secure the loyalty of the working classes to the social order through the expansion of the capitalist press. The new market driven press would be an effective instrument of social control by removing what many portrayed as a key source of political unrest and civil disorder: ignorance. Education and enlightenment through a free press will drive out politically dangerous ideas and promote the national interest:

> The larger we open the field of general instruction the firmer the foundations on which the order, the loyalty and good conduct of the lower classes will rest. (Palmerston, quoted Curran and Seaton, 1991, 27)

> The freedom of the press was not merely to be permitted and tolerated, but to be highly prized, for it tended to bring closer together all the national interests and preserve the institutions of the country. (Gladstone, quoted Curran and Seaton, 1991, 27)

A sea change had occurred since the previous decade when in earlier debates about the stamp duty the reformers lost to the traditional argument that repeal would open the floodgates to more and more unacceptable publications. The reformers arguments appealed to the fear of radicalism, arguing that cheap newspapers owned by 'more temperate and disinterested friends of the people who would lend themselves to their real instruction' and would be an important educational weapon against trade unionism. Francis Place, secretary of the repeal campaign suggested to a select committee in 1832 that if the stamp duty had been repealed earlier, 'there would not have been a single trades union in either England or Scotland'. Grote, a leading campaigner, argued in 1834 that the absence of a cheap capitalist press contributed to: 'a great deal of bad feeling that was at present abroad amongst the labouring classes on the subject of wages' because of 'the want of proper instruction and correct information as to their real interests'. These campaigners were not arguing for '...libertarian principle but the need for a more positive approach to political indoctrination'. (Curran and Seaton, 1991, 26)

At the same time as these parliamentary proceedings were occurring the government was engaged in the attempt to impose more stringent

enforcement. Between 1830-36 1,130 cases were prosecuted in London alone
(Curran and Seaton, 1991, 13). By 1836 the government was arguing that the
existing law was ineffectual and new more repressive measures were introduced. Many of the reformers who argued for repeal also voted in favour of
the new measures thus illustrating, according to Curran and Seaton a degree
of ambivalence towards repeal at this time. As a result, the clandestine radical
press disappeared but some unstamped publications became official, stamped,
publications and these not only flourished but broke many circulation records
because they had high ratios of readers per copy ratios thus reaching very
large, national readerships. These publications were financed by sales alone
and therefore could be run by people committed to the rights and interests of
diverse sections of society, and independent of the influence of advertisers.
They were influential in representing radical ideas about unionism, organised
action, about movements in other parts of the country (Curran and Seaton,
1991).

The appeal to the concept of a free market in the press was of course
embedded in wider political change as the class and wealth structure of
Victorian society gave new political strength to the industrial middle-classes.
These reformers were under no illusions but that it was they who would stand
at the reins of a liberated press bringing enlightenment to the masses. Milner
Gibson, president of the association for the repeal of 'Taxes on Knowledge',
made these arguments clear, saying that repeal would create 'a cheap press in
the hands of men of good moral character, of respectability, and of capital' and
give them 'the power of gaining access by newspapers, by faithful record of the
facts, to the minds of the working classes.' (Curran and Seaton, 1991, 29).
Others were reassuring that journalists too would be drawn from social strata
some way above the working classes, and their quality would improve as more
were attracted to working for a free press.

This debate was of critical importance. It resulted in the repeal of various
duties and restrictions but it also revealed the model of the emerging capitalist press held by the reformers, many of whom had a direct interest in and
experience of the press. Reform arguments impressed all but a small group of
traditionalists that the free market would work to control the radical press and
to educate the working classes appropriately in ways in which direct state controls could not. Today a similar debate would find proprietors stressing the
autonomy of working people in making up their own minds; the idea of the
press educating the public through its readership would be unlikely to figure
in their arguments.

The liberal idea that the press in a free market provides a mechanism for
the balanced representation of opinion is greatly undermined by Curran and
Seaton's analysis. Two structural elements in the market have meant that right
wing interests have usually been in the ascendancy: increasingly large capital
costs required to start up a newspaper and the trend for advertising revenue to
become a critical factor in newspaper accounts. Both these factors restrict the
opportunities for putting radical or critical ideas in to the public debate. As the
new middle classes increased their influence and commercialisation developed, the latter half of the nineteenth century and the early twentieth century
saw a rapid decline of the radical press.

The growth of advertising was an important factor in the changing financial structure of the press and even well-established newspapers were forced to close if they failed to attract such revenue. A limited circulation among the wealthy was regarded as worth much more than a large circulation among the poorer classes. 'This combination of economic and political discrimination by advertisers crucially influenced the development of left-wing journalism.' (Curran and Seaton, 1991, 41). To survive, a newspaper, no matter how radical, was forced to move up-market to attract advertising, to attract alternative funding (eg the *Daily Herald* was funded by the Labour Party and the TUC in 1922), or to remain with a small, limited audience. Whereas the left-wing press declined, income from advertising facilitated the growth of many new magazines, journals and newspapers appealing to more specialised audiences, drawing in advertising revenue, and newspapers went through a massive growth from annual sales of 85 million in 1851 to 5,604 million in 1920.

The inter-war years saw a consolidation and concentration of ownership on a large scale. It was during this period that Baldwin said of proprietors that they were 'aiming at ... power, and power without responsibility ...' (cited in Curran and Seaton, 1991, 49). Economic and competitive pressures created an environment in which rising costs forced attempts to increase circulations in a constant spiral, with ever-growing dependence on advertising revenue. Newspaper content changed. Political and public affairs coverage declined as 'human interest' stories grew in prominence in favour of entertainment and to separate papers from parties. Only newspapers appealing to small, élite audiences were protected from this trend by the greater advertising revenues they could raise in proportion to their readership. Curran and Seaton sum up the significance of this period in the following way:

> Their main significance lay in the way in which their papers provided cumulative support for conservative values and reinforced opposition, particularly among the middle class, to progressive change. (61)

The Second World War – reversing trends

The Second World War represents an ironic turn in the saga of press freedom according to Curran and Seaton because the restrictions imposed both through necessities such as newsprint rationing and through the controls adopted by a government wary of criticism helped to create the conditions for a radicalising of the press, at least in the area of social policy. They cite the press coverage given to the Beveridge Report as an example of the leftward move in some areas of opinion which helped to produce a shift to a social democratic consensus culminating in an election victory for the Labour Party in 1945. The recommendations of the report were not supported by Tory politicians and the Minister had hoped to publish it quietly. Press attention caused enormous publicity and the report was transformed 'into a cornerstone of the new consensus'. This reverse case, illustrating the influence of left wing newspapers, demonstrates how the press can enlarge and sustain public debate even in the face of official opposition.

The onset of war was an uncertain time for the government which was unsure of public support and wary of criticism. The government's position was uncertain through 1941 and 1942. In 1940 stringent regulations had been introduced which created a regime in which newspapers could be closed (eg the *Daily Worker* and *The Week*). Later in 1941 the Home Secretary, Herbert Morrisson, was reporting to the House on the closure of the *Daily Worker* when Nye Bevan responded by describing how the proprietors of the *Mirror* and the *Sunday Pictorial* had been seen by two members of the cabinet, Clement Attlee and Lord Beaverbrook (owner of the *Express* that later attacked the *Mirror*), and told that their editorial line was subversive, and that if they didn't change then compulsory censorship might follow. A few weeks later Bevan asked Churchill why, if he thought the newspapers were acting improperly, he didn't prosecute instead of using 'this weapon of secret terror.' Churchill responded by saying that the questioner seemed to doubt that the government had the right to have such confidential discussions:

> Such an idea is altogether foolish and has no relation whatever to the way in which affairs are conducted in this country. (*Hansard*, Feb 6, 1941, cited Hoch, 1974, 62)

Churchill's reply was cheered by fellow MPs. Hoch describes this remark as '... one of the most accurate assessments of British society ever made'. (Hoch, 1974, 62)

Later the same year the *Daily Mirror* published a famous cartoon with the caption 'The price of petrol has been raised by one penny (official)'. This depicted a torpedoed sailor adrift on a raft in the open sea. According to Curran and Seaton, this cartoon was misconstrued by the government who were sensitive to charges of allowing profiteering by oil companies, whereas in defence the *Daily Mirror* claimed it was a comment about the loss of life incurred in the transport of oil to Britain by sea (Curran and Seaton, 1991). Churchill ordered an investigation into the newspaper's shareholders, and the compiling of all the paper's 'unpatriotic' remarks (Hoch, 1974). The political attack on the *Daily Mirror* (circulation 1.9 million), which was echoed in sections of the press (eg Beaverbrook's *Sunday Express* made many insinuations about the *Mirror*'s owners that they were Zionists, or connected to American isolationists), '... was thus a pre-emptive strike against the government's principal critic. It's purpose ... was not only to silence the *Daily Mirror* but also to intimidate the rest of the press into adopting a less critical stance.' (Curran and Seaton, 1991, 77).

However, when Herbert Morrisson attempted to enforce the 1940 regulations in 1942, which allowed the suppression of a newspaper for publishing matter calculated to foment opposition to the war, and to close the *Daily Mirror* the opposition was fierce and the move was defeated. At the same time a public campaign to lift the ban on the *Daily Worker* was also successful and after 1942 all attempts to directly control the press were rejected. The liberal ideal remained quite strong in this debate and provided a check to the more authoritarian forces in the government. (Curran and Seaton, 1991)

New regulations introduced in 1942 restricted the amount of advertising that newspapers could carry, thus formalising the situation that had already arisen from newsprint rationing, instituted in 1940. This had already helped to level the playing field and these measures further helped to reduce the dependence of the press on advertising. By reducing the proportion of advertising income allowed, publishing costs went down. Advertising revenue also tended to be redistributed more evenly because there was such a shortage of space. The press could aim at a more working class readership, and sell more copies. For example, sales revenues of London daily newspapers rose from 30 per cent of total revenue in 1938 to 69 per cent in 1943 and space devoted to public affairs doubled in most daily newspapers during the war years. Advertisers became less particular about editorial policies, and editors could direct their opinions to a more homogeneous audience. These effects, combined with the general experience of life in war conditions, tended to radicalise the press, making it less entertainment centred, and more concerned with political and public affairs. (Curran and Seaton, 1991)

Post-Second World War

The period after the Second World War was marked by a slow return to pre-war market conditions and a steady growth in affluence. The increased availability of newsprint and a large increase in advertising revenues re-established the unequal competitive pressures with predictable effects. By the early 1970s the *Daily Herald, News Chronicle, Sunday Citizen (Reynold's News), Empire News, Sunday Dispatch, Sunday Graphic* and *Daily Sketch* had all ceased publication for similar reasons. They had low penetration of the middle class market without the compensation of a sufficiently large mass working class market. Curran and Seaton point out that although the working of the market was beyond the manipulation of any one party or organisation the demise of the first three newspapers in the list deprived some 9.3 million readers of their 'left of centre' newspaper.

The reasons for their closure are clearly illustrated. In 1960 when the *News Chronicle* closed it had a circulation of 1,162,000, more than five times that of the *Guardian* and in 1964 when the *Herald* closed, it had a readership of 1,265,000 or nearly five times the readership of *The Times*. In other words, there was not a massive haemorrhaging of readership. Greater losses occurred in advertising revenue as advertisers adjusted their rates to the 'purchasing power' of the different readerships they were trying to reach. The *Daily Herald*'s advertising revenue fell from 11 per cent of the national spend to 3½ per cent, while its circulation fell from 11 per cent to 8 per cent; a much smaller decline. The *Herald* in 1945 had attracted more advertising revenue per 1000 copies than the *Mail* or *Express* but by 1964 this had shrunk to less than half. Similarly, the *Sunday Citizen* obtained only one tenth of the advertising revenue per 1000 copies of the *Sunday Times*. In these circumstances the market leaders were able to speed the elimination of their weaker rivals using expensive marketing techniques, many of which had no link to their role as newspapers, for example competitions, give-aways and special marketing techniques.

The effects of the change in market conditions after 1945 also had a marked effect on the composition of newspapers as they returned to the 'more normal' post-war market conditions. The following table summarises some of these changes for a selection of national newspapers.

Table 2.1: Changes in newspaper composition between 1945-1976 (Curran and Seaton, 1991, 114–115)

Per cent of Total Space as:		DH/Sun	D.Mr	D.Ml	Tel
Advertising	1946	17	16	18	35
	1976	40	42	36	48
Per cent of Editorial Space					
Human Interest, News and Features	1946	18	34	22	22
	1976	34	33	27	15
Sport	1946	20	29	19	11
	1976	30	28	23	18
Other*	1946	14	31	17	12
	1976	24	25	22	19
Public Affairs, News & Features	1946	45	25	39	49
	1976	14	13	20	30

Other: Consumer and women's features, horoscopes, cartoon strips, quizzes, competitions, arts, entertainments and other features.

Between 1946 and 1976 the proportion of space devoted to advertising more than doubled in most cases, almost all sections of editorial space increased with the exception of public affairs, which showed massive relative declines, between 39 per cent and 69 per cent. In other words the recreation of free market conditions in the post war period almost exactly reproduced the structure of newspapers in the pre-war period. It should be noted that it was not the case that the percentage reduction in the space devoted to public affairs meant that all newspaper readers have less column inches of newsprint to read on these issues. The large increase in size of national dailies means that in most cases readers in 1976 obtained as large or a larger coverage of public affairs, albeit amongst an enormously greater coverage of almost all other content. However, this was not the case for the 9.3 million readers of the *Daily Herald*, *News Chronicle* and *Sunday Citizen* who transferred to the *Sun* or *Daily Mirror*. They clearly lost the chance of reading the news presented by a paper with their chosen perspective but they also lost out on the detail and scope of the public affairs coverage.

The post war press was still firmly in the hands of traditional proprietors although journalists became stronger and developed a professional consensus on resistance to proprietorial pressure. However, from 1974 newspapers become more partisan (as British politics became more polarised), and this partly reflected the character of the new generation of proprietors. Murdoch's papers became more right wing as he did, and he imposed these views regardless of the views of his readers, eg the switch of the *Sun* from Labour to Tory in the 1974 election, becoming a partisan Thatcherite paper even when over half its readers were Labour supporters. Murdoch of course, also brought a highly interventionist style of management to his newspapers whilst espousing a hands-off approach.

Another example of the new style of proprietorship was the *Daily Star*, launched in 1978, and which started out as a relatively radical paper because it was aiming at a 'down-market' mostly labour supporting audience. Victor Matthews, head of the Express Group between 1977-1985 and whose views on editorial freedom were that 'by and large editors will have complete freedom as long as they agree with the policy I have laid down', rejected the idea that the paper should support Labour in the 1979 election. Later after the Tory victory, the paper published an article critical of the government's first budget. Matthews angrily rejected it, telling the editor 'There aren't any poor. You can take my word for it. There are no poor in this country.' The *Daily Star* became another Tory tabloid, supporting the Tories again in 1983 even though only 21 per cent of its readers did so (Curran and Seaton, 1991, p90).

Since 1945 the national press has become concentrated into fewer hands. By 1988 Murdoch, Maxwell and Stevens controlled 57 per cent of total daily circulation. Regional ownership and control also increased with the market share of the five leading five publishers trebled their market share 1947-1988. This centralisation and concentration is part of a wider trend. The top five media companies in each media sector control around 40 per cent book sales, 45 per cent ITV transmission, 50-60 per cent recorded media sales, and 75 per cent of daily and *Sun*day papers and many companies are linked through cross-ownership of newspapers, film companies, book publishers etc. Between 1969-1986 nine multinational conglomerates bought over 200 magazines and newspapers with a total circulation of 46m. In reverse, there is now no popular national newspaper in Britain which does not have or is not controlled by a major interest outside the media.(Curran and Seaton, 1991).

The globalisation of trade and manufacture, the revolution in satellite and cable communications, coupled with the revolutionary changes in data storage and manipulation have made possible the rapid development of global conglomerates. However, while the structure of press ownership has followed these trends it has made relatively little difference to the concentration of press ownership which reached a peak in the 1960s.

Table 2.2: Concentration of Newspaper Ownership. Per cent circulation controlled by three largest corporations. (from Curran and Seaton, 1991, 91)

	1947	1961	1976	1988
National Daily	62	89	72	73
National Sunday	60	84	86	81

Post war proprietors like Rupert Murdoch and Robert Maxwell have been able to interfere with day to day decisions made by editors as well as monitor their progress and fire and replace them when they thought it appropriate. To be sure the size, global range and variation within their vast corporations have meant that they have not been able to give their newspapers the concentrated, almost fanatical attention which characterised the pre-war magnets (Beaverbrook, Northcliffe etc.) but the levers of power have remained unaltered and available. Some proprietors have taken a more hands-off approach and have preached the doctrine of press independence. However, this has been a position untested by any radical change by any major newspaper editor. In fact when proprietors have wished to intervene and change policies and editors, even promises of non-intervention given at the time of the take-over failed to prevent them. Murdoch's undertakings of non-interference at the *Times* lasted a few months but it took a little longer to get rid of Harold Evans, who fought a personal battle to retain independence and the editorship. (Evans, 1994)

Quality newspapers have maintained and even increased their commitment to serious political coverage but the polarisation between quality and popular was not based on differences of readership preferences for different types of content – market research found that readers of all types preferred the same types of stories (Curran and Seaton, 1991). But extending their readership to a wider audience only represented a marginal gain in advertising income for the quality press because their advertisers were willing to pay for the smaller, élite audience.

Thus the section of the press that provided the most detailed news and analysis catered for a privileged audience and largely reflected its class interests. Although market research showed that there were substantial audience minorities within the mass market these were not enough to sustain low circulation, serious newspapers, because they lacked attraction to advertisers.

> What newspapers have been available for consumers to buy has been shaped through the medium of advertising by inequalities of income and wealth in society. This has resulted, in turn, in a press structure which has helped to sustain and legitimate these inequalities. (Curran and Seaton, 1991, 118)

Conclusion

This short synoptic history of the press has focused on the extent to which the press has fallen short of the liberal ideal and how it still retains massive in-built structural impediments to achieving the open debates that a 'free' press should provide. The pattern of media ownership and the influence brought to bear on the workings of the media by proprietors renders the media a restricted zone for the achievement of a free and critical debate in which many voices are represented.

However, it is important not to overlook the achievements of the press. Many of these achievements, the coverage of the Vietnam War, the prediction and coverage of famine in Africa, the coverage of man-made environment disasters from spillages to almost undetectable toxic or environmentally damaging substances (eg CFCs) have had substantial effects on public opinion and eventually political action. Media organisations, newspapers, television companies etc. can themselves be seen as sites of conflict and struggle in which talented, ambitious or socially motivated individuals and groups struggle to establish the truth as they see it against the institutional version of truth which is often shaped by powerful and interested groups. This struggle has often gone unnoticed just as the products of the media have often gone unmonitored and subject to only weak periodic appraisal by Royal Commissions and by watchdogs preoccupied with palliating public concern about decency, privacy and violence.

In this volume we argue for a radical reappraisal of the function of the media in general and the press in particular. The argument has two major elements. The first is that our society is now facing unprecedented uncertainties including dangers and threats to its future, risks that cannot be underestimated. Second, although we know something about the environmental threats that hang over us from a variety of sources – the media, scientific research, campaigning groups – the wide and critical public debate about these issues, which liberalism says is a necessary condition for determining the future course of public policy, is not taking place. For this the media, and in particular the press, bear responsibility.

Curran and Seaton's analysis is that the liberal theory of the press is a myth, and never had much reality, although as a set of guiding aspirations it has informed many political debates on the press, and it has influenced many proprietors to the extent that they have often felt it necessary to pay lip-service to the idea, even if in practice they have rarely followed its precepts. In their view the press has always been used by politically dominant élites to restrain radical ideas.

The investigation in this volume will examine the content and structure of the press coverage of significant public policy issues. We will also examine its impact on public opinion, as well as an investigation into the relationship between press coverage and what we are proposing to call 'cultures of understanding' about the environment. It is clear that the media help to shape, perhaps manipulate, the consciousness and preoccupations of the public and many aspects of culture and political life. This is a major responsibility and power that needs recognition and much greater understanding than we have at present. Our investigation aims to uncover the intimate link between press coverage of significant issues and the influence that it brings to bear on public understanding.

Later in this book we will clarify what we mean by the notions of collective intelligence, cultures of understanding and the concept of public education. In the next chapter we will advance the argument, using the environment and development debate as an example, that the next two or three decades is a critical period in our history as we collectively face major political choices. What we shall show is that in spite of the potential for disaster that looms, the evidence is not presented to the public through the forum of the press, nor is the press active with respect to this important aspect of the public policy agenda.

3

The Social and Environmental Context

Doom or boom, intelligence and cultures of understanding

Introduction

The contemporary picture of the UK press that emerges from an examination of its history and present structure, is not reassuring. It is certainly not in line with liberal theory in which the press acts as a forum for unfettered public debate, in which perspectives and ideas reflecting the interests of all major sections of the public are represented. Nor does it pass the test of uncovering the whole truth about important national events. All too often we find out later, that the public has been badly misled and the press has either been lied to or connived in the deception. The reasons for this unfortunate situation stand out starkly from the historical accounts that we have examined. The press is dominated by powerful international corporations which are in turn controlled by relatively few powerful individuals. These individuals wish to maximise their penetration of the media market and also influence the direction of national and sometimes international politics. While they pay lip service to editorial and journalistic freedoms they appoint editors who will carry out their policies and ensure that the newspaper reflects their views (see Bower 1988, Shawcross 1992, Evans 1983 and Coleridge 1994). In some areas of news which do not reflect on contemporary issues of importance or where the proprietor and editor have no particular interest there is undoubtedly considerable journalistic freedom and there is undoubtedly a contest within even the most tightly controlled editorial/journalist teams for journalists to extend their freedom.

The silver lining to the dark cloud which represents the contemporary British press is the excellent work done by many of its reporters and journalists in exposing corruption, secret government manipulation of publicly stated policies and campaigns on behalf of individuals who have been unjustly dealt with by the courts, government or powerful corporations. Nevertheless this professional expertise is sometimes exercised under considerable adverse pressure and there have been notable occasions when the dog has not barked. There is also considerable variation within the UK national press, some newspapers have outstanding reputations for news coverage while others seem to regard news and public debate about important issues as an intrusion in their main tasks of entertainment, diversion, influence and profit. When we begin to examine the quality of the press coverage of the selected events it will be important to remember that in June 1992 the so-called quality press was read by about 24 per cent of the newspaper reading public and this represented only 15 per cent of the total population (MORI Omnibus Poll June 1992).

In this chapter we ask the question, does this matter? We acknowledge that there are powerful traditional arguments which could lead to the answer that on the contrary it is important that the present situation should be left undisturbed. The evidence from this perspective is that we have managed well in the past with an imperfect press and no doubt an imperfect media in general. Maybe we should review democratic theory instead. This view was illustrated by the Parliamentary exchange between Nye Bevan and Winston Churchill, recorded in Chapter 2. Churchill was in fact saying that government in the UK is normally carried out by powerful élites that reach private agreements. More recently in their defence of the Arms to Iran policy, ministers and civil servants were saying that government needed secrecy, and maximum flexibility to take unpleasant decisions that go beyond what public opinion would countenance, in the interest of the nation!

We realise that this argument has a great deal of resonance with the views of many people who prefer private brokerage to public debate. However, this élite consensus, concept of government will only hold public confidence while the manipulation of public affairs works smoothly and traditional solutions seem to work. As Giddens (1991, 1994), Beck (1992, 1995), Beck *et al* (1994) and others have pointed out, this is no longer the case. The concept of manufactured uncertainty captures the self imposed nature of the massive loss of public confidence that is currently being felt in government and other major institutions. Giddens' answer is to encourage dialogic democracy in which new openness and participation in debate develops new levels of trust and legitimacy.

We will attempt to use this broad framework to follow through a case study of the UK press and its reporting of environment and development issues. It is through this case study that we hope to answer the question, does it matter? The last three chapters of the book will be given over entirely to the case study. In this chapter we will be examining the new social context in which, we will argue, the press has a vital role to play in helping to develop a more educated and intelligent public, which can in turn develop new relationships and new trust in the major institutions of government.

Our choice of environment and development issues as portrayed by the press rested on a number of considerations, many of which will be described at a later stage in our discussion. At this point it is important to note the centrality of environment and development issues to the phenomenon of manufactured uncertainty. It would be impossible to list all the environment issues that have impinged upon or threatened the certainties in our lives over the last 3 or 4 decades. Even a superficial list will remind us of the fundamental reappraisal that has taken place since, to take an arbitrary starting point, Rachel Carson wrote the 'Silent Spring' in 1962. Issues that have disturbed traditional certainty include:

- The partial destruction of the ozone layer by CFCs.
- The greenhouse effect and global warming, produced by industrial, agricultural and household gases, CO_2, methane etc.
- Acid rain produced by SO_x and NO_x gases from cars and industry.

- Pollution of drinking water in aquifers by fertilisers.
- Increased asthma and respiratory disease from air pollution in cities - motor cars and industry.
- The depletion of fish stocks through over fishing (consumption).
- Famines caused by wars and climatic change in North East Africa and elsewhere.
- 13 million child deaths per year, caused by malnutrition and often preventable disease.
- The re-occurrence of 'eliminated' diseases in new virulent forms eg TB, malaria etc.
- The occurrence of completely new diseases, such as AIDS, contamination of the food chain with BSE, Creutzfeld-Jacob Disease (the human variant of BSE), Lassa Fever, E. Coli 0157, etc.
- The widespread destruction of important habitats and natural resources - tropical forest, wetlands, mangrove swamps etc.
- The rapid increase of population in highly populated areas and areas least able to support more intensive farming.
- The increasing differentiation between rich and poor nations and between rich and poor within nations.

It will be important to note that almost all of the issues listed here are self-inflicted, often as a result of the material progress made by the dominant nations and their élites and the successful expansion of the human species into almost every habitat on the globe. Yet these are all problems for which there are no clear definitive solutions. Almost all of these issues therefore can be described by the concept of manufactured uncertainty.

Carson's book represents the first major disclosure that manufactured products, (chemicals) produced specifically for improving agriculture and aiding farmers in their fight against pests, animal disease and weeds were beginning to invade the natural habitat and damage all life including birds, fish and human beings. Carson lists a wide range of chemicals, many of which have since been banned or subject to substantial control. Nevertheless chemicals used in agriculture and industry continue to enter the food chain and a great deal of uncertainty remains about their effects including issues as varied and dramatic as the extinction of marine mammals and the declining sperm count of North American and European males. Carson targeted chlorinated hydrocarbons such as DDT, Chlordane, Dieldrin, Aldrin and Endrin, organo-phosphates such as Parathion and Malathion and arsenic compounds. Since Carson wrote her book we can add substantially to this list including Polychlorinated Biphenols (PCBs) and Chlorinated Fluorocarbons (CFCs). Carson was particularly concerned with poisonous chemicals entering the food chain, being concentrated in animal fat (including human fat) by predation and by feeding contaminated milk to mammalian young (also including human milk).

The effects of other chemical substances are now known to extend to the destruction of the ozone layer (CFCs etc.) and to altering the composition of the atmosphere sufficiently to affect enhanced global warming (the greenhouse effect). The ozone layer absorbs ultra violet B radiation which causes skin cancer in humans and damages some plants. By thinning the ozone layer, CFCs have substantially increased the rates of this kind of cancer. The international banning of this chemical must be regarded as a marked success, although there is evidence that the ban has been breached quite substantially.

However the effects of global warming with its attendant redistribution of climatic zones and the increases in sea level which threaten low lying, highly populated areas are far less certain and far more difficult to control. Control of global warming involves the need for massive changes in power generation, transportation systems, agriculture and animal husbandry. These areas of our social life are far more intractable because they are central to our successful efforts to improve the quality of life; that is, to all social and economic progress. Effective change here looks like involving every aspect of our social life and productive systems and will not be solved by banns and controls based on technical fix innovations with little accompanying impact on style of life.

In addition to these problems the constant increase in the world's population places increased strain on all resources and effectively magnifies the effects of the differentiating forces within the global economy. So while the successful nations (USA Europe, Japan, the emerging Asian economies), constantly improve their standard of life many of the so-called developing nations see theirs lag further behind as improvements in production are swallowed up by a rapidly increasing population. In the mid-sixties the poorest 20 per cent of the world's population took a mere 2.3 per cent of global income; today that figure is even smaller, 1.4 per cent (Elliott, 1996).

It should be emphasised that the increased affluence for some has been accompanied by increased poverty for others. When this development is accompanied by the emergence of new resistant strains of once 'defeated' or 'controlled' diseases like tuberculosis, malaria and new emerging diseases like Aids, another area of manufactured uncertainty develops. These diseases are now progressing back from areas of poverty or the social margins where partial or underfunded treatment exacerbates or develops the problem, to affluent families in Western cities. Even within these affluent contexts the 'new' diseases, which are in a sense a product of poverty and neglect, are almost untreatable.

This list is unfinished, it is illustrative. It nevertheless could be characterised as doom-mongering and unnecessarily pessimistic. In this chapter we will first confront the doom versus boom controversy, this will be followed by a discussion of the evidence relating to one environmental and development issue, global warming. We will argue that the nature of these new problems places a maximum stress on all our social institutions because our problems frequently stem from the success of our major manufacturing, distribution and financial systems and the extent to which they have been widely adopted; not their failure. How do we guard against success? How do we reverse the momentum of several centuries of struggle and achievement? This problem will require substantial changes in our abilities to re-think re-educate and re-direct our intelligence. This is discussed in the latter sections of the chapter.

Doom or boom

We recognise that despite the considerable literature on the new problems and uncertainties confronting the human race there is a small but respectable literature that dismisses almost every problem as a figment of the imagination of a successful and profitable 'doom' predicting industry.

From earliest times prophets of doom have achieved fame and fortune by persuading the rich and powerful that supernatural forces more powerful than earthly princes will destroy or damage them unless they are appeased in some way. Victor Clube (an astrophysicist at Oxford) points out that 'the sight of something flaming in the sky was enough, in pre-Enlightenment days, to put people in a dangerous mood; to expect the fall of emperors, the collapse of nations, the destroying angel of the Apocalypse, the End of Everything' (Radford, 1994). Is it not possible that the dire warning about global warming, pollution and even AIDS are just another variant of this kind of scare mongering, dressed up in modern scientific clothes. Certainly, as Radford points out, US scientists and cold war warriors were able to persuade Reagan to invest millions of dollars in the failed Strategic Defence Initiative (Star Wars) which was designed to destroy Soviet missiles in space. Some then continued to try to get the US government to invest billions of dollars in a programme to deflect or destroy asteroids of the kind that are believed by some to have destroyed the dinosaurs.

Perhaps a more relevant version of this debate occurs within the academic community between the Malthusians and the Cornucopians (Tierney, 1990). Malthusians like Paul Ehrlich point to the common sense notion that exponential rises in population are likely to outstrip the likely increases in food production and cause famine. In fact Ehrlich extends this argument to all limited natural resources and predicted multiple crises as populations increase. Writing in 1968 in 'The Population Bomb' he predicted 'The battle to feed all of humanity is over. In the 1970s the world will undergo famines - hundreds of millions of people are going to starve to death'. He goes on to point out that 'vast agricultural surpluses are gone' and that 'nothing can prevent a substantial increase in the world death rate'.

The book sold three million copies and Ehrlich became a celebrity scientist. Some years later he broadened and updated the argument in 'The End of Affluence' and predicted an even larger disaster. 'Due to a combination of ignorance, greed and callousness, a situation has been created that could lead to a billion or more people starving to death'. An age of scarcity would soon be upon us. However, as Tierney (1990) points out, while the world population did grow in line with Ehrlich's prediction none of the dire consequences followed. Death rates did not rise, in fact they fell and food production increased faster than the population. To add insult to injury Julian Simon, a Cornucopian economist who had attacked Ehrlich's thesis, challenged Malthusians to name any 5 natural resources that would become scarcer in the next 10 years. Ehrlich had taken up the challenge and named chrome, copper, nickel, tin and tungsten. By 1990 all of these metals had become relatively and absolutely cheaper and Ehrlich lost $576 on the side bet!

Julian Simon's Cornucopian thesis clearly deserves careful consideration. It is counter intuitive and relatively unpopular but these are not sufficient reasons for dismissing it. Cornucopians gain most strength from the studies carried out by economists who traced the price of natural resources back as far as records are available and calculated the cost to the average worker of a particular commodity. A book published in 1963 by H J Barnett and C Morse demonstrated that in practically all cases an average worker could buy more with a day's pay than at an earlier period. Things were getting less scarce and people were better off as the population grew. Their explanation derives from the adaptability and ingenuity of mankind. As shortages develop so producers find ways of locating new resources, recycling old ones, finding substitutes or economising and using less to do the same job. This ability to adapt we can see derives from our intelligence - the ability of humankind to identify and solve relevant problems.

The question now becomes, if the Cornucopians are right and things will be even better in the future than they are now, why should we worry about the future? Would not it be simpler and sensible to let the future look after itself? We do not hold that view. However, we do not argue for Ehrlich against Simon, we take the view that while Simon is nearer a true appraisal of our present situation, both Ehrlich and Simon make serious mistakes in their method of interpreting the future.

Both Ehrlich and Simon use a simple interpolative methodology. Ehrlich projects population trends and resource depletion trends to discover a crisis 10 or 20 years in the future. Simon goes a step beyond this and notices that these ultimate crises almost never happen. Instead innovation or substitution takes place specifically to avoid the threatened crisis. Simon's mistake is then to suppose that this will always happen. In making this step Simon is repeating an error to which economists are prone. Instead of directing his research towards discovering more explicitly what enables this adjustment to take place and therefore ensuring that the conditions which have enabled capitalist societies to adjust in the past to highly volatile situations are still healthy and improving or at least in place; he goes out on a limb to predict a future of inevitable improvement, a cornucopia.

We would criticise Simon's simplistic picture of inevitable improvement on a number of counts:

1   It is in part an illusion which does not take into account the major problems of applying economic accounting procedures developed in industrialised capitalist countries to countries in which traditional agricultural communities predominate. These are often primary producers whose export products are getting cheaper. In addition their subsistence economies frequently require a greater input of labour as wood and water become scarcer and their land less fertile.

2   It does not take into account the differentiation produced by capitalism, within and between countries. Simon therefore underestimated the damaging effects of structural poverty. These can be seen as damaging some groups and nations directly but also as a major drag anchor on affluent society as it becomes more prone to crime and vulnerable to new diseases. In

the extreme case it is likely that a price will have to be paid as war and civil unrest also spreads beyond ghettos and impoverished nations and makes the absorption of refugees or military intervention a necessity.

3   It does not take into account the massive increase in pollution and environmental stress that will occur as the underdeveloped world struggles to emulate the 'success' of the 'successful' industrial world. Simon extends his 'more is better, the future is always bright' to almost every issue. For example, he claims that population increase will always be dealt with because more people will produce more goods and there will be a greater pool of intelligence from which to draw new ideas and innovations to solve emerging problems. In the USA some 7 per cent of the world's population consume some 35 per cent of the world's resources. If the world population were to remain constant, and the USA were to stabilise their consumption of resources then the rest of the world would need to extract and consume 4-5 times the present rate of resources in order to emulate that success.

4   It does not take into account our historical knowledge that major civilisations have decayed and in some cases disappeared. It would seem over optimistic to assume that our own civilisation or major parts of it are simply incapable of comparable decay.

5   Finally and most importantly it neglects the work of Hirsch (1977) a fellow economist who pointed out that absolute measures of commodities are not reliable indicators of progress. There exists a whole range of things that people value, for example, living space, clean air, quick clean comfortable and efficient transport, clean water etc. which are not the same as the commodity or service that is conventionally expected to supply them. This is because those goods and services are not indefinitely elastic, they are governed by what Hirsch called the positional economy.

A good example of the working of the positional economy is illustrated by the motor car. At one time the motor car provided the relatively rich with a clean, efficient, comfortable and quick means of transport. As motor cars became cheaper and widely available those possessing it changed their position i.e. lost their advantage over others. As car ownership became common place and more and more cars crowded onto an expanding but relatively fixed road network, motor cars increasingly failed to deliver any of these qualities. Indeed in many parts of urban Britain they moved from a clean, efficient, comfortable and quick to a slow, stressful, inefficient and polluting form of transport. It is now clear that motorised road transport in the form of the motor car is not only failing to deliver what it was intended to deliver but it is also spoiling our countryside and causing ill-health through asthma, cancer and other bronchial/lung diseases.

The progress from clean, efficient, comfortable and quick to slow, stressful, inefficient and polluting is now being experienced in many walks of life, for example, sea bathing, drinking water and additives and pollutants in foods. In some cases they can be put right simply by generating a political will, by raising public consciousness and by making new regulations or by making public money available. The removal of smog from city centres, the cleaning of some rivers and beaches are examples of these solutions. In other cases technical advance makes polluting industrial products unnecessary, as was hoped to be the case with CFCs and asbestos. Nevertheless in each of these cases considerable damage was done and many people currently suffer from or have died from the effects of these pollutants, either directly, through asbestos or indirectly through skin cancer. Also some are much more difficult to control in this way.

Clearly these problems of affluence are more common in advanced industrial countries than in 'so-called' developing countries. However, they are startlingly obvious and well developed in even the least wealthy of countries. For example, no-one who has visited the growing cities of India, Thailand and Mexico etc. could fail to recognise the above scenario. In fact many developing countries are experiencing these problems of 'affluence' in an acute form long before they have solved the problems of mass poverty and underdevelopment. Hirsch's analysis therefore links with Giddens' notion of manufactured uncertainty and our notion of the failure of success. In these cases the central processes and drives of modern industrial society, the very basis of its continuing development, are the processes that are damaging the environment and threatening future development.

It follows that Simon's methodology is fundamentally flawed. within our analysis we will always attempt to take into account the constraints of the positional economy and attempt an interpretation of the meaning of economic trends which takes into account concepts like the individual and collective interest and the unintended consequences of social action.

If these methods and frameworks of analysis are adopted it follows that we are neither Cornucopians nor Malthusians. We take the view that our continued existence/development depends on the balance between our ability to adapt and change our methods of production (Simon) and the rate at which problems arise from our inability to control the growth of our civilisation and the demands it makes on threatened and deteriorating natural systems. (Ehrlich).

It follows that our well being and continued development is now and will always be, in the balance. While *homo sapiens* exists on the earth in such large numbers, and demand such a large slice of the resources and products of that earth to satisfy their needs, our society will need to be able to define, analyse, understand and solve our problems. We anticipate that many of these solutions will involve more than changing from one commodity to another, eg from leaded to unleaded petrol, they will require quite substantial changes in life style. In other words we will need to substantially improve our intelligence in all senses of the word. We will need to improve our information flows and our abilities to take intelligent, democratic decisions.

We will argue that as our capitalist system becomes even more successful and more and more people are freed from the drudgery of traditional society and partake in the delights of a power-hungry consumer society so the stress on natural systems will increase and solutions to the problems created will need to be invented more and more frequently. This, is almost the same as saying that manufactured uncertainty will increase and that 'success' has 'failure' built into it.

Many of these changes will not be popular. Quite recently the government has been studying a recommendation that the price of fuel is made to double in the next 10 years. This kind of interference with the market will be resisted by many, as counter to the best interests of our economy, which should be free from artificial constraints and regulation. This kind of issue is already affecting our water supply, sea bathing, the air we breathe and the food we eat and will multiply into almost every aspect of our life as we try to bring the pollutants that we routinely produce into balance with natural systems that control the composition of the atmosphere, the ozone layer and global warming.

If these decisions are to be taken in time. If the issues are to be understood by the majority of people and decisions taken by the democratic process. If they are to be taken on the basis of a full and open debate in which the best available information is made available and properly interrogated. Then we will need to improve our methods of debate. We will need to study the way our press, television and other forms of mass communication actually work. Do they inform or do they distort the information that should be made freely available? What is their impact? Do they influence public opinion, change attitudes and shape our culture or are they largely irrelevant? Can we go as far as saying that they not only do all of these things but that they also affect our ability to define, analyse understand and solve pressing problems? In short affect our intelligence.

At this point we need to divert slightly to examine more closely one of the issues listed earlier in the chapter.

Long term, diffuse and uncertain problems

One of the most serious medium-to-long term problems facing our civilisation is in our view global warming. We have chosen this issue because it possesses all the classic features of manufactured uncertainty and because by looking briefly at some of the issues or debates associated with it we can illustrate the nature of the problems we face and the need for a more active and positive approach towards spreading an understanding of them and to seeking solutions.

Global warming falls into the same long term, diffuse, uncertain category of problems as environmental pollution by toxic chemicals. David Price of the US Public Health Service, described these as follows:

> We all live under the haunting fear that something may corrupt the environment to the point where man joins the dinosaurs as an obsolete form of life. … And what makes these thoughts all the more disturbing is the knowledge that our fate could perhaps be sealed twenty or more years before the development of symptoms. (Carson, 1962, 188)

In the case of global warming the symptoms have begun to emerge. The scientific community became aware of the threat of global warming in the late seventies. As a result of a major conference in 1985 the message spread out into the community of environment and development charities (NGOs), governments and international organisations. In 1988 the Intergovernmental Panel on Climate Change (IPCC) was set up by the United Nations to proved an authoritative, consensus view. It involved most of the major scientists who were researching this topic, from around the world. The IPCCs first report published in 1990 warned of the dire effects of global warming. This report was sufficiently influential to persuade governments to negotiate a Climate Change Convention which was signed at the Earth Summit in Rio de Janeiro in 1992. The first full meeting of signatories has since taken place in 1995 in Berlin and the next Earth Summit took place in New York in 1997. The second IPCC report was released in April 1995 and published in April 1996.

This sequence of events could only have occurred in the context of a relatively high level of governmental awareness. Almost all governments (150) have signed the convention which has committed industrialised nations to stabilise their emissions of carbon dioxide at the 1990 levels by the year 2000. This is well below the 60 per cent reduction of CO_2 emissions recommended by IPCC scientists. In addition they will attempt to reach agreement in New York to reduce levels after the year 2000. They have also signed the 'precautionary principle', which states 'where there are threats of a serious or irreversible damage, lack of full scientific certainty should not be used as a reason for postponing [precautionary] measures'. Nevertheless politicians and others are aware that spending money on a merely threatening event or danger (that might not happen) is a politically risky business. If large amounts of money are diverted from popular projects, whether they be tax cuts or the rejuvenation of public services, to implementing costly or restrictive measures or building sea walls from which the sea then retreats, the careers of politicians involved can be damaged. In matters of this kind it is therefore essential that not only is the public informed but they become involved in a debate that brings forward proposals and possible solutions that obtain majority or consensus support. Clearly the media would need to be centrally involved in such a development. To justify this involvement media professionals would need to know that the problem involved major implications of national and international importance.

It is therefore important to divert slightly from an examination of the press coverage of these events to examine the possible dangers and uncertainties spelled out by the scientists examining global warming.

Global Warming

Global warming is believed to be occurring because human activity has increased the concentration of the main greenhouse gases (carbon dioxide and methane) by 30 per cent and 145 per cent respectively in the last 200 years. Figure 3.2 illustrates the growth of CO_2 in the atmosphere and Figure 3.2 illustrates on a longer time longer time line the growth in the consumption of fossil fuels.

The progress of global warming is uncertain because of the complex interdependence of massive systems (atmosphere, oceans, biomass, industry, agriculture etc.). However, if this increase in greenhouse gases were alone responsible for global warming the earth's average temperature would have risen by 1°C. The actual rise is somewhat less (0.4°C in 30 years) and this reduced level is now believed to be the result of the cooling effects of other industrial pollutants which reflect sunlight (IPCC Reports 1990 & 1995).

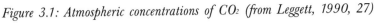

Figure 3.1: Atmospheric concentrations of CO₂ (from Leggett, 1990, 27)

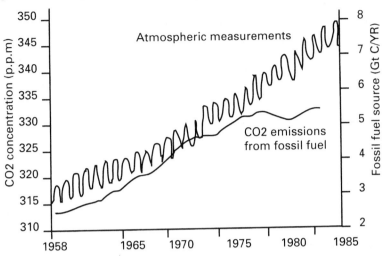

Figure 3.2: Growth in fossil-fuel consumption since the Industrial revolution and current world energy consumption. (From Leggett, 1990, 28)

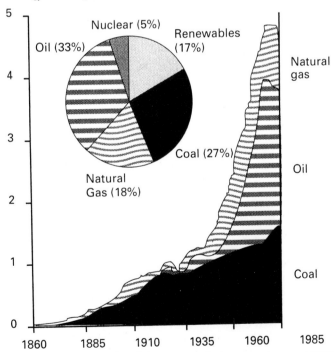

Nevertheless, the evidence for the increases in temperature grows year by year. The past century has been the warmest for the last 600 years. The four warmest years have occurred in the 1990s and nine of the ten warmest years have occurred since 1980. The security of the link between these rises in average temperature and the concentration of CO_2 also increases as research from a variety of fields produces the same result. Figure 3.3 illustrates the relationship over a time line of 160,000 years.

These fields of research vary from the isotopic analysis of 'fossilised' air bubbles trapped in glacier ice for up to 150,000 years to the construction of complex computer programs designed to model the earth's atmosphere using the most up to date average temperatures from around the world. Despite this convergence and consensus some uncertainty remains and this is magnified when the effects of the predicted rises in temperature are calculated.

Figure 3.3: Correlation between CO_2 concentrations and temperature during the past 160,000 years (Leggett, 1990, 64)

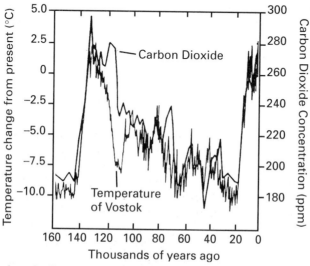

The predicted effects of global warming centre on the changes in climate that might be produced and the effects of melting terrestrial glaciers and in particular the Greenland and Antarctic ice sheets. Depending on the rate at which these ice sheets melt the IPCC predict a rise of sea level between 15 centimetres and 95 centimetres in the next century. However, if the West Arctic Ice Sheet also collapsed the rise could be up to six metres, although this is regarded as a remote possibility. However, even the 'most likely' outcome of a rise of 50 centimetres would cause incredible disruption and flooding. Many inhabited coral atolls would almost certainly be destroyed. Large areas of fertile delta would be inundated in particular in Egypt, India, Mozambique, Pakistan, Thailand and Vietnam, low lying coastal areas (lagoon coasts) would be flooded in Western Africa and elsewhere. Vast populations measured in 10s and possibly 100s of millions would be displaced. Major cities all over the world including rich cities like Tokyo, Shanghai, Hong Kong, New Orleans, London, Hamburg, Venice and many, many others would be badly affected and would need to engage in massively expensive sea defences. The cost would be enormous but at least these cities would have the resources to protect themselves, unlike many other affected regions.

The effects of climate change will also bring massive disruption on a regional scale and this will be accompanied by local changes which will affect rainfall and evaporation. For example, much of the corn-belt in the USA would probably receive less rain and crops would fail. Similarly the IPCC predict that much of the grassland in Africa will deteriorate into desert. The flow of many major rivers on which large populations depend will deteriorate, the Indus by 43 per cent, the Niger by 31 per cent, and the Nile by 11 per cent. Water which is already the cause of international conflict will become a major cause of disputes.

The results of this world-wide co-operation by thousands of scientists came together in the report published by Cambridge University Press priced £150.00. Hardly a publication available to a large public. Most newspapers covered the event of its publication with a single article. Its contents were not considered newsworthy by the majority of editors. We do not challenge this professional judgement in relation to the editorial and commercial contraints that affect editors. However, we do challenge a system that prevents people from getting news about events that will affect everyone's future. It is presently a widely held belief that news about the environment is all doom mongering, unpopular with audiences and readers and unlikely to sell newspapers or increase audiences.

The first report published in 1990 was reported quite differently and helped raise public concern about the environment to new heights. It is interesting to note that the predictions and calls for action in this second report have not changed a great deal. Some uncertainties have been removed and some estimates have been changed in a downward direction. The central recommendation that the polluting of the atmosphere by CO_2 and other greenhouse gasses will have to be reduced by 60 per cent in order to prevent massive damage and dislocation has remained unchanged. In the intervening period almost no progress has been made in moving towards ways of implementing this recommendation and the public debate of the issue has almost died.

It is almost as if the institutions for informing and educating the public within democracies are unable to deal with a topic that challenges the practices and habits of news reporting developed over many decades. Practices and understandings that depend on the reliability of the major institutions within our society, government, major companies and research institutions to solve the problems that arise on a day to day or year by year basis. News derives from the very practice of diagnosing problems, debating them and solving them or shelving them (Downs, 1972). In most cases shelving problems does not threaten the whole of the world's climate or the existence of many societies. It may on occasion radically effect the life chances of disadvantaged or weak groups within or between societies. There are of course predictable patterns as to which problems are solved and which are shelved.

The scale and depth of the dangers within the estimated progress of global warming are of a totally new dimension and have completely overwhelmed the capacities of major institutions to deal with it. The problem has been recognised and posed by scientists in research institutions. They have no solutions to the problem. The problem has been passed on to governments who have in turn pushed it back to scientists, engineers and experts in a wide range of institutes and major companies. There are still no obvious solutions and a great deal of uncertainty. The major problem, the generation of CO_2, is a by-product of our manufacturing industry, our transportation systems and our agriculture. It is a measure of our success as advanced industrial countries. Economically successful nations have higher rates of CO_2 emissions.

In Figure 3.4 the *per capita* energy consumption (TEP/Capita) is closely associated with production (GDP/Capita). For instance, the USA consumes about 6 times the energy *per capita* of Brazil and nearly 24 times the energy *per capita* of India. In broad terms the OECD countries consume twice the energy of the Less Developed Countries (LCD) but have about a fifth of the population.

Figure 3.4: Indicators of energy consumption per capita and per unit of product (1986) (Leggett 1990, p. 172)

	Total population (millions)	Total energy consumption (MTEP)	TEP/ Capita	TEP/ US$1000	GDP(US$) /Capita
OECD	818	3,855	4.71	0.38	12,119
USA			7.2	0.41	17,480
Japan			3.2	0.20	12,840
FRG			4.5	0.30	12,080
France			3.6	0.28	10,720
UK			3.8	0.46	8,870
Italy			2.5	0.24	8,550
LDCs	3,830	1,915	0.5	0.59	680
Brazil			0.8	0.55	1,810
India			0.2	0.80	290
Mexico			1.2	0.78	1,860
Korea			1.4	0.60	2,370
China			0.6	2.12	330
CPEs	475	2,040	4.3	0.61	6,749
USSR*			4.9	0.62	7,340
GDR*			5.9	0.56	10,234
Czechoslovakia*			4.8	0.55	8,500
Total	5,123	7,810			

TEP/US$1000 refers to 1985.
(Sources: British Petroleum Statistical Review of Energy, World Bank, Report on World Development (1988); Handbook of Economic Co-operation and Development;
Note: OECD = Organization for Economic Co-operation and Development;
LCDs = less-developed countries; CPEs = centrally planned economies.

The realisation that CO_2 has this damaging effect has emerged just at the time when major sections of the worlds population in India and China have achieved growth rates equivalent to 'take off' to advanced industrial status, with the necessary concomitant of greatly increased CO_2 emissions. They have already expressed their opposition to any ideas that would slow their growth and deny their populations the advantages already enjoyed by advanced industrial actions. In these circumstances the media find the topic unpopular, boring and difficult to reconcile with their competitive pre-occupation to reach bigger audiences. They have therefore shelved it.

In order to investigate this problem further we need to look at and understand the bonds between newspapers and their audiences and the kinds of consideration that determine the role that newspapers play in our society.

The press, intelligence and cultures of understanding

The central function of the press is to convey news to the general public. Modern discussions of the press from Lippman to contemporary press barons link this function with the need for an informed public within democracy. Without an informed public it is argued corruption will gain ground, problems will multiply, the public will be alienated and revolution, rebellion or autocracy could result. However the mechanisms through which 'news' is converted into an informed public and results in good decisions, clean government and a healthy democracy are rarely examined. In this section we will discuss two concepts that we feel can be reshaped or defined to assist in understanding this process: intelligence and cultures of understanding.

The notion of intelligence was once closely linked with the press. Early newsletter writers during the Stuart period, for example the writers of the Marprelate tracts, were known as intelligencers. It now seems strange to associate the modern tabloid reporter or paparazzi with the notion of intelligence. Later in 1655 one of the news publications permitted by the Commonwealth was called the *Publick Intelligencer* (Siebert, 1952) However, the concept of intelligence has developed in a number of divergent ways. For example the conveying of secret information, or spying, the complex mental process of understanding and the conveying of public information, tidings or news. This last meaning has largely fallen into disuse[1] but it is possible to appreciate the appropriateness of its use as the title of a newspaper. Information is a necessary ingredient to the development of understanding and therefore to intelligence in its broadest sense. The mistake is to confuse a necessary condition for understanding events and issues with a sufficient condition. Acquiring evidence is part of the process of understanding which then continues through a process of testing and the re-examination of evidence. It is therefore possible to see intelligence as a quality produced by applying a method for developing understanding. An intelligent understanding is one that accords with the evidence, produces the possibility of solutions or a guide to future action and is contingent, that is, dependent on a continuing process. This is essentially the definition of intelligence that we will use in our discussion of the link between the press, intelligence and cultures of understanding.

It is interesting to note that because we have defined intelligent understanding as a process, the quality of intelligence can be applied to collectivities as well as individuals. We will therefore need to distinguish between individual and collective intelligence. This follows simply because collectivities, whether they be governing bodies of public or private corporations, take decisions. It does, however, produce two interesting and important consequences. It has the implication that individuals can be cajoled or forced to act in ways that are seen by them at the time or in retrospect as being unintelligent, by organisations that take decisions that are binding on them. This is

---

1   The last newspaper using *Intelligencer* as its title ceased in 1801 (Oxford Dictionary).

why as individuals we always have an irreducible 'interest' in any organisation to which we belong or subscribe and which can affect our actions or the actions of others that will affect us. Secondly it means that any judgement about an individual's interest or the problem confronting them must take into account the collective interest(s) or contexts in which they act. This contextual aspect of intelligent understanding is best seen in the case of the 'whistle blower' who takes the decision that the broader public interest, at some crucial point, overrides the sectional interest of the organisation of which they are a part. They perform an essential, but often dangerous function, in any democracy. Adams (1984)

The above definition of intelligence is somewhat at odds with another development of its meaning. Intelligence has also been used to convey a quality of mind or faculty. This in turn has led to the development of tests designed to measure it and to the use of these tests within education and occupational selection. We will not be concerned with this usage. Indeed we would prefer to use the term talent to cover these concerns. A talent is an ability, partly learned, partly genetic, to understand and work within established systems of ideas and symbols, for example, academic disciplines, the arts and sport. It can therefore, in some degree, be measured because there are high degrees of agreement within these systems as to what constitutes knowledge or excellence. We would place intelligence, outside of this framework. Indeed it is possible to see this most clearly when highly talented individuals use their talents unintelligently.[2]

It follows from this discussion that intelligence as we have defined it, cannot be measured. This raises the questions, of what use can it be and what purpose is there in associating it with the press (and generally, the media). The first point to make is that while intelligence cannot be measured it is quite properly open to judgement. Secondly, the quality of these judgements within any society will depend in the quality of the relevant information available to people making these judgements and the quality of the cultures of understanding that support public debate. In order to pursue these questions it is necessary to develop our definition further.

We have defined intelligence by identifying a process and by locating intelligent understandings of problems, events and issues within that process. We can go further by pointing out that it is possible to locate the development of intelligence by locating that process wherever it occurs or should occur. We would argue that this is especially important and relevant to newspapers. For example, if a newspaper fails to report or give prominence to news which includes evidence that would seem to challenge a preferred editorial view or which might affect sales, there is direct evidence of a practice that will diminish intelligent understanding and promote a partial or distorted understanding. Something we normally describe as ignorance.

At this stage it is important to remember that full information is a necessary but not sufficient condition for intelligence to develop. Even if full information is available it can be expected that important differences of understanding will emerge and many of these differences will not be capable of solution within

2   It does not follow from this argument that there is no role for intelligence within established disciplines. Intelligence can be applied in any setting and the possession of a talent can greatly assist in the development of intelligence.

existing limits of knowledge. Further differences of understanding will occur because of the different perspectives and cultures of understanding that are established and ongoing within all societies. Individuals come to new events and to emergent problems with very different interests and therefore with very different frameworks for interpreting and evaluating news.

We will use the term 'perspective' to indicate a view from a particular position in society and the term culture to indicate the values, attitudes and in some cases practices that have developed around particular positions in society (Lacey, 1971). We can illustrate these key concepts by describing two contrasting individuals. A person born into a wealthy family will experience directly the advantages of wealth in terms of the material possessions, the education, etc. that wealth can buy, that is he/she will necessarily view events in society from a position of high status and wealth. He/she will therefore have a different perspective from someone born into poverty.

However, within society there are many shared values deriving from common conditions and aspirations and these interact with perspectives in the formation of cultures. It follows that while the person born into a wealthy family will tend to adhere to a set of beliefs and practices that protects and increases their wealth and interprets poverty as the fault of the individual within the context of a state provision of relief that is already adequate and costs too much, it is not inevitable for this to occur. Cultures are more open to individual choice, collective concerns and the operation of intelligence. It is clear that since the 2nd World War the way in which the wealthy have related to and acted towards the poor has changed substantially and part of this change has been cultural change in which the press has played an important part.

Newspapers (and the rest of the media) operate at the level of culture formation. They provide the matrix in which information is provided, the public debate occurs and celebrities are created, take part and sometimes fall from view. It is possible to view this discourse as a simple hustings in which powerful groups promote their own myths and deride the myths of others in order to gain in power and wealth (Bailey 1977). However, it is also possible to see in this debate a process of understanding that constitutes the development of intelligence. Using our definition of intelligence it is possible to make judgements about the quality of debate in any sector of the media. It is important to note that within education, researchers have begun a similar endeavour to analyse and characterise the press' contribution to public debate (MacLure & Pettigrew, 1995; Wallace, 1993). In particular it is possible to explore the extent to which participants in that sector are being sufficiently informed and opened up to a broad understanding, in order that they can develop (if they so choose) an intelligent understanding of what is going on, their own interests and the collective interest. This stance is in line with Giddens' notion of dialogical community but our approach also addresses the issue of agency.

It is at this point that Lippman's pessimistic analysis points to the impossibility of the omnicompetent citizen and the fatal flaw within modern democracy can be re-addressed. If newspapers can be shown to be instrumental in the maintenance and formation of cultures of understanding then at least we have in our hands a lever for improving the quality of debate, the quality of understandings and the intelligence of the proposed solutions to our problems. Much of the remainder of this book will examine the evidence for and against this influence.

Even Lippman recognised the necessity of specialisation within the process of informing the public. His own proposal for a specialist group of social auditors was, in essence, a proposal for one such 'trusted' specialist group. The issue for the general public is not therefore 'how to comprehend all the evidence about all the problems facing society' but in most debates it will be which specialists/celebrity commentators/politicians/spokespersons to trust. As part of this judgement they will need to be capable of interrogating the debate in order to recognise the quality of the arguments based on evidence, their own interest and the broader interest of society. They will need to be able to make a balanced, in some cases, contingent judgement based on their previous experiences of expert opinion and unintended consequences.

It is important to recognise that these are skills that can be taught during formal education and built upon during adulthood by observing and participating in well conducted debates. In addition they are attributes than can become valued and recognisable elements of cultures and sub-cultures. This collective recognition of intelligence as an important set of qualities would both promote their acquisition and make cultures of understanding open to criticism and improvement. In other words there are a number of recognisable mechanisms already developed within society within which it is possible to work towards virtuous spirals of improvement and deeper understanding as opposed to laissez-faire policies of stagnation or even decay and the growth of ignorance.

We will pursue those issues within our investigation of the press. This will involve investigating the quality and quantity of information made available, the emphasis given to its presentation and the openness or directedness with which the information has been presented. However before presenting the results of our investigation we need to look more closely at a central concept in our investigation, cultures of understanding.

Cultures of understanding

In order to derive a working definition of cultures of understanding, we have built upon the tradition of sub-cultural work that emerged in the USA in the 1950s and 1960s and flourished in the UK in the 1970s. We have chosen this tradition because it rests on a relatively simple definitional structure. It also raises the questions as to what constitutes a sub-culture and what conditions are necessary for its formation. In addition, this definitional structure is adaptable to the very different social situation which we are investigating, the diffuse cultures of understanding shared by newspaper readers.

The research tradition to which we refer is exemplified in the work of Merton (1957), Becker *et al* (1961), Cohen (1955) and Homans (1951). The definition on which we will build was developed by Merton in his discussion of the socialisation of medical students.

> ... the process by which people selectively acquire the values and attitudes, interest, skills, and knowledge - in short the culture - current in groups to which they are, or seek to become, a member.

It was Cohen who provided an insight into the general factors that under-pinned the process of formation of a sub-culture while studying 'delinquent boys'. He listed three factors or stages that would be required:

1   The existence of a number of people (usually groups but in our case dis-persed collectivities) with common problems. Usually this problem is structural and intractable, it will not go away. It gives rise to similar expe-riences and a common perspective;

2   The groups (or dispersed collectivities) need a means of communication which enable the problem(s) to be shared and recognised;

3   The emergence of an agreement that the understandings and solutions to the problem that derive from this communication constitute a useful and meaningful response, even if the original problem fails to go away.

Later, Becker (1961) and others made use of these insights in a study of med-ical students. He summarised the progress made in the following way:

> Subcultures develop when a number of people are faced with common problems and interact both intensively and extensively in the effort to find solutions for them. This intensive interaction in an isolated group produces a particularly meaningful and essential array of these under-standings and agreements we call ... culture.

The study by Becker *et al* was carried out within a single institution and involved close observation and much direct discussion with students. He recorded rapid personal change as students took on the personae and values of doctors but his research also made clear the informal interactions that helped sustain the formal progress towards professional status. The process was complex with many contradictory pressures which caused tensions and difficulties.

Homan's work on the other hand is essentially a synthesis of a number of small group studies from factories to street corner groups. He added the essen-tial element of *sentiment* to the process described so far. He noted the feelings of security, satisfaction and attachment that derived from these agreements and structures. This attachment through sentiment makes the individual to some extent dependent on them.

It is possible to see similarities between Homan's notion of sentiment and attachment and Silverstone's more recent application of Winnicott's notion of transitional objects to the media and particularly television (Silverstone 1994). Silverstone links his analysis to a number of social scientists who see society as a defence against anxiety, uncertainty and the threat of chaos. Social analysts following this trail have frequently borrowed heavily from developmental psy-chology to demonstrate that the development of adult independence is in one sense, a transfer or extension of dependence from mother and family to a dependence on community and culture. Society is therefore defended (main-tained) by individuals as a defence against a much deeper, fundamental fear; the fear of chaos and uncertainty.

> The institutions that we have inherited and which still struggle to main-tain; family, household, neighbourhood, community, nation (increas-ingly vulnerable perhaps and increasingly open to challenge as a result

of social and technical change) are those institutions that have historically been the containers of, and provided the resource for, our ability
to sustain that defence.

Silverstone correctly interprets television as being newly integrated into
the process of defence and emerging as both a defence and substitute for the
institutions listed above. We would add that newspapers have been integrated
over a much longer period and they have undoubtedly lost some of their significance. Nevertheless they retain an important role and among the older
generation they still hold a more important role in some respects than
television. (Shaw 1996, 146)

Silverstone's contemporary analysis is important because it demonstrates
the deep origins of the dependence of viewers (and readers) on the media.
When this insight is added to the practical and clarifying definition of cultures
described earlier we have the framework for our research. These early char-
acterisations of culture clarify the rather mystical and mysterious concept that
Silverstone employs and also renders the concrete representations of cultures
and sub-cultures open to some kinds of empirical investigation and evaluation.

We noted that Becker sees the process of sub-culture formation as proceeding within relatively isolated groups through intensive and extensive interaction.
We extend this definition from small groups to large dispersed collectivities by
recognising that small groups and institutional sub-cultures interact with those
larger dispersed cultures that we wish to describe and that are to some extent
contained within them. The relationship between some occupational groups
and newspaper readership illustrates this point. A university lecturer in education seen reading the *Sun*, a Conservative MP seen reading the *Guardian*
(Nicholson, 1996) or a building labourer seen reading *The Times* would provoke
comment and some censure from his/her colleagues[3] and there are constraints
within families, voluntary groups and clubs which are very similar.

We would argue that in addition to the attachment through small groups,
individuals relate directly to the national scene, through macro cultures of
understanding. In order to feel part of this larger entity, individuals need a
flow of information from areas of national life that are outside their direct
experience. National life is therefore in some senses defined by the flow of
information in the media. It legitimately includes fashion, sport, scandal, the
bizarre, the horrific, the amusing as well as news about governments, foreign
wars, the economy and the environment etc. Partaking in this flow of information enables individuals to feel part of the larger community and they can
confirm this in conversations with friends, family and even with strangers.
News, therefore, solves important problems of identity and provides a framework for communication; two elements in the definition of culture. We take
the view that, despite the influence of other media, newspapers retain the ability to interact intensively and extensively with specific audiences and develop
and maintain cultures of understanding within these audiences.

The service that newspapers provide is therefore to render the news available within a cultural idiom that is more than just acceptable to its readers. It

3   These examples are collected from personal experience and Emma Nicholson's recent book.
    Secret Society (1996)

does so in ways that satisfies sentiment by increasing the security and well-being of its customary readers. New events need to be understood and made to fit existing explanations or patterns of belief. The narrative is carefully adjusted so that it is both accessible and acceptable. The account provides evidence to the reader that he/she is part of a central strand of British life with like-minded people situated in a wide range of institutions. This close interactive relationship is mediated by authority figures who appear within the newspaper and by reporters and editors.

Cultures of understanding are therefore seen here as substantial phenomena linked to the identity and security of the readers for whom they form part of the process of defining reality.

Cultures of understanding and the press

In restricting our research to the press, we are open to the criticism that we are neglecting television. Many would argue that television has already grown in influence to the point that it has surpassed newspapers and that we should have directed our research at television. While we acknowledge the current importance of television, and increasingly the Internet, and in addition envisage a future in which the electronic media will continually gain in importance, we do not accept the argument that this invalidates our research.

We chose to study newspapers because the electronic storage of newsprint has made possible, for the first time, the interrogation of millions of articles by computer. Research that at one time took teams of researchers weeks to accomplish can now be done in an afternoon, by a single researcher. We would not have embarked on the study at all if we were not convinced that newspapers retained an important influence within the media. It could be that within the next few decades that this influence will be lost. However, unless we make use of the present window of opportunity to understand how and why it is effective we will not be in a position to meliorate similar conditions for unregulated influence being established in world-wide media networks by powerful media moguls and their empires.

Newspapers differ from television in two important but diminishing respects. Since it is likely that television will change to resemble newspapers in these respects, rather than the reverse. Newspapers are in these respects a precursor of television.

The first important difference is the partisan nature of much newspaper reporting. Most national newspapers are closely tailored to particular interests and major social groupings, while others have no voice. This characteristic is likely to maximise the influence of individual newspapers with their readers. It also means, given the large majority of right wing newspapers, that their collective effect within the media can be very large, when they act in unison.

The second major difference with television is that newspapers exist within an open, weakly regulated, capitalist free market. Television on the other hand is still subject to licensing constraints involving undertakings with respect to quality, balance and education. In fact as we have seen in Chapter 2, the open market for newspapers is restricted by massive constraints in terms of starting-up costs and capital. The free market is interfered with through cross subsidies within media empires and in addition, factors like advertising revenue interfere with the open competition in news and news presentation. Finally the lack of regulation (quality, balance and education) means that competition for sales can displace news presentation as a major reason for buying a newspaper and replace it with games of chance (scratch cards), give-away competitions, purveying sex and other distractions.

While it would appear that the last set of differences might diminish the influence wielded by a newspaper, it is important to remember that we are interested in the extent to which newspapers shape cultures of understanding. If by restricting news and filling their pages with other 'interests', newspapers influence their readers understanding of the world, we would still consider this as an important power to influence readers (Zaller, 1992).

We take the view that the relationship between any section of the media and its audience is extremely complex. The messages and images published in newspapers and broadcast through television and radio are not intrinsically more or less effective in influencing their audience. Meanings are constructed by the members of an audience in a particular context. They are often contested and can sometimes have effects quite contrary to those intended or expected. The study of this process has only just begun to reveal the kinds of factors that are brought to bear in particular contexts. Burgess *et al* (1991), Harrison and Burgess (1994), for example, demonstrate the contested nature of news consumption in a dispute over the development of a local marshland site for a theme park. The detailed analysis of the preceptions of bias, the interpretation and reconstruction of meaning of statements made by major protagonists, make clear the active and complex nature of communication. Our approach is intended to complement this detailed understanding of process and map the broad movements of opinion within readerships and relate them to the output of particular newspapers.

Conclusion

Within this chapter we have brought together three disparate strands of our argument to form a coherent framework in which to investigate press influence. In the first section we argued that the predictive, 'doom and boom' debate, about the future was irrelevant to understanding the context in which future public debates would be held. The key ideas brought forward from this discussion were 'uncertainty' and the ability to remain flexible and alert to new developments on a truly world-wide basis.

In redefining intelligence to mean the ability to apply a method for understanding problems within a world characterised by growing uncertainty, rather than a relatively fixed individual attribute, we put in place the second leg of our tripod.

Finally, by recasting the debate about newspaper influence in terms of cultures of understanding and how newspapers maintain and restructure them in the process of supplying news, we hope to redirect research into press influence and link it to an assessment of the adequacy of the press, in particular with respect to their coverage of environment development issues. In the next chapter, two of those three strands will provide a framework for assessing research carried out on press influence in the USA.

4 Public Opinion and Media Influence in the USA

Introduction

In chapter three we have outlined a set of concepts and ideas that will provide a framework or model for our analysis of the effects of the press on public opinion and the significance of these effects for our democracy and for solving present and future problems. In chapter three we pointed out that the nature of these problems had changed in the decades since the Second World War and the seriousness and multiplicity of challenges threatened the future of our society as we now understand it. The discussion in chapter three makes clear how important an improved intelligence, shared by the majority of citizens, will be in attempting to solve or come to terms with many of these highly intractable problems. It is very likely that substantial changes in culture, technology and styles of life, if not deterioration in some aspects of our present standards, will be necessary. In order that these changes are understood and that these emerging difficulties are not heaped on those sections of society least able to fend for themselves, an open and informed debate will be necessary. The development of trust and the construction of institutions and forums for such a debate will not be an easy matter. At the present time there is no agreement about the part played and the effects of media on the current formation of public cultures of understanding.

In chapters one and two we reviewed the dissatisfaction felt by some social analysts about the structure of the press (media) and the many barriers, and distortions that influence the selection of news that reaches publics in societies served by a so-called free press. However, these analyses are disputed and in particular they do not establish what level of influence the press (media) has in forming public opinion and public understanding. Powerful interests that control large sections of the media are still able to argue that there is no proof within these studies that the media can have a direct and manipulative effect. They argue the free market case that newspapers are judged by their readers (customers) who can exercise choice. If they do not like the way that the newspaper reports the news they can change their newspaper. Newspapers that do not respond to customer demand will go broke. Hence the newspapers that are available at any time are the result of customer choice, they are presenting the news in ways that customers want. To change things would be to court disaster. If unnecessary change were to be indulged in by a single newspaper it would spell commercial failure and if the free market were interfered with it would undermine press freedom and damage the role of the press in ensuring the openness and effectiveness of our democracy.

This is a very compelling argument. For most of this century it has satisfied the major political parties who, when they are in government, are the only organisations in our society (other than the multinationals that own the newspapers) able to bring about change in the press. On occasions when the trend to monopoly control of the press has damaged the free market argument the resulting enquiries have usually expressed concern but done little to remedy things. On occasions since the war when the government has felt threatened by press activity it has usually been through the invasion of privacy. Any move to limit the press in this respect does indeed run the risk of damaging one of its major functions, the uncovering of malpractice in government. The last Conservative Government came very close to legislating on this issue (the 'last chance saloon') but then withdrew from the fight when the press retaliated by uncovering an avalanche of Conservative and ministerial 'sleaze'.

Our approach will be different. We will seek to demonstrate that the academic tradition from Lippman to Herman and Chomsky and Curran and Seaton has been correct in fearing the press' power to influence the public. We argue that the power possessed by the press (media) is to a large extent 'irresponsible' and we argue that the demonstration of this power to influence is the first step in establishing a well informed debate about the future of the press (media) in our society.

In the late 1980s a new method for establishing the power of the media in the formation of public opinion was beginning to emerge. By this time opinion polling organisations, in particular in the USA, had accumulated long runs of opinion polls on a wide range of issues from the role of women and racial attitudes to polls about presidential candidates and current political issues. This stock of evidence enabled researchers to compare changes in public opinion and media output. At first media output needed to be scanned by large teams of researchers but more recently it has been possible to use computer techniques for accessing articles and this has enabled a variety of studies which measure the effects of media output to take place.

In this chapter we will review three studies from the USA by Page and Shapiro (1992), Fan (1988) and Zaller (1992) which come to rather different conclusions about the nature of public opinion. We will start by examining the work of Page and Shapiro. In particular we will focus on the arguments that they put forward within their recent book the 'Rational Public' (1992). Within this book they replace Lippman's somewhat pessimistic view of the American public with a remarkably optimistic vision of collective decision making. It therefore acts as a challenge to the arguments being developed in this book and is in many respects out of line with the other two studies. Nevertheless it is an important study based on the policy preferences of Americans recorded by opinion polls since the 1930s. However, before critically appraising the 'Rational Public' we look briefly at some of their early work in which they establish evidence of press influence.

The rational public and media influence

In the 1980s Page and Shapiro (1984, 1987, 1989) were concerned to advance the debate within political science within the USA about the effects of the mass media on public opinion. They were aware that many of the contradictory results of studies in this field (Chaffee 1975, Kraus & Davis 1976, McGuire 1985) were due to faulty, short-term quasi-experimental designs or due to omitting to take into account the contextual factors relevant to opinion change. They list these as follows, 'the information is (1) actually received, (2) understood, (3) clearly relevant to evaluating policies, (4) discrepant with past beliefs, and (5) credible.'

By bringing together a vast dataset of opinion poll questions since 1935 and by identifying 80 pairs of policy questions that were asked several times, over intervals averaging about 3 months, they are able to design a robust study to investigate press influence. For each of these 80 cases (about half of which recorded significant change) the team coded all news stories from archival news summaries. They also coded the sources of news into 10 categories which ranged from presidents and their administration to unfriendly foreign states and individuals. The news items were coded with regard to their relevance, salience, pro-con direction and the president's popularity. This enormous effort of data accumulation and coding (which alone represented 10,000 hours of work), despite problems of interpreting complex regression equations and random errors inevitably introduced in the coding exercise, yielded important results.

The research had been focussed on the sources of news, not the role of the media in presenting it. It demonstrated that within the American context some sources were generally much more influential than others. The news summaries presented by trusted commentators, experts and popular presidents were associated with measurable positive gains in the acceptance of the views that they put forward. In the case of news commentators these were very large. In the case of some sources, for example interest groups involved in demonstrations, there were negative movements in opinion while others like unpopular presidents had very little impact.

Causal inferences from this research must be drawn with considerable care. There were clear interactive possibilities. For example, popular news commentators might well achieve their influence by reflecting powerful and popular strands of public opinion. Nevertheless the explanatory power of Page and Shapiro's regression equations is such that their work must be seen as demonstrating a clear, probably interactive relationship between news flows and public opinion.

Page and Shapiro's (1992) book, however, develops this important early work in an unexpected direction. Having produced a robust demonstration of a link between the mass media and the formation of public opinion they appear to be deeply concerned with two arguments developed around public opinion polling and the pessimistic implications of their work for democratic theory.

The important and pessimistic argument developed by Lippman had been adopted by political scientists in their interpretation and research into opinion polls and their significance for the American political system. The first element in the argument was to demonstrate that opinion polls could appear stable while disguising a substantial amount of fluctuation and change on the part of individuals. The second element[1] was to demonstrate that poll questions were often asked about issues on which respondents were largely ignorant. The implications of these arguments is that the American public closely resembles Lippman's early description of it, that US democracy is a 'sham' and that it can be manipulated by powerful interests. Page and Shapiro confront these implications with the idea of the 'rational public'.

> The main argument is that the collective policy preferences of the American public are predominantly *rational*, in the sense that they are real – not meaningless, random 'non attitudes'; that they are generally *stable*, seldom changing by large amounts and rarely fluctuating back and forth; that they form a *coherent* and mutually consistent (not self contradictory) patterns, involving meaningful distinctions: that these patterns *make sense* in terms of underlying values and available information; that, when collective policy preferences change, they almost always do so in *understandable* and, indeed, predictable ways, reacting in consistent fashion to international events and social and economic changes as reported by the mass media; and finally, that opinion changes generally constitute *sensible* adjustments to the new conditions and new information that are communicated to the public. (xi)

This must be one of the longest, most complex, definitions in the literature. It does nevertheless sum up the argument presented by Page and Shapiro. It makes sweeping claims which the authors believe they have substantiated using the evidence from opinion polls.

Before we look at the evidence presented by Page and Shapiro we will take up some of the issues that emerge directly from their definition of a rational public. It is clear that they ignore most of the problems and arguments raised by Herman and Chomsky, Curran and Seaton and others. In particular they do not confront the documented evidence of a systematically distorted profile of reporting from war zones although they do admit to it later in the book. However, they do confront Lippman and it is clear that they regard their book as a complete destruction of Lippman's arguments about the weakness and prejudiced nature of American public opinion.

Interestingly enough Page and Shapiro agree with Lippman's hypothesis about the impossibility of the omnicompetent citizen. They also have little difficulty in accommodating the arguments and evidence developed by Converse (1964) that the average American citizen is not only very poorly informed about many of the issues about which he/she is expected to vote but that on most of these issues he/she hardly has a consistent opinion at all. They reproduce evidence which shows that on some important issues less than 40

---

1   There are many others, including of course that the wording of a question on the same topic could alter poll responses with essentially the same meaning by 20 or even 30 per cent. (Bourdieu 1993) We will not be concerned with this particular critique because nearly all the work discussed in their book is based on the repetition of identical questions and the measurement of change. Nevertheless it poses interesting questions about the meaning of some polls (see Bourdieu 1993, Zaller 1995 and others).

per cent of respondents give consistent responses to opinion polls on three occasions over a period of four years. eg public ownership of power and housing (24 per cent) and school desegregation (37 per cent). Hardly issues of little concern. They also accept findings that show that at the 'height of the Reagan administration's Iran contra scandal – when Oliver North and John Poindexter and others had testified extensively in television hearings – the ABC News/Washington Post poll found that barely half of the public knew that the United States was supporting the rebels rather than the government in Nicaragua'. (p11)

In fact this poll represented a high point on the poll sequence which began in 1983 when only 29 per cent of the American public realised that the USA government was supporting the rebels, against the Nicaraguan government. A similar poll revealed that only one third of the public could locate Nicaragua in Central or Latin America.

Page and Shapiro simply sweep aside the arguments that follow from this demonstration of ignorance and inconsistency at the individual level and assert that collective opinion is not to be considered in the same way as individual opinion. While individuals' opinions fluctuate collective opinion can be stable, while individuals are ignorant the collective opinion is rational.

> ...we maintain that public opinion as a *collective* phenomenon is nonetheless stable..., meaningful, and indeed rational in a higher, if somewhat looser, sense ...it is reasonable, based on the best available information... (14)

In a section entitled 'from individual ignorance to collective wisdom' Page and Shapiro point out how, in their view, this transformation comes about. The first point they make is that as soon as opinion is collected from a large group and accumulated, this very process tends to 'cancel out' the distorting effects of random error and eliminates the effects of 'real but effectively random opinion changes by individuals'. They invoke a process which they call 'collective deliberation' which means that the collective is more attentive to new information and arguments than individuals can be.

This process can give rise to a real, stable, informed public opinion because while an individual will fluctuate as he or she receives or misses new bits of information they have a 'true' or long-term preference which could be ascertained by averaging their opinion over a long period. Page and Shapiro argue that in the absence of this means of ascertaining pubic opinion the cross sectional survey of a large enough sample works because the individual fluctuations are cancelled out in the collective response.

The points made by Shapiro and Page are not new. They derive from the theory of sampling. However, they do not enable the authors to claim that as a result of producing a stable result from a fluctuating field of opinion that public opinion is well informed, or rational or anything else. It is merely a representation of collective opinion at a given time – it can be more or less strongly held, more or less polarised, more or less well informed and more or less rational. The stability of measurement does not tell us anything about these other attributes.

The issue of whether public opinion is rational or not must be made on other grounds. The grounds must include at least an assessment of whether the information on which the opinion is based is reliable or not, balanced or biased, relevant or not to the real problems faced by the community and whether or not other more important problems are being neglected or suppressed. By glossing over this issue and totally neglecting the approach of Herman and Chomsky, Page and Shapiro are unable to pass comment on the rationality of public opinion. What they demonstrate instead is that American (USA) public opinion follows the dominant messages produced by the American media which in turn depends heavily on news releases from government and large powerful corporations and other organisations.

An indication of the extent to which Page and Shapiro are prepared to go to deal with this issue is contained in their dismissal of the demonstrated ignorance of American voters.

> Perhaps it was not essential in the 1980s for citizens to keep the confusing situation in El Salvador and Nicaragua straight, so long as they understood that the United States had been trying to overthrow a leftist government south of the border and to defend other governments against leftist insurgencies. (12)

This quotation indicates that Page and Shapiro are aware that the propaganda model is at work in this situation but that they feel it is a 'rational approach'. This seems to us to be an indefensible position.

Much later in the book in a chapter dealing with the education and manipulation of public opinion and after they have made their claims about a rational public, they explicitly face up to this issue. This is illustrated in the following quotations.

> Our findings that media-reported statements and actions strongly affect Americans' policy preferences, and that government officials can influence public opinion by controlling certain international events, raise important questions about democratic theory. (355)

> The stability and coherent patterning of public opinion that we have found, and the public's capacity to react sensibly and responsibly to new information, are of little consequence if that information is regularly deceptive or false. (355)

> The possibility that the public is systematically misled in its policy preferences also threatens the main thrust of our argument about the rationality of public opinion. (355)

It is important to notice at this point that Page and Shapiro insert 'regularly' before deceptive in the second quotation and systematically before misled in the third quotation. This enables them to admit to cases of deception without conceding their argument that the American public is in the main 'rational'.

It is not until page 367 in a book of 398 pages that Page and Shapiro eventually bring together some of the incidents and areas of policy in which the American public have been misled or deceived. In the fifteen pages which Page and Shapiro give to these issues they record in a matter of fact, condensed account major issues and policy areas of enormous importance in which the American public were misled or are habitually misled. They create a hole large enough to bury their theory of 'rationality' completely out of sight.

We can only summarise some of the most prominent deceptions referred to by Page and Shapiro.

They include the missile gap during the late 1950s, the Tonkin Gulf incident off North Vietnam in August 1964 and the Soviet arms scare of the late 1970s. These are listed as successful deceptions designed to mislead the public 'each played a part in a major shift in US foreign policy with far reaching consequences'. The 'missile gap' presented by various conservative journalists and senators, followed by John Kennedy first as presidential candidate then as president, was totally untrue. Evidence exposing the deception was suppressed by Defence Secretary MacNamara until Congress had approved a programme to build one thousand ICBMs. This policy probably led into the Cuban missile crisis. The Tonkin Gulf incident in which two American destroyers were allegedly attacked by North Vietnamese PT boats was the key event in justifying US overt military action in North Vietnam. In one case the attack was provoked by electronic stimulation of North Vietnamese coastal radar to give the impression of an armed attack and in the other case the report emanated from an incorrect report from an inexperienced sonar reader. The second attack never took place and no damage was inflicted in either. The draft of the Tonkin Resolution had been prepared in advance. Finally the 'window of vulnerability' in the late 1970s, like 'the missile gap' and 'the bomber gap' before it, never existed and even after the evidence was available the 'Reagan administration continued to report it's rhetoric of vulnerability long after the revised estimates were widely known'. The public was nevertheless 'misled and probably manipulated' into support for more military spending.

These events are described in detail and linked to changes in public opinion, but Page and Shapiro list or briefly describe many others in which control over events, the information about the events and a strong influence over the media have led to deception and major changes in public opinion. They include in their list events involving Libya, Grenada, Panama, perhaps KAL007, major events in the Cold War, Greece, Korea, China and the Soviet Union. In addition they list covert actions by the CIA that the public did not learn about; the overthrow of Mossadiq in Iran (1953); the overthrow of the leftist, Arbenz of Guatemala (1954), the attempt to overthrow Sukarno of Indonesia (1958), the Bay of Pigs adventure in Cuba (1961), the overthrow of Patrice Lumumba in the Congo, the 1965 military coup in the Dominican Republic and many others in Afghanistan, Ethiopia, Chile, Cambodia, Angola and of course Nicaragua.

In domestic policy the list is shorter but they conclude that 'the government, organised interests, or both are sometimes able to dominate public discourse and provide the public with misleading information over long periods of time'. The evidence in the rest of the book shows clearly that when this occurs public opinion is usually affected. The list includes the structuring of the Social Security Act to discriminate against blacks, the withholding of reports that questioned atomic safety, the support of deregulation and campaigns against social welfare programmes. In addition, Page and Shapiro include concealing covert operations against groups opposed to or unpopular with the government, for example Martin Luther King and other civil rights leaders, the infiltration and disruption of anti war groups, (Nixon) and the harassment of opponents of Central American policies (Reagan). They conclude,

> Many of the instances of misleading information we have discussed, and others as well, seem to fit into consistent patterns. That is, they appear to represent not just isolated incidents of deception by particular individuals or groups, but general tendencies in the whole body of political information that is provided to the American public ... (375)

> We believe that the American public many be regularly exposed to certain kinds of misleading or biased information and interpretations that affect preferences concerning a wide range of foreign and domestic policies. (p376)

The major dimensions of the pattern of deception and bias that are listed by Page and Shapiro, are summarised as the ethnocentric bias, anti Communist bias, a pro-capitalist slant, a minimal government bias, a pro-incumbent and pre-status quo bias and a partisan bias. In other words this analysis which starts by proclaiming a rational public in the USA ends by agreeing with Lippman and Herman and Chomsky that on a whole range of issues that relate to the interest of powerful institutions the press operates in line with the propaganda model. It is difficult for Page and Shapiro to concede this much and then continue to argue for a rational public because a misled and deceived public which has often responded by believing the deception and absorbing the bias can hardly be described as rational. Page and Shapiro therefore go further than the earlier examples of authors who simply demonstrate how the public have been systematically and effectively misled because they demonstrate the accompanying changes in public opinion. However, this presentation of the evidence remains flawed because of the contradictions in the theoretical arguments that they present.

We will therefore continue to look for confirmation that the media is deeply influential in shaping public opinion by examining the work of David Fan. We will then explore the issue of collective rationality within the theoretical framework developed by John Zaller.

Infons, ideodynamics and influence

David Fan's thesis is simple and direct: it is that information controls public opinion. His disciplinary background is in physics and he approaches the subject by using a mathematical model to predict opinion change. In other words he uses units of information (infons) received by the public via Associated Press (AP) dispatches. By coding these items of information relevant to specific issues, for example defence spending, for directionality, salience and quality he attempts to predict changes in public opinion. The resulting graph of opinion change can then be compared with the actual graph as measured by opinion polls.

The modelling procedures are complex and involve a number of simplifying assumptions so that the data can be used in mathematical equations, For instance, while each infon has it's own characteristic content score, most AP infons for any one issue will have similar impact over time characteristics. Fan reckons that most people do not have the time or resources to consider seriously all the questions that related to defence spending. Nevertheless, since 90 per cent of the population usually has opinions on this matter but lack the time to relate them to each other, each infon is assumed to be an independent message. In addition each infon is characterised as having a one day half life. This means the persuasive effect drops to 50 per cent after one day, 25 per cent after the next day and 12.5 per cent after the next and so on.

These kinds of assumptions are necessary for mathematical modelling. In addition the computer scoring of news texts to record infon scores for or against the selected issues required a second set of assumptions, for example the deselection of paragraphs which contained reference to non-American troops, for example Arab, Druse, Christian etc. All of these procedures involve introducing approximation or error into the process and there are times when the possible dimension of error seems to negate the process itself. However, it is important to remember that these errors are unlikely to strengthen any relationship that might exist. They inevitably contain a strong random element and this is likely to weaken the demonstration of similarity between the predicted opinion change and the opinion change measured by opinion polls. In the absence of built in assumptions that are likely to increase this relationship, the test of Fan's hypothesis rests in the examination of the predictive strength of his model; an empirical test or as Fan puts it;

> It is the empirical testability of ideodynamics and it's success in six out
> of six cases which permits the suggestion that this parsimonious model
> is both robust and highly predictive.

Fan chose six issues on which to base his investigation. Five issues were chosen with marked opinion change since this would be the most challenging test for his model and one was chosen for which opinion remained fairly stable. The chosen issues were: the level of defence spending (1977-84); whether more American troops should be sent to Lebanon, following the withdrawal of Israeli troops in 1982; the political popularity of the democratic candidates during the primaries for the democratic presidential candidate (1983-84); whether the economic climate was improving or worsening (1981-84); whether unemployment or inflation was more important (1977-80) and whether or not to favour aid to the contras in Nicaragua (1983-86).

Fan's methodology involved taking an opinion poll on the chosen subject as a starting point and then computing the changes that would subsequently take place by coding and weighting the AP press releases according to their content and direction. In addition the methodology involved making simplifying assumptions, only some of which have been discussed here. The results are striking. All the curves produced by this method of coding press releases show a striking similarity to the path of public opinion measured by a series of opinion polls. The graph of the computer prediction and the poll result for defence spending is reproduced here because there is no other simple way of presenting the results. All of the results were statistically significant at the <0.001 level but it is doubtful whether this assessment is a useful way of assessing significance.

Figure 4.1: Opinions on defence spending from AP dispatches scored to favour more and less defence spending only. Opinion poll points are shown as squares. (Fan 1988, 79)

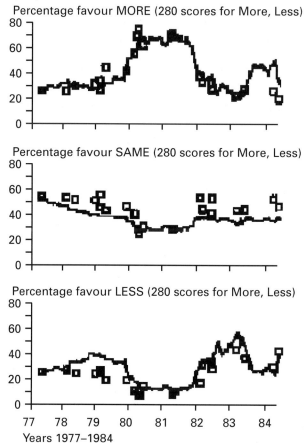

Fan points out that the rise in opinion favouring more defence spending in 1979 was due to the great increase in information favouring this position. The drop in support in 1981 was not due to any drop of articles in support, the change was associated with an increase in 'opposing messages'. Since Fan's model computes change for each group, i.e. favour more spending, favour the same and favour less spending, it is well able to handle all eventualities.

The claim made by Fan is substantial 'that opinion can be computed from an analysis of the content, repetition, and timing of the messages arriving at the population'. Before Fan's work there had been strong claims backed by good evidence that the press was able to set the agenda for public discussion and there were studies reporting strong correlations between opinion change and media messages (Neuman 1987, Noelle-Neuman 1984, Page, Shapiro & Dempsey 1987, Graber 1984). Fan takes this a step further and demonstrates that it is possible to model and *predict* opinion change based on a study of media messages. He therefore shows that the press is able to mould public opinion within agenda items.

His discussion of the significance of his finding is, like most of his book, terse and difficult to assess. However, he sees the public as almost totally dependent on the messages sent to them via the press (media). He portrays the press as a monolithic, trusted conduit for stories which then determine public opinion. Public opinion is therefore passive, changing colour in a chameleon like response to different coloured lights shone on it by the press. He therefore sees the need for competing élites which successfully transmit different sides of a story – thus checking the power of the other élites.

However, even in this competitive situation Fan rather glumly records that 'for its part, public opinion may just reflect the messages sent, whatever they may be'. In other words the élite with the best access to the public and able to saturate the press output with its version of events will control public opinion. There is little room in this view of the formation of public opinion for the notion of a 'rational' public.

There is in our view an important half truth in Fan's position. His design omits the factor of choice. The public is able to exercise some autonomy by choosing its sources of news. However, Fan's research is limited in its ability to support or test the significance of this view. Some of the simplifications in his design, disguise or gloss over issues of considerable importance. In the first case Fan takes a single source, the AP wire service as representing the messages received by all members of the public. This may or may not be a good approximation of the structure of the press in the USA, with a regional or city press highly dependent on the wire service for news, on the issues that he studies. It is not a good model for the UK press with a relatively small number of national newspapers who are likely to have their own correspondents and exhibit quite widely differing house styles, political bias, coverage and readerships. It would not therefore be easy to generalise Fan's model and findings to the UK. In the USA the press is seen as a relatively neutral conduit for élite generated news items but in the UK this assumption will need to be tested.

In the second case, Fan's computer model is not a pure prediction. It uses the poll scores to calculate constants that are then used in the computation of the curves. For example, the 'modified persuasability constant was 0.6 per AP paragraph per day' for the defence spending computation, while the same constant for the democratic primary (in which the options were Mondale, Glenn, others and no opinion) was 1.5 per AP paragraph per day. The fit between the opinion poll and the computed curve is therefore engineered rather than predicted in a strict sense. The concept of persuasability is not seen by Fan as problematic. It is something to be calculated and then applied. This procedure glosses over a vast number of issues that need to be carefully examined and understood if we are to understand the relative influence possessed by élites and the press and on the other hand the opportunities it offers for improving debate and understanding, about the increasing number of issues that threaten our well being.

In our view, these limitations do not detract from the essential achievement. Fan demonstrates the close dependence of the US public on information derived from the press. It is important to note that the very different methods employed by Page and Shapiro and Fan demonstrate a similar relationship. However Page and Shapiro label this finding 'rationality' while Fan sees it (in so far as he theorises at all) as almost total 'dependency'. In our own work we will attempt to explore the nature of this relationship more thoroughly and demonstrate the existence of diffuse and diverse cultures of understanding that provide the opportunity for different rationalities, some dependence and some exercise of autonomy, doubt and independent intelligence.

Before moving to research carried out in the UK and to our own research, we need to examine the work of John Zaller whose work throws considerable light on the nature of the indicators we are using, public opinion polls and the way in which the public makes up its mind about an issue. In other words, the nature of public opinion.

Understanding public opinion: the RAS model

Zaller's work on the 'Nature and Origins of Mass Opinion' covers exactly the area that we wish to examine. It can be characterised by four general statements:

- how people form political preferences
- how news and political arguments diffuse through large populations
- how individuals evaluate this information in the light of their political values and other dispositions
- how they convert their reactions into attitude reports in mass surveys and voting decisions in elections.

Zaller is a political scientist and differs from Fan quite fundamentally in his approach. He is not concerned with the mathematical modelling of the 'intricacies of human information processing'. Instead he builds a model, drawing on psychology and political science which describes the aspects of information processing that have 'reference for understanding the dynamics of public opinion on major issues'.

Zaller is concerned with understanding public opinion as it is measured and used in political debate. He builds into his model the insight from Lippman that citizens vary in their habitual attention to politics and hence their exposure to political information and argument. However, he goes further and argues that people are only able to react critically to the arguments or slants contained in the news that they encounter to the extent that they are knowledgeable about the issues being reported. This is an important insight which he explores in his analysis of data. It clearly modifies Fan's rather deterministic mechanical model and also substantially challenges Page and Shapiro's notion of 'rationality'. In so far as rationality implies judgement then Zaller makes it clear that knowledge is essential if critical judgement (and therefore rationality) is to be part of the process of opinion formation.

In addition, Zaller makes clear that all issues are not equal. People do not typically carry around in their heads fixed attitudes on every issue that an interviewer from a polling organisation happens to ask them about. Issues will differ, some will be well trodden paths with well known parameters and content, others will be vague and hardly considered issues on which opinion is weakly held. Despite these differences the process of expressing an opinion is similar. According to Zaller respondents will construct an opinion statement from ideas and information that are available to them and appear most salient. In the case of new issues or issues for which they have little concern or time to consider, the selection and formation of opinion will be most uncertain in terms of what is salient, what can be drawn upon and how it relates to the issue under consideration. It is clear from the discussion so far that Page and Shapiro's notion of rationality dissolves even further as the process of opinion formation is clarified. Clearly the stability of a set of opinions about an issue could be as a result of wide spread ignorance or wide spread detailed knowledge. These are quite different states of affairs and quite different 'rationalities' with different consequences.

Zaller constructs a model to explain the nature of public opinion and the processes by which it comes about. He does this by constructing four axioms that form the basic structure of his model. He then proceeds to test these axioms against a wide range of evidence. In doing this he introduces new or supplementary functions or 'operational models' which are built from the axioms but contain according to Zaller 'no significant new substantive claims about public opinion'.

In this section we will critically examine the axioms and some of the evidence and elaboration of the models. In particular we will be assessing the part played by the UK press (as opposed to the USA press) in this process of building public opinion and suggesting an amended version of Zaller's operational model for the British situation. The four axioms that constitute Zaller's model are as follows:

> A1 *Reception axiom:* The greater a person's level of cognitive engagement with an issue, the more likely he or she is to be exposed to and comprehend – in a word to receive – political issues concerning that issue.

Zaller stresses that in his view opinion formulation is essentially a cognitive process, that is the acquisition of information and its conversion into opinion statements. In addition he cites evidence that people who score higher on tests of political knowledge are substantially more stable in their attitude reports than others. On the other hand those who are most 'interested' in politics are more likely to vote but not more likely to be stable in their attitudes. This axiom is best understood in relation to A2. The emphasis here is on comprehension and the ability of the individual to understand rather than simply receive.

> A2 *Resistance axiom:* People tend to resist arguments that are inconsistent with their political predispositions, but they do so only to the extent that they possess the contextual information necessary to perceive a relationship between the message and their predispositions.

Zaller sees this axiom as incorporating a great deal of theory and research. In particular it relates to Converse's notion that few people understand how political ideas and events relate to each other. Most people are dependent on 'experts' or 'trusted others' to do this for them. They are therefore dependent on trusted sources (McGuire 1969). In a large number of instances people rely on cues about the source of the message in deciding what to think about it (Petty & Cacioppo 1986). The exceptions occur when their own experience, expertise or interest gives them a basis for independent thought (Axiom A1).

Unfortunately, Zaller argues, this kind of involvement is rare in the USA where 'the stakes are high but people find it hard to stay interested'. He cites a substantial body of research to support this. The example of support for the contras in Nicaragua, used by Zaller, Fan and Page and Shapiro, is taken a step further in one small study cited by Zaller in which the sample was divided into two groups, doves and hawks, by administering a set of questions on how they valued military strength, aggressive posture and opposition to communism. In addition political awareness was measured using a set of simple knowledge testing questions.

Figure 4.2: Comparison between responses to questions about aid to Contra rebels (Zaller, 1993, 25)

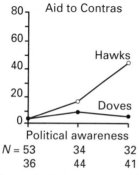
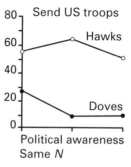

$N = 53$ 34   32
          36   44   41

If you had a say in making up the federal budget, would you like to see spending for aid to the Contras in Nicaragua increased, decreased, or kept about the same?
[Percent favouring increased spending.]

Would you strongly favour, not so strongly favour, or strongly oppose sending US troops to Central America to stop the spread of communism?
['Strongly favour' and 'not so strongly favour' have been collapsed]

The difference in the shape of the two responses is marked. When in the second case a cue, ('stop the spread of communism') is given within the question the difference between all of the groups of doves and hawks increases but the increases are much larger between those where political awareness is relatively low. It confirms the view that political knowledge relevant to the dove/hawk distinction was the necessary ingredient in the first case to enable those with high awareness to make the 'right' choice.

We have stressed Zaller's second axiom because we feel that the part played by knowledge or in our terms 'understanding' is crucial. The fact that the body of research underpinning this aspect of Zaller's discussion is substantial is also of importance. We will be using this aspect of Zaller's model substantially in our own approach.

Zaller's third axiom is probably of least significance for our discussion at least in the form that he expresses it.

A3 *Accessibility Axiom:* 'The more recently a consideration has been called to mind or thought about, the less time it takes to retrieve that consideration or related considerations from memory and bring them to the top of the head for use'.

It is difficult not to agree with the general sense of this axiom. It would appear to be related to Fan's assumption of a 24 hour half life. However, it is important to note that 'related considerations' are often a difficulty for uninformed respondents. It would appear that cues are again relevant here. This aspect of accessibility and memorability are examined in our research reported in Chapter 8, although there the focus is the physical or actual accessibility of news via the readers' chosen newspaper. We will therefore adapt this axiom and change it from one that seems heavily reliant on the psychology of memory to being more dependent on accessibility via a particular newspaper the nature of the report and the memorability of the event.

The final axiom relates directly to the way survey questionnaires elicit public opinion.

A4 *Response Axiom:* 'Individuals answer survey questions by averaging across the considerations that are immediately salient or accessible to them.' (p49)

Zaller almost apologises for the simplicity of this axiom and acknowledges that far more complex psychological models exist with from 4 to 43 stages or postulates. Zaller defends his model by pointing out that opinion polls do not represent 'true attitudes' but are best described as 'opinion statements' that reflect the respondents feelings at the time and the amount of consideration that he/she is prepared to give to the question at that point.

It is important to note that this axiom explains why voting behaviour and/or a second subsequent opinion poll question may well elicit a different response from an individual. It will depend on what considerations he/she brings to bear in the new circumstances. Where the flow of information has remained fairly constant it is highly probable that individual changes will be near to random and the result of the poll will be about the same. (this is Page and Shapiro's rationale for misleadingly using the term 'rational public') However, if the flow of information changes or the nature of the action changes (i.e. voting compared with answering a question) it is likely that the considerations that are salient will also change. It is probable that this will occur in a non random way and give rise to change in outcome.

Zaller summarises his model as the Receive-Accept-Sample or RAS model and we will refer to it in this way in our discussions later in the book.

Conclusion

These three very different approaches to public opinion agree on one important aspect. Public opinion and the messages conveyed by the media are closely associated. The strength and consistency of this empirical finding is impressive. It holds across the three very different approaches to this issue. In addition each study is in its own way robust and based on very large datasets or a wide range of researches (Zaller). To find this relationship so substantially demonstrated in the US literature by researchers with such different research origins and value orientations to the data and evidence is very important.

This, however, is often where agreement ends. We do not intend to draw out in detail the agreements and disagreements of these complex explanatory models. We will focus on the most important that affect our concerns.

The most important single difference is undoubtedly Page and Shapiro's central thesis that despite evidence of the individual fluctuations within polls repeated over relatively small time scales and the frequently demonstrated ignorance of the public on matters of substantial importance, the collective response of the public can be regarded as rational. We have argued that Page and Shapiro's thesis self destructs when the evidence contained with their own book is properly related to it. However, when the work of Fan and Zaller are added to the argument the notion of the 'rational public' disappears without trace. Fan's demonstration of the dependence of public opinion on the frequency and direction of news items on issues of major importance poses the unanswerable question: how can so dependent a public be rational?

Zaller takes the argument further in a theoretical sense by showing that the ignorance of the American public and the superficial judgements made by them in polls (and elections) can be explained by a simple robust model of decision making. A central strand of this model is based on a demonstration that those sections of the public that know most about an issue are the most stable in their opinions; it is the ignorant who fluctuate as they bring the most recently supplied and remembered news items to bear on the problem.

This series of studies raises issues of direct relevance to the concerns that we were addressing under the notion of 'cultures of understanding'. It is clear that instead of simply explaining away ignorance, fluctuating and superficially held opinions and the dependence of public opinion on the media, as rational opinion, it is important to understand more about these phenomena and make judgements about the possibilities of remedial action. It should not escape our notice that Page and Shapiro's argument is very similar to that put forward by powerful press interests in this country. That is, that the public by exercising choice is in control of its own destiny. It is informed as much as it wants to be and any interference would be rejected by the public as interfering with its independence and the rationality of the market.

The evidence and the arguments produced by the three US studies go some way towards damaging the adequacy of this free market model. They certainly demonstrate dependency and widespread ignorance. However, they fail to link individual members of the public or even recognisable groups with their news sources. They therefore treat the media as a relatively undifferenti-ated whole and the public is shown as responding to the messages passed on by a relatively neutral media. This model of the media may or may not fit the USA. It certainly does not fit with the UK press. We will now proceed to look at research in the UK that has focussed on these issues.

5 Evidence for Cultures of Understanding

Introduction

It follows from our discussion of sub-cultures and socialisation theory that cultures exist because they help people to solve problems. One problem that every individual has to solve on a day to day basis is how to interpret the news. Especially in a democracy every individual feels that they need to understand something about the most important domestic and world events that form a context for their lives and may on occasions impinge directly upon them.

Lippman writing in the 1920s pointed out that when communities were small, knowledge relevant to local decision making could circulate freely. As societies have grown larger and become integrated into a global system, the complex task of making news available in forms that interest and engage the majority was in his view almost impossible. The power of relatively small élites to distract the public with news about celebrities and freaks or to dominate the news with a self interested version of events had already given rise to a press structure and public dependency that we can recognise today.

Our discussion of Lippman's concerns about the low level of public interest in important issues and events and the great and growing complexity of these events throws up the problem of the impossibility of a public made up of omnicompetent individuals.

Page and Shapiro attempt to overcome or explain away this difficulty by posing the notion of the 'rational' public. In their view we do not need to concern ourselves with the ignorance or inconsistency of individuals within the public (even if this amounts to a majority) because the public as a whole is rational. However, our examination of Page and Shapiro's arguments reveal that the theoretical justification of this claim is extremely weak and the long list of important occasions and issues over which the US public was misled, places the problem squarely back on the agenda.

Fan shows, in the US context, that the flows of information (using the Associated Press wire service) do determine what the public think. Fan is particularly rigorous in demonstrating that the direction of articles (for or against various issues) determines the direction of public opinion not just the agenda of issues. Zaller goes beyond Fan's research in a broad theoretical sense to show that there are general rules governing how the members of the public form their opinion. In particular his model demonstrates the inappropriateness of the notion of a rational public. The public respond most readily to information that is most recently and memorably available. Only a small proportion of the public have stable and worked out ideas on most issues. The majority trawl back fairly superficially for relevant information. They are therefore highly dependent on the flow of information provided by the media and on the interpretation of trusted public figures.

The picture that emerges is one of a 'dependent' public rather than a 'rational' public. This dependence supports our view that it makes sense within the UK context to explore public opinion as a series of overlapping cultures of understanding each sustained and dependent upon a major national newspaper. Clearly these kinds of cultural entities will be diffuse and changing but they will have at their core an array of beliefs and ways of looking at the world that need to be sustained by interpreting and presenting (or suppressing) world and domestic events in ways that do not disturb their central 'myths'. Using terms developed by Bailey (1977) the job of the newspaper becomes that of defending and maintaining the myths of the culture of understanding of its readers, enticing into readership similarly minded individuals and deriding the myths of opposing groups.

Even within this simplified process of communication the complexity of world affairs and the speed with which events move onto the world stage and need to be understood mean that most individuals will not often have time to explore and work out their own response. They will be dependent on trusted commentators within the media (newspaper) and on trusted public figures who are in turn supported by their chosen newspaper. It follows that if a public is restricted in its choice by factors outside its control (see Chapter 2) and various configurations of belief and ways of looking at the world are no longer supported by a newspaper, for example those supported by the *Daily Herald*, the *News Chronicle* and *Today*, they will weaken and disappear. In so far as there are similar newspapers available, individuals will migrate to them and strengthen similar cultures of understanding but when there are not there will be cross pressure and new alignments which constitute substantial social change.

In other words there is an important argument to consider that the quality and variety of newspapers in any society is a crucial indicator of the health of its democracy. Without a proper representation in the press particular points of view will not be supported, the evidence that sustains them will not be collected or widely reported and the strength and cohesion in the 'unrepresented' cultures of understanding will be slowly dissipated.

There is an important argument to be made that the share of the press supporting the Thatcher election victories and governments of 1979, 1984, 1989 and the Major election victory and government of 1992 played a part in substantially changing the structure of British politics. It could be argued that it required a major realignment of the Labour Party, which was needed to gain some support from a predominantly right wing press, to give the party any chance of an election victory.

The press and political culture

In his recent publication based on the seventh *Guardian* Lecture at Nuffield College, Martin Linton (1995) presents a series of graphs which demonstrate how changes in the spectrum of national newspapers has affected support for the major political parties.

Figure 5.1: Parties' press share in postwar elections (Linton 1995, Table 6.1)

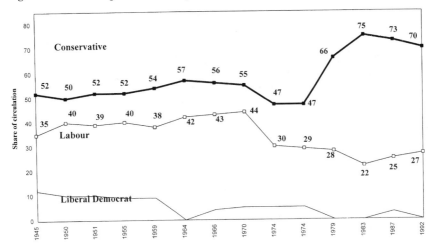

The graph demonstrates two distinct configurations of support in the period since the Second World War. The period between the 1945 and 1974 elections and the period between the 1979 and 1992 elections. The share of the vote obtained by the Labour Party shows a close association with the share of the press supporting the party at elections. This is demonstrated in the following graph.

Figure 5.2: Labour press share/vote share (Linton 1995, Table 6.3)

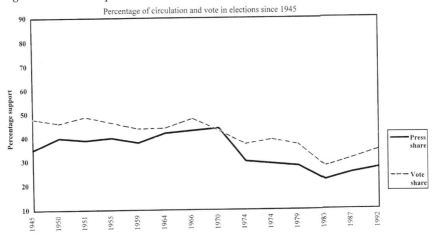

This declining share of the vote was reflected in a series of election defeats as illustrated by the next graph:

Figure 5-3:   *Winners and losers in postwar elections (Linton 1995)*

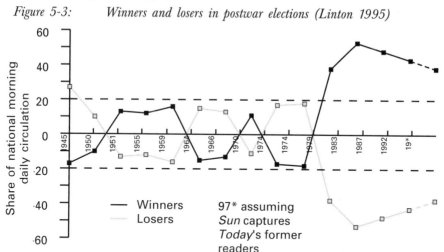

The two horizontal lines drawn on the graph show that up to the 1974 Election the Conservative Party enjoyed an advantage of less than 20 per cent (between 11 and 18 per cent) in press coverage. Since shortly before the 1979 election when the *Sun* declared in favour of the Conservative Party and until the election of 1997, the Conservatives have enjoyed an advantage of between 38 per cent and 53 per cent in press coverage. During this period they did not concede defeat in an election despite periods of deep unpopularity in mid-term. More recently the *Sun* defected to New Labour and other national dailies took a more sympathetic line. The superficial judgement that this change in the level of press support contributed to the defeat of the Conservatives has yet to be tested by detailed analysis.

However, it is most important to note that this interpretation of the power of the press to influence the outcome of elections is strongly contested. Peter Kellner, an experienced journalist who is widely respected for his interpretation of poll data on elections, calls it the 'myth of media potency' and explains its continued existence in terms of the interests it serves (1995). He argues that it gives the losers an alibi and for the proprietors it proves a handy myth in the poker game of politics. It enables them to gain more influence than their weak hand merits.

We will be examining this claim in more detail and the academic work on which he bases his position at the end of this chapter. In the early part of the chapter we will attempt to recast the debate about press influence by examining the evidence and establishing the existence of, cultures of understanding. Using this concept we will reinterpret the evidence for press influence on the way the public voted in the 1992 election. Finally we bring this analysis to bear on the claims made by Peter Kellner. We find that the two positions have more in common than the polarity that the participants claim.

The array of national newspapers that existed in the period 1990–1992 contained a substantial right-wing bias but they served fairly distinct readerships. This is not to say that their spheres of influence did not overlap or that they were not in competition. The newspaper market was in fact characterised by intense competition prior to News International's decision to reduce the price of its newspapers and subsidise them from the growing profits of Sky Television. Nevertheless the first duty of each newspaper was to its existing readers and by looking at their characteristics we can gain an insight to the cultures of understanding sustained by the various newspapers.

Cultures of Understanding

Cultures of understanding do not spring into existence simply because a newspaper publishes news in a particular way. Any newspaper will need to take careful note of the different world views, skills, abilities and perspectives of potential readers and construct their paper to appeal to a definable targeted audience. In addition all cultures are affected by major structural dimensions within society so that social class, gender, region, ethnicity, age, and other similar factors will determine some of the major constraints affecting the way newspapers report the news and reflect society. The following tables illustrate the way the British press is segmented into 3 major groups serving audiences with 3 distinct social class profiles.

Table 5.1: Social class profiles of newspaper readers by newspaper, MORI Omnibus Poll Jan 1990 to Dec 1992 (33 months)

Social	Quality Broadsheets				Middle Market Tabloids			Popular Tabloids					
	GDN	IND	DTL	TMS	DML	EXP	TDY	DMR	Sun	Star	DRD	NONE	TOTAL
Class	%	%	%	%	%	%	%	%	%	%	%	%	%
A + B	46.8	48.6	50.5	52.3	25.5	23.2	18.2	7.7	6.3	4.8	8.0	16.9	19.0
C1 + C2	44.3	44.2	41.9	38.7	58.4	59.0	59.5	54.7	52.4	49.6	50.8	51.6	52.0
D + E	9.0	7.2	7.6	9.0	16.1	18.0	22.3	37.5	41.3	45.6	41.2	31.5	29.0
N=	2878	2758	4182	1596	6589	5302	1962	11098	12488	2705	3448	23190	78196
N%=	3.7	3.5	5.3	2.0	8.4	6.8	2.5	14.2	16.0	3.5	4.4	29.7	100.0

A second way to present this table and which illustrates the distinctive social class distributions of these readerships is to record those four social class groups that constitute over 80 per cent plus of the readership.

Table 5.2: Four social class groups which constitute 80 per cent plus of a newspaper's readership.

GDN	IND	DTL	TMS	DML	EXP	TDY	DMR	Sun	Star	DRD	None
A	A	A	A								
B	B	B	B	B	B	B					
C1	C1	C1	C1	C1	C1	C1	C1	C1	C1	C1	C1
C2	C2	C2	C2	C2	C2	C2	C2	C2	C2	C2	C2
				D	D	D	D	D	D	D	D
							E	E	E	E	E

There are other broad characteristics that distinguish individual groups for example, the *Daily Telegraph* has the oldest age profile of readers the *Daily Mail* is the only newspaper which has regularly more women readers than men and the *Telegraph* has the highest imbalance between the sexes (3:2, M:F). Women are more represented in the tabloid readerships but the largest concentration of women is in the non reader group (55–58 per cent).

These broad characteristics will explain many of the concerns, interests and values of each readership group but it is the detail and distinctiveness of each group that most describes its basic character, the values, knowledge and concerns through which it understands the world, its culture of understanding. This can be examined by analysing the central question of the MORI Omnibus Poll: 'What would you say is the most important issue facing Britain today?' This question evokes a single response but a supplemental question: 'What do you see as other important issues facing Britain today?' captures a wider range of an individual's concerns. These concerns reflect the basic values of each readership and the level of concern produced by the most recent news selection received from the newspaper, and of course other sources.

The Omnibus question is coded into 28 categories of response, including 'don't know' and 'other'. By looking at the different degrees of concern between readership groups we can see on the one hand general differences, which reflect basic values and long term concerns and on the other specific differences which may reflect basic concerns but which can on occasion be put down to newspaper influence. At this point we are examining the broad characteristics of the cultures of understanding of each newspaper, later we will examine changes that occur in these broad general patterns to gauge the degree to which newspapers can influence or manipulate their own readerships and their understanding of the 'news'.

It is important to remember that the issues/concerns discussed here rise and fall. Some like the environmental pollution fell from being mentioned by 30 per cent of those questioned in July 1990 to 5 per cent in December 1991 while unemployment rose from 18 per cent in March 1990 to 44 per cent in August 1991. Other issues like Northern Ireland hardly ever achieved a 5 per cent level of response during the whole of this period. In this chapter we will not be focusing on these changes or the general level of concern, but on the comparative differences in the amounts of concern shown by the various newspaper readerships on each of these issues. We will do this by ranking the levels of interest or concern of the various readerships and by looking at the average ranking over the whole period (1990–92).

The table characterises the cultures of understanding of the eleven national newspapers listed. The method of presentation highlights overall differentiation and does not make clear the more subtle differences within the three grouping. Nevertheless some startling and important differences emerge, which need to be examined in more detail.

The issues/concerns can be grouped into 3 broad categories; issues of most concern to predominantly working class readerships; concerns most relevant to middle class readerships and issue which are 'mixed' on this class dimension. The 3 groups of issues are as follows:

Table 5.3: Table Presenting Issues of Most Concern over the period 1991–92 (Unless otherwise stated the newspaper readership demonstrates the highest or lowest concern for each issue listed against it.)

	Most Concern	Least Concern
Guardian	Education, Housing, Nat. Health Service, Nuclear fuels and weapons, Pollution/ Environment and 'Other' issues suggested.	Least 'Don't Knows', Crime, Inflation and Taxation.
Independent	Northern Ireland (Pollution/Env, second to *Guardian*) (NHS & Education second to *Guardian*)	Least 'Don't Knows', Drug abuse. (Crime and inflation second to *Guardian*).
Daily Telegraph	Common Mkt, Defence, German unification, Northern Ireland, Pound/Exchange rate, Race/race relations and Trade Unions.	Devolution, Housing, Local Gov./Poll tax, Pensions and Unemployed
The Times	Economic Situation (Common Mkt second to *Daily Telegraph*).	Aids, Nuclear Energy/Fuels, Scottish Assembly and Trade Unions.
Today	(Pollution and Environment, highest Tabloid.)	Northern Ireland and Nuclear weapons.
Daily Mail	Crime, (Race/race relations, second to *Daily Telegraph*).	Privatisation.
Express	(Trade Unions, & Pound/ Exchange rate, second to *Daily Telegraph*).	Scottish Assembly
Daily Mirror	Privatisation, Pensions (Nuclear power/fuels, second to *Guardian*). (NHS, third to *Independent*).	Devolution, Scottish Assembly
Sun	Aids, Tax, highest 'Don't Knows'	National Health Service (Economic situation TUs and least 'Other suggestions', second to *Daily Record*).
Star	Inflation, Local gov./ Poll tax (Unemployment second to *D.Record*)	(Pollution/Env, second to *Daily Record*).
Daily Record	Devolution, Drug Abuse, Scottish Assembly, Unemployment.	Common Mkt, Defence, Economic Situation, Education, Pollution/ Environment, Pound/ Exchange Rate, Race relations, TUs and least 'Other' suggestions.

Predominantly Middle Class readership concerns:	Common Market, Defence, Economic situation, Education, German Unification, Pollution and the Environment and 'Other' issues.
Predominantly Working Class readership concerns:	Aids, Drug Abuse, Local Gov./Poll Tax, Pensions, Unemployment and 'don't know'.
Concerns which are 'mixed' with respect to Social Class response:	Crime, Devolution, Inflation, Nuclear Power/Fuels, Pound/Exchange Rate Nuclear Weapons, Race Relations, Scottish Assembly, Privatisation, NHS, Taxation and Trade Unions.

The core of middle class and working class issues are relatively unsurprising. It is well known that foreign news, education and the environment are middle class concerns. Also it is relatively unsurprising that issues which impinged hardest on the working class like drug abuse, poll tax, pensions and unemployment are high concerns with working class readerships. The interesting exceptions appear mostly within the 'mixed' group. Taxation for example is both a class and an ideological issue. The middle class are in general more concerned with taxation as an issue. However, among the middle class group the *Guardian* readership shows the least concern and among the working class group the *Sun* readerships shows the most concern of any newspaper.

Similarly concern about the National Health Service which was running at a high level during this period would seem to be an especial concern of working class people, since they must depend on it with out recourse to private medicine. Nevertheless the newspaper readerships show a marked tendency to split along the political affiliation of the newspaper. The *Guardian, Independent* and *Daily Mirror* readers show a high level of concern about the health service while the *Sun, Star, Daily Record* and *Daily Telegraph* readers show a low concern. It would seem possible that these levels of concern could be influenced by newspaper coverage of NHS matters. Similar evidence of newspaper influence appears with respect to Housing, Nuclear Power/Fuels, Privatisation etc. These distinct elements within the cultures of understanding of readerships would be unlikely to be as constant and distinct as they appear within the data, unless nurtured by appropriately selected or emphasised news flows.

The argument about whether newspapers cause or merely feed these differences is beginning to appear as a false dichotomy. Our argument will be that newspapers feed these differences and by doing so ensure their circulations are maintained. However, by doing so they also have the power to manipulate, exaggerate or minimise differences. This power is not usually capable of producing sudden changes or surges in public opinion unless coupled with unusual events like war, dramatic discoveries or scandals, nevertheless this power to sustain selected cultural items over long periods represents an important power in shaping national cultures, national debates and ultimately the kind of society in which we live.

One strand of these cultures of understanding which must be considered is how adequate newspapers are in providing the knowledge and skills relevant to understanding the major problems that we face. One simple, but on its own inadequate, measure of the quality of these cultures is to examine the 'don't know' and 'other' suggestions in response to the MORI question. A 'don't know' response speaks for itself. It describes the ability of individuals within newspaper readerships to make the first and fundamental decision about what elements of their society are causing them concern. Without the ability to take this first step any citizen is substantially handicapped in making decisions about policies, priorities and any collective action. A 'don't know' to the supplemental question also suggests a limited scope.

The survey is typically organised so that the pollster merely has to code against a pre-defined list of issues. These represent the most frequently occurring issues mentioned by respondents and typically account for over 80 per cent of all responses. Less frequent responses are recorded as 'other' suggestions.

These can be seen as a measure of the richness of a culture of understanding. It reveals that people in this group are able to refer a wider range of issues, outside the common list that emerges from the averagely informed, and stands opposed to the 'don't knows'. We would expect the 'other' suggestions and the 'don't know' rankings to be lists in which the newspapers are ranked in the opposite direction from each other. This expectation is confirmed by the following table in which two per centages are illustrated against the 'don't know' column. These are the mean percentages of 'don't know' responses to the first question and the mean per cent responding 'don't know' to the supplemental. The 'other' suggestions are based on the total of all 'other' suggestions, in response either to the main question or to the supplemental.

Table 5.4: 'Don't Know' and 'Other Suggestions' average ranking Jan 1990 to Dec 1992 (33 months)

	Don't Know	1st Question	2nd Question	Other		
	Avge Rank	Avge %	Avge %		Avge Rank	Avge %
SUN	2.3	6.5	11.7	GDN	2.5	31.0
NONE	3.3	5.3	9.5	IND	2.7	30.2
DRD	3.7	5.6	12.4	DTL	3.3	28.1
STAR	4.1	5.6	11.7	TMS	3.6	28.4
DMR	4.7	4.2	8.6	DML	5.6	23.0
EXP	6.6	3.3	8.4	EXP	6.6	21.7
TDY	6.8	3.2	7.0	NONE	7.2	20.5
DML	7.3	2.8	5.9	TDY	7.5	20.2
DTL	9.1	1.6	4.9	DMR	8.7	18.2
TMS	9.2	1.4	5.2	STAR	9.0	17.5
IND	9.6	1.2	2.6	SUN	9.8	16.7
GDN	9.8	1.2	2.4	DRD	11.1	13.3

It follows that 6.5 per cent of *Sun* readers could or would not indicate a single concern and almost 12 per cent could not think of more than 1. At the other extreme less than 2 per cent of *Guardian* readers were unable to indicate one major concern and only 2.4 per cent could not think of more than one. By contrast the extent to which these readership groups could think of a wider range of issues than the typical list contained in the survey is evident and almost exactly the reverse of the first list.

Another indicator of the quality of cultures of understanding in the broadest sense can be achieved by examining the collection of issues/main concerns listed in Table 5.3. The *Daily Telegraph*'s list holds few surprises. Its readers were most concerned among newspaper readerships about the common market, defence, German unification and Northern Ireland indicating a fairly narrow patriotic culture. The picture appears complete when the Exchange Rate/pound, Race relations and Trade unions are added to the list of major concerns. However, the list of issues for which they demonstrate the lowest relative concern, Devolution, Housing, Local government/poll tax, Pensions and Unemployment seems to indicate a remarkable lack of concern with other peoples' problems, even those within the UK. It is interesting to compare this finding with a recent description of *Daily Telegraph* readers as seen by the editor Charles Moore in an article for the *Guardian*:

> *Telegraph* people love their country, of course, but they are interestingly unpolitical. They want facts and good jobs and things which definably improve the quality of life. ... Our readers are good people but not goody-goody, like some readers I won't name. They don't have a nasty itch to set the world to rights. (*Guardian*, 13/5/96)

Moore's assessment is incredibly accurate. It is not disinterested: 'I have never seriously wanted to work for any papers except the ones which now compose the *Telegraph* group.' His identification with the values it promotes is complete 'I love the *Telegraph* because it has the qualities I most value in friends'. He is also confident about the place its values have in the national picture,

> The character of the *Telegraph*, which is closely related to the better aspects of the British national character, is what has made it the leader of the British quality daily market for more than 50 years.

It would be easy to deride these sentiments or dismiss them as advertising puff. It is also important to make a critical note of how a desire to improve 'the quality of life' expressed by Moore does not extend to other peoples' housing, pensions or unemployment as demonstrated by the MORI data. It would nevertheless be a mistake not to note the sincerity of a true believer, who both serves and shapes the values of over 2 million readers. Part of this equation is the power to influence powerful others. The *Telegraph* reader knows he or she is part of a cultural élite and their views and values matter to people with power.

> Conservative governments take the *Telegraph* seriously, and so, interestingly, does Tony Blair. This sense that the *Telegraph* matters can make one arrogant ...

Moore's recognition of the *Telegraph* as something more than 'merely a paper that people buy', is a recognition that a newspaper plays a crucial role in maintaining a culture of understanding. 'The *Telegraph* is like the *Guardian*, because it is a paper that people love'. It is when a newspaper moves away from this close relationship that it looses both circulation and influence. Moore recognises this and incorporates those paper he sees as successful in this relationship within his own reading. 'At work by 9.30 I look at the other papers; the *Mail*, the *Sun*, the *Guardian* – the papers which best understand their readers; the others not much'.

Establishing the existence of a complementary set of notions among newspaper editors and journalists which relate closely to our concept of cultures of understanding is not difficult. The terminology and mind set of this professional perspective is very different from the understandings that we wish to pursue. Nevertheless the structural dimensions of the concept of cultures of understanding are contained in a number of interviews that we conducted with journalists and in numerous descriptive and analytical publications on the press. The quotations below each contain descriptions of the readership and how they are viewed by experienced professionals in the press:

> *The Times* has quite a strong influence. Certainly what *Times* readers are interested in is the countryside and certainly the prominent display in *The Times* of a contentious planning application, for example , can have a prominent effect on its outcome. And a real effect. And similarly, you have got to realise that different papers have different audiences, *The Times* is basically directed at an audience of policy makers, not entirely obviously, but that's the thrust of its direction … that's what it is trying to be on a daily basis. These are the issues and what should we be thinking about them. My experience is that it can have a very real influence. (Interview March 1992: Mike McCarthy, Environment Correspondent, *The Times*)

> But we have survived and are growing again, despite Murdoch's price war, because there is such a thing as an *Independent* reader. It is dangerously easy to talk rubbish about newspaper readerships. But you, the people responsible for our existence, seem, to us to be sceptical, intelligent, hungry for argument and information, suspicious of conventional wisdom; a wry and insubordinate regiment of modern Britons. So thank you for that: as soon as you become easier to please, this newspaper has lost its purpose. (Andrew Marr, *Independent*, 7/10/96)

> … one of the great virtues of the *Daily Telegraph* is that we do have this attitude that we report bombs, bullets and how many dead, how many people were displaced by this dam, how many people are starving in this rainforest, who was shot yesterday, instead of abstracts, and that is the way that we talk to our readers, who are dismissive of things that are not concrete, because they are busy business men, they are farmers, who deal in specifics, that's the kind of readership we have. A lot of hard headed people who you have to talk to in largely factual terms, and you will get through to in talking in factual terms. (Interview March 1992, Charles Clover, Environment Correspondent, *Daily Telegraph*).

Much of the published work on newspapers and their readerships uses descriptive, historical or linguistic analysis. We are therefore presented with interesting case studies of examples of when particular newspapers were successful or unsuccessful in forging a close dynamic relationship and influencing or not influencing its public.

Matthew Engel (1996) points to Lord Northcliffe's failure to persuade *Daily Mail* readers to change their bread eating habits and eat brown bread; to Lord Rothermere's failure to persuade them to support the Blackshirts and to Lord Beaverbrook's failed campaign for Empire Free Trade in the *Daily Express*. On

the other hand he describes Northcliffe's successful exploitation of xenopho-
bia prior to the first World War, the *Daily Mirror*'s ability under Cudlipp to
express the views of working class people during and after the second World
War with its sales reaching 5.2 million and Murdoch and Lamb's successful
exploitation of sex, irreverence and robust humour within the *Sun* to rest the
initiative from the *Mirror* and overtake the *Mirror*'s sales in 1976. The failures
are explained by Roy Greenslade (1996) as attempts to impose 'barmy ideas'
against the grain of public opinion. Other expressions used to describe this
relationship for example by Jeremy Tunstall (1996) include the *Mirror* 'losing
touch' with younger working class people, the management of the *Star*'s disastrous move into soft pornography, a 'serious lapse of judgement' and the
Sun's management 'did indeed understand their ten million readers'.

Political influence: a special case

Greenslade has no doubt about the *Sun*'s political influence in the 1970's and
80's. He points to the papers own admission immediately after the 1992 general election 'It Was The *Sun* Wot Won It' and refers to Engel's persuasive text.
Unfortunately as we have seen there are just as many examples of commentators denying the effects of the press on its public as there are confirming it. In
fact the *Sun* revised its position the very next day and denied that it had influenced the outcome of the election in any way. Rupert Murdoch had apparently
intervened in no uncertain terms to deny the existence of a power that could
be embarrassing to a newspaper proprietor if the claim was legitimised by its
acceptance by an editorial team. In addition a number of academic studies of
the 1992 election result confirm the relatively slight effect of individual newspapers in the short term. Peter Kellner, writing in the *Sunday Times* uses the
study reported in Labour's Last Chance to argue that 'media power is a handy
myth' and he quotes the result of the study by Curtice and Semetko to conclude: 'There is no evidence in our panel that there was any relationship
between vote-switching during the election campaign and the partisanship of a
voter's newspaper'. This is the most damaging finding in recent years to the
slowly growing academic consensus within the study of British politics that
newspapers make a difference to the way that their readers vote.

Although voting is a rather special case with respect to newspaper influence it is perhaps the most important decision that newspaper readers take as
a result of following long campaigns, transmitted to the public largely via the
media. If newspapers were shown to be ineffective in influencing the public
during this process it would severely damage the credibility of an active role
for newspapers in building cultures of understanding. There is of course the
argument that as television increases in importance, and when a decision (how
to vote) becomes very salient and is debated at great length, the electorate will
be less influenced by press bias, especially if the major contestants in the
debated have equal access to television. Nevertheless at the present time we
would expect that newspapers retain a power, through their expertise in developing and maintaining cultures of understanding to differentially influence
their readerships.

Using this approach we would expect to take a long term view, not just the
period of the election campaign and to look for differential effects of individual

newspapers, not just the effects produced by a group of newspapers. The variation between newspapers is likely to be affected by the skill of the journalists; the closeness of the relationship (strength of culture of understanding) between journalists and readers; the nature of the needs and the nature of the readership. This last point refers to Zaller's finding that well informed readerships are less likely to be swayed on matters that they are already well informed about. Taking this approach we expect to be able to show that for large-scale, well designed studies the academic study of press influence on voting shows a consistent result. During elections in which the conservatives have had the support of the great majority of the press, this has constituted an important but not necessarily decisive electoral advantage.

The early study of the role of the press in influencing voting behaviour Lazarsfeld and Berelson (1944) did not demonstrate a direct effect. Instead they found that the media confirmed people in the opinions which they already held and where change took place it was indirect, through the agency of opinion leaders to sections of the population. However, as Curran and Seaton point out (1991, 256-61), Lazarsfeld and Berelson admit that 58 per cent of the changes in opinion '…were made without any remembered personal contact and were very often dependent upon the mass media.' Following an intensive review of the study by Becker and Combs (1975), Curran and Seaton argue that Lazarsfeld and Berelson's study can be interpreted in a different way to show that the media raised interest, fixed opinions and informed that electorate, This interpretation brings the study in line with other early studies, for example Hovland (1949, 1959), which showed that where social attitudes are deeply entrenched the impact of the media is small but where prior experience has not been significant the media can be very influential. We would also take the view that establishing and maintaining the existence of a particular set of cultural values and in particular political views, with the option of strengthening them at critical moments like elections, constitutes an important social and political power.

Despite a large number of studies and much speculative writing which included the opinion that measuring the influence of newspapers on their readers presented insurmountable methodological problems (Seymour-Ure 1968) academic opinion has remained divided. However in 1969 Butler and Stokes published 'Political Change in Britain', which used a panel study of voters and demonstrated some clear effects that have been confirmed in a large number of studies since (Crewe and Harrop 1983, Miller 1991, Newton 1991, Mughan 1995). These studies demonstrated that voters were more likely to stay loyal to their initial choice of party if they read a newspaper that supported that party. If they switched party they were more likely to switch towards the party that their daily newspaper supported sometimes by ratios of 3:1 and if they started out the campaign as 'don't knows' they were more likely to decide to support the party of their newspaper sometimes by ratios of 2:1.

This gradually accumulating evidence supported a growing body of opinion among academics on the importance of press influence on public opinion. Unfortunately most of these studies were based on small samples because panel studies which retain the same respondents each time the survey is conducted are expensive and it is difficult to ensure that the original respondents are traced and questioned. Miller's sample, for example, which began the study with 3100 respondents shrank to 772 respondents who were interviewed on 3 occasions. This loss of respondents does not necessarily invalidate the studies, it does however limit the analysis that can be done on the effects of individual newspapers and limit the confidence with which one can generalise from the results. Nevertheless these studies represent a substantial body of evidence from within the UK that British newspapers influence public 'opinion' even at times when media coverage reaches an almost saturation point and when television might be expected to free readers from their dependence on newspapers. These conclusions have not gone unchallenged.

Curtice and Semetko's analysis of the 1992 election (1994) seems to contradict this run of research findings and throw doubt on this general conclusion. However, we will argue within this chapter that Curtice and Semetko's conclusion is wrongly interpreted. We will use a subsequent and more extensive analysis carried out by Martin Linton (1995) and our own investigation of opinion poll results prior to the 1992 election to substantiate our reappraisal.

The argument for political influence

Martin Linton was particularly concerned to overcome the limitation of small samples which prevent the analysis of the effects of individual newspapers. In the absence of a single poll with a regular sample of 10,000 he amalgamated the monthly MORI (2000 respondents) and ICM (1500 respondents) polls and calculated the voting swings on a quarterly basis. This gave him the desired quarterly figure for a sample of 10,000. The second important feature of Linton's research is that he begins his analysis in January 1990 and uses quarterly averages for a 5 year period. This detailed and extensive treatment of the voting profiles for individual newspaper readerships reveals that each newspaper has a characteristic profile and that while the major differences occur between newspapers supporting the Labour and Conservative parties some equally surprising differences occur between conservative papers.

Linton's data also includes the polls taken at the time of the election. He is therefore able to calculate trends up to the actual election; to the point of voting. Our own data is restricted to the MORI Omnibus Poll which does not include a poll at the time of the election. The election poll is important to Linton because he is specifically interested in the effects of newspapers on the election outcome. Our purpose is different. We are centrally interested in evaluating the evidence for or against the existence of cultures of understanding. Our focus is therefore on the content of these cultures and the mechanisms by which they are sustained and manipulated. Nevertheless Linton's finding that newspapers do have an effect is an important piece of evidence supporting our arguments.

Linton lists the swings to the Conservative Party over four quite different periods, the swing since the poll tax, the last 3 months of the campaign, the period from the announcement and the swing during the last week of the campaign.

It is the case that selecting four arbitrary periods over which to measure swings produces some consistent results. The first 4 newspapers in columns 1 and 2 are the same although not similarly differentiated but there-after the lists look very different. It is also important to note that an analysis which included groups of conservative newspapers in a single category (see Curtice and Semetko) would combine papers that were sometimes associated with large swings, the *Sun* and the *Daily Mail* with newspapers that were sometimes associated with small swings the *Daily Express* and the *Daily Telegraph*. The best picture is obtained by looking at the changing political affiliation of readers of competing newspapers with similar social class readerships over the whole period.

Table 5-5:   Swings to Conservatives (based on Linton 1995)

1		2		3		4	
Swing to Conservatives since Poll Tax	%	Swing to Conservatives in last 3 months	%	Swing to Conservatives during the campaign from week of announcement to final result (4 weeks)	%	Swing to during last week of the campaign	%
Daily Star	19	Daily Star	8	Daily Mail	14	Independent	12
Sun	16	Sun	8	Daily Express	8	Today	12
Daily Mail	15	Daily Mail	5	Daily Telegraph	8	Daily Mail	10
Today	13	Today	5	Independent	7	Times	9
Independent	12	The Times	5	The Times	5	Daily Star	7
Daily Mirror	9	Guardian	5	Today	5	Sun	5
Guardian	9	Independent	3	Daily Star	3	Guardian	4
Daily Express	8	Daily Telegraph	2	Sun	2	Daily Telegraph	3
The Times	7	Daily Express	0	Daily Mirror	0	Daily Mirror	3
Daily Telegraph	3	Daily Mirror	0	Guardian	0	Daily Express	2

Figure 5-4:   Sun, Star and Mirror (Linton 1995, Table 5.6)

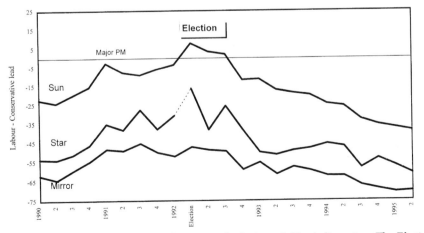

Conservative (+) or Labour (-) lead in voting intention

This graph introduces an additional point on the horizontal (time) dimension. The Election result is included as a point on the same basis as the quarterly results.

The table shows two episodes when the *Mirror* readers responded quite differently from the papers backing the Conservative Party. The first in the point at which Mr Major takes Mrs Thatcher's place as leader of the Conservative Party. The *Sun* and the *Star* record pro conservative swings in their predominately labour readerships of 20+ per cent while the *Mirror* records a movement of about 16 per cent. The second point is the election itself where both conservative papers produce distinct pre-election swings of more than 5 per cent which is not reproduced in the *Mirror* readership. There is of course plenty of evidence in the newspapers themselves of the widely different treatment of these two events. Linton reproduces some of them. In the period immediately before the election the *Sun* released an amazing mixture of accusations, some humorous, some apparently deadly serious; on immigration, the health service, Kinnock and the shadow cabinet and deriding most of Labour's election promises. Typical of those stories would be the poor textile worker who was terrified that a minimum wage would cost her job, the young couple who were convinced that their baby was saved because their local hospital had become a trust, and the list of celebrities and super stars who would immediately leave Britain if a Labour government was elected. The more general accusations included the threat that Labour's immigration policy would open the 'floodgates' cause race riots and allow fascists to be elected to Parliament. Labour would allow 'extreme Left-wing councils to spend money like water', replace our proud democracy 'which has taken 800 years to build' with 'an ever more restructured, centralised, socialist, superstate' and finally introduce soaring taxes, mortgages and inflation. The mix of humour, outrage and apparent fact all attacked Labour in what amounted to a major campaign in favour of the conservative party.

It would be surprising, given the work by Fan and Zaller, if some people reading this newspaper were not affected to some degree by this outpouring. Especially since paler versions of the same stories were being published by most newspapers and were being picked up by television which inevitably reflected 'the spin' given to them by the press and the conservative party. The effect of reading the *Sun* newspaper is therefore best gauged by comparing newspapers like the *Sun* and the *Mirror* comparing and contrasting their coverage of major events and observing the resulting relative effect on their readership.

Linton's analysis is clear in its conclusions. Figure 5.5 plots the differences in the conservative lead between *Sun* and *Mirror* readers and is in his view conclusive. The graph shows that despite a general swing to the conservatives the *Sun* has produced a much bigger movement, amounting to a change in lead of about 15 points.

Linton's study represents a major piece of evidence for the view that the press has a substantial role in influencing public opinion prior to elections and that individual newspapers have different effects. Linton's data-base was constructed from a combination of polls. We now pursue the same issue using the MORI Omnibus Survey.

The MORI Omnibus Survey and press influence

The large differential effects of the kind described by Linton as produced by newspapers are rarely the outcome of a balanced rational argument. They are

Figure 5-5:   *Sun on baseline of Mirror (Linton 1995, Table 5.7)*

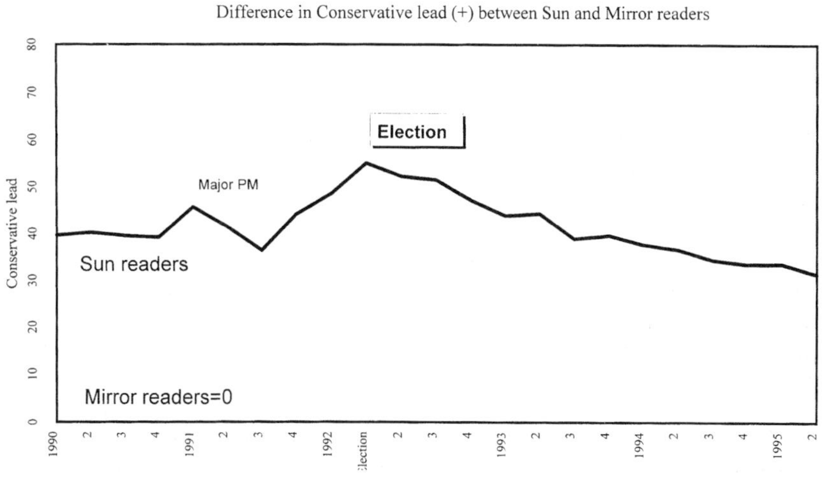

Difference in Conservative lead (+) between Sun and Mirror readers

achieved by a broad attack on a wide range of issues that is both comprehensive, long term and unremitting. In a post election letter to the *Sunday Telegraph*, quoted by Linton, Alastair McAlpine, former Treasurer of the Conservative Party recognised this when he congratulated the people that he saw as the main orchestrators of the conservative election victory.

> The heroes of the campaign were Sir David English, Sir Nicholas Lloyd, Kelvin MacKenzie and the other editors of the grander Tory press. Never in the past elections have they come out so strongly in favour of the Conservatives. Never has the attack on the Labour Party been so comprehensive. They exposed, ridiculed and humiliated the party, doing each day in their pages the job that the politicians failed to do from their bright new platforms. This is how the election was won ... (*Sunday Telegraph*, 12/4/92)

This broad approach of deriding the myths of opponents and building or legitimising the myths of the party supported by the editorial team produces and maintains the characteristics of the cultures of understanding of different newspapers. The period before an election is in many senses an exceptional period. The campaigns mounted during this period will only be successful if they are developments of broad patterns of belief and understanding established over much longer periods of time.

One of the keys to gaining support for a political party is the belief that people hold about the future prosperity and economic stability of the country. All members of a society have access to the same economic statistics and all have their own subjective experience of managing their own household affairs. People differ in their economic circumstances and the economic record of the conservatives has been to cause greater economic differentiation between social classes and the sub class of under or unemployed. However, individuals translate their subjective experiences through a set of beliefs and understandings that are partly sustained and built up through their newspapers.

It follows that newspapers of the political right will attempt to develop confidence in the conservative government by encouraging their readers to believe in an improving economy and a brighter future. In addition they will build up the reputation of Conservative leaders and denigrate Labour leaders. It is important to see how successful they are in creating these views and agreements among their readers. It might be expected that due to the increased economic differentiation produced by a series of conservative measures, the more working class the readership the more difficult it would be to persuade them that economic conditions were improving. The following table illustrates this point.

Table 5.6: Average Rank Order of Newspaper Readership. Highest Rank denotes those readerships most persuaded that economic conditions are improving or that they were satisfied with Thatcher/Major or dissatisfied with Kinnock/Smith (1990–1992).

Economic Conditions Improving		Satisfied with Thatcher/Major		Dissatisfied with Kinnock/Smith	
DTL	1.8	DTL	1.6	DML	2.2
EXP	2.7	EXP	2.0	EXP	2.5
DML	3.0	DML	2.8	DTL	3.2
TMS	3.3	TMS	4.4	TDY	5.4
TDY	5.1	TDY	5.5	SUN	5.6
IND	6.8	SUN	5.6	TMS	5.7
SUN	7.2	NONE	7.2	IND	7.3
NONE	7.5	IND	7.5	NONE	7.4
DRD	9.4	STAR	8.8	DRD	7.8
STAR	9.9	DMR	10.5	GDN	9.5
DMR	10.5	GDN	10.9	STAR	9.8
GDN	10.7	DRD	11.2	DMR	11.7

The two most interesting cases are the *Guardian* and the *Sun* readers. The *Sun* readers are more working class in composition than the Non Readers, yet they are more persuaded that economic conditions are improving. The *Guardian* readers are as middle class as the other broadsheets although they are more likely to be employed in the public sector. They are the most convinced that the economy is not improving.

Clearly the tabloids are more focused on personalities and it is here that we see the strongest effect of newspaper influence. For example, the *Sun* readers express satisfaction with economic conditions at a higher level than would be expected from the economic position. They are ranked 7, above groups with much bigger proportions of affluent readers who have benefitted more from government policies. However, their positions in the 'personality' columns is even more out of line with expectations based on the class position of their readers. The *Sun* readers are ranked 6 in their satisfaction with Thatcher/Major and 5 in their dissatisfaction with Kinnock. During the period between the elections the *Mirror* and the *Sun* worked hard to deride the personalities of their opponents and to support and to build up the strengths of the parties they supported. The differentiation between the *Sun* and the *Mirror* in these three fields represents a measure of their success in influencing their respective readerships. In the interpretation of economic conditions the differentiation is 3.3 ranked places, in satisfaction with Thatcher/Major it increases to 5.3 ranked places and in dissatisfaction with Kinnock it increases again to 6.1 ranked places.

These different patterns of belief and understanding are sustained by fairly consistent streams of selected and interpreted news. They also provide the context within which individuals make up their minds about which party to vote for.

Our analysis of the MORI monthly omnibus opinion poll political data uses a comparative strategy. It takes as a central marker the 30 per cent of poll respondents who tell opinion poll interviewers that they do not read any national newspaper. Despite this lack of direct influence there are at least two ways in which they could be indirectly influenced by newspapers. They might associate with people who do read them and who pass on information or views. They might read local or regional newspapers or journals or watch television programmes that are in part influenced by what the national papers say. Nevertheless they provide us with a large sample of respondents who are not directly influenced by one particular national newspaper. They therefore provide us with a general measure of public opinion against which it is possible to gauge the swings produced by the range of individual national newspapers. Unfortunately Linton does not use non readers in his analysis. We will use a different approach from Linton to produce statistically stable measures of opinion for individual newspapers. We will do this by locating periods of stability and change among the non readers and by combining the results of the monthly polls that fall into each of these periods.

Periods of stability and change

The selection of periods of stability or change inevitably contains an arbitrary element and in addition it is influenced by external events, in particular the general election in April 1992. We have taken a minimum period to be 4 months in order to achieve total analytical samples of around 8000. The selection of periods for analysis is based on the next table of Labour/Conservative leads from the non-reader group. These are based on the Omnibus Poll question: 'How would you vote if there was a General Election tomorrow?'

The total time period is Jan 1990–Dec 1992 and is based on 34 months. No Omnibus Poll was conducted in June and September 1990. In March 1992 the regular Omnibus Poll was replaced by a specially commissioned poll for the *Times* which asked a wider range of political questions in the run-up to the election. Many of the questions are identical to the usual Omnibus Poll including the one above, and so the voting intention figures for March 1992 have been used to complete this table. (Throughout Table 5-7 to Table 5-13 a minus sign means a Labour lead.)

Table 5.7: Monthly Leads Conservative/Labour of the non-reader group Jan 1990–Dec 1992 (34 months)

Period 1: January 1990-November 1990. A stable period with a large Labour lead.

Mean Labour lead 15.3 per cent.
Throughout most of 1990 the Labour lead varied between 11.3 and 20.3 percentage points. In November 1990 Margaret Thatcher was removed from office and replaced by John Major. This produced a considerable swing to the Conservatives who took a small lead in Dec 1990 of 2.5 points. This brought to an end the period of a large consistent Labour lead.

	Period 1 (P1)										
	Jan	Feb	Mar	Apr	May	Jun	Jul	Aug	Sep	Oct	Nov
Con	21.3	20.0	17.6	17.7	20.0	n/a	19.6	20.7	n/a	19.5	20.7
Lab	32.6	35.2	37.9	36.5	37.4	n/a	35.7	33.1	n/a	33.8	32.9
Lead	-11.3	-15.2	-20.3	-18.8	-17.4	n/a	-16.1	-12.4	n/a	-14.3	-12.2
N	354	312	359	340	373		522	356		369	360

Period 2:   December 1990–March 1991. John Major's honeymoon.

Mean Conservative lead 0.96 per cent
During this period the Omnibus Poll records a small Conservative lead or a very small Labour lead (1.3 points). It is not until April 1991 that opinion moves back to supporting Labour in a more substantial and stable way.

Period 3: April 1991-December 1991. A stable period with a small Labour lead

Mean Labour lead 4.9 per cent
During this period the Labour Party is generally in the lead with an advantage ranging with 4 and 8 points. However, in September the lead slips and demonstrates considerable vulnerability.

	Period 2 (P2)				Period 3 (P3)								
	Dec	Jan	Feb	Mar	Apr	May	Jun	Jul	Aug	Sep	Oct	Nov	Dec
Con	32.6	33.1	27.1	27.1	24.2	22.5	24.2	24.4	26.5	26.2	24.9	25.9	24.0
Lab	30.2	30.2	27.4	28.4	28.5	29.1	28.4	29.9	33.8	25.9	31.37	29.88	29.79
Lead	2.5	3.0	-0.3	-1.3	-4.3	-6.7	-4.2	-5.5	-7.3	0.3	-6.5	-4.0	-5.8
N	408	407	364	350	340	356	348	365	371	320	382	543	542

Period 4: January 1992-April 1992. The General Election period.

Mean Labour lead 2.25 per cent[1]
The polls taken during the election period fluctuate between a Conservative and a Labour lead. They include three polls taken during March, for which a mean value is reported in the table.

1   It is important to note that we do not use these poll results to estimate the outcome of the General Election. It would appear that these results overstate the strength of the Labour vote. This does not concern us here, nor does it affect our comparative analysis.

Period 5:   *May 1992-August 1992. Post-Election calm and transition to*
Labour lead.

Mean Labour lead 0.63 per cent
This is the most arbitrary of our analytical periods. It continues the
fluctuating pre-election pattern with two months of Labour lead and two
months of Conservative lead. In fact, if periods 4 and 5 are treated
together the analysis that follows is hardly changed. However, we have
maintained the difference so that period 4 comes closest to resembling
the election period used in the studies by Linton (1995) and Curtice and
Semetko (1994).

Period 6:   *September 1992-December 1992. The re-establishment of a*
Labour lead.

Mean Labour lead 10.6 per cent
In this final period the Labour vote recovers and the Conservative vote
declines to 1990 levels at the end of this period. The cycle is complete.

	Period 4 (P4)					Period 5 (P5)			Period 6 (P6)			
	Jan	Feb	Mar	Apr	May	Jun	Jul	Aug	Sep	Oct	Nov	Dec
Con	28.5	22.7	20.5	32.7	29.3	33.4	26.1	30.1	25.1	22.5	22.7	19.0
Lab	29.3	26.6	24.9	32.4	30.4	27.6	33.6	29.7	32.6	30.0	34.8	34.2
Lead	-0.9	-3.9	-4.5	0.3	-1.1	5.8	-7.5	0.3	-7.5	-7.5	-12.1	-15.2
N	406	345	745	454	420	451	602	350	407	364	400	356

It is clear from our examination of Linton's work that the various newspapers covered the events leading up to the election in radically different ways.
In the analysis that follows we are able to trace the way that the voting intentions of individual newspaper readerships change in the periods up to the
General Elections and afterwards. We look at three groups of newspapers,
popular tabloids, middle-market tabloids, and broadsheet, and for each group
we include the figures for non-readers in attempt to monitor the change that
was being produced by the political debate in all other media outside the influence of a particular national newspaper.

Popular tabloids: *Sun, Daily Mirror* and *Daily Record*

In the following tables, the pattern produced by each newspaper reflects the
general trend described by the non-readers, but there are interesting differences.

Table 5.8: Average leads for designated periods: Sun, Mirror, Daily Record *and*
Non-readers

	P1	P2	P3	P4	P5	P6
None	−15.33	0.96	−4.88	−2.22	−0.63	−10.58
Sun	−16.92	1.65	−5.58	1.83	3.72	−10.28
Mirror	−51.86	−38.15	−38.97	−39.69	−39.29	−49.98
Daily Record	−44.27	−40.12	−34.83	−34.79	−35.80	−45.72

These average figures can be used to calculate change or average swings
for each newspaper audience. This will give us a picture of the differential
effect of reading a particular paper.

Table 5.9: Changes in leads between Conservative and Labour for designated periods Sun, Mirror, Daily Record *and Non-readers*

	P1-P2	P2-P3	P3-P4	P4-P5	P5-P6	P1-P4
None	16.29	−5.84	2.66	1.59	−9.95	13.11
Sun	18.57	−7.23	7.41	1.89	−14.00	18.75
Daily Mirror	13.71	−0.87	−0.72	0.40	−10.69	12.17
Daily Record	4.15	5.29	0.04	−1.01	−9.92	9.48

Note: The small change from Jan 90 to the election period is reported in column P1-P4. The relative increase in Sun readers' reported intention to vote Conservative over the 'none' group readers is therefore 18.75 − 13.11 = 5.64

Sun readers show much bigger changes than either *Daily Mirror* or *Daily Record* readers. They exhibit the largest pro-Conservative swing after Major took over the leadership and despite a large reaction during the period of Labour recovery (P2-P3), record the largest pro-Conservative swing during the election period (P3-P4). Over the period up to the election it would appear that the *Sun* was relatively successful in increasing the intention of its readers to vote Conservative by an average of 5.6 points more than the non-readers (P1-P4). The *Daily Mirror*, on the other hand, was relatively less successful in damping this trend by an average of 1 point. In this respect, the *Daily Record* was more successful with a damping effect of 3.6 points, although this may also reflect the special circumstances of the Scottish context in addition to the newspaper's coverage. We can also see that in the post-election period there is a large scale return back to the pre-election pattern in voting intentions (P5-P6), something that occurs in all readership groups.

The results for these newspapers are therefore in line with expectations. The readers of popular tabloids show a differentiation of voting intentions in line with the direction and vehemence of their election campaigns, in their chosen newspaper.

Middle-market tabloids: Daily Mail, Daily Express, Today

Table 5.10: Average Leads for designated periods: Daily Mail, Express, Today *and Non readers*

	P1	P2	P3	P4	P5	P6
None	−15.33	0.96	−4.88	−2.22	−0.63	−10.58
Daily Mail	26.96	41.39	40.05	42.20	40.12	20.87
Daily Express	27.43	43.24	37.74	40.28	47.22	24.46
Today	−4.04	13.65	7.83	6.74	1.72	0.44

It would appear that the *Daily Mail* was more influential than the *Daily Express* in persuading its readers to change their voting intentions in favour of Conservatives. Both papers were associated with larger swings than occurred among Today readers. Today appears to have had very little influence on its readers as the next table illustrates. Its pro-Tory election campaign did not apparently go down well with its initially pro-Labour readership. Today readers responded enthusiastically to John Major in the Spring of 1991 (17.7 point change in column P1-P2) but then demonstrate considerable disillusionment with repeated swings back to Labour (P2-P3, P3-P4, P4-P5 and P5-P6).

Table 5.11: Changes in leads between Conservative and Labour for designated periods: Daily Mail, Express, Today *and Non readers*

	P1-P2	P2-P3	P3-P4	P4-P5	P5-P6	P1-P4
None	16.29	−5.84	2.66	1.59	−9.95	13.11
Daily Mail	14.43	−1.34	2.15	−2.08	−19.25	15.24
Daily Express	15.81	−5.50	2.54	6.94	−22.76	12.85
Today	17.69	−5.82	−1.09	−5.02	−1.28	10.78

Today's pro-Tory election stance was not therefore influential with its readers who record a pro-Conservative change of 2.3 points less than non-readers (P1-P4) by the time of the election. It will be important to bear this result in mind when we examine the effect of a more recent change in editorial policy of the *Today* newspaper.

Broadsheets: Guardian, Daily Telegraph, Independent

The social class composition of the broadsheet readership samples is so different from the social class composition of the non-readers sample that their readers, who can be expected to be relatively well informed on most of the major issues of the campaign at the beginning of this period would be expected to demonstrate lower swings (Zaller 1995). This turned out to be the case in two instances but in the first column of Table 5.13 (P1-P2) the Independent was a notable exception.

Table 5.12: Average Leads in per cent for designated periods: Guardian, Daily Telegraph, Independent *and Non-readers*

	P1	P2	P3	P4	P5	P6
None	−15.33	0.96	−4.88	−2.22	−0.63	−10.58
Guardian	−51.57	−41.96	−48.44	−45.89	−46.34	−51.14
Daily Telegraph	41.40	53.41	44.89	48.83	47.96	39.31
Independent	−17.49	3.28	−6.95	−8.88	−7.76	−17.63

Table 5.13: Changes in leads between Conservative and Labour for designated periods Guardian, Telegraph *and* Independent *and Non-readers*

	P1-P2	P2-P3	P3-P4	P4-P5	P5-P6	P1-P4
None	16.29	−5.84	2.66	1.59	−9.95	13.11
Guardian	9.61	−6.48	2.55	−0.45	−4.8	5.68
Daily Telegraph	12.01	−8.52	3.94	−0.87	−8.65	7.43
Independent	20.77	−10.23	−1.93	1.12	−9.87	8.61

As expected the *Guardian* readers show the smallest swing to the Conservatives (P1-P4). However, although the *Telegraph* readers respond well to John Major's leadership accession they show a surprisingly high level of disillusionment and do not recover much lost ground during the actual campaign. Independent readers show an unexpected change from the general profile. They were clearly very impressed with John Major and relieved by Thatcher's departure. They demonstrate the largest swing from Labour of any newspaper readership group in the period P1-P2. However, their disillusionment is also considerable and they demonstrate a substantial swing back to

Labour which continues in the pre-election period, the only readership group to do so in this section of the press. Despite this disillusionment they still record the largest pro-Conservative movement among the broadsheets in the total pre-election period (P1-P4). It is important to note that the 8.6 point change is considerably less than the change recorded by non-readers. The overall result therefore conforms to Zaller's model.

The broad pattern of the changes in readership voting intentions presented here confirms Linton's claim that newspapers do influence the way that their readers vote at elections. It also points to an overall advantage for the conservatives at the last election because they were supported by a press that reached 70 per cent of the newspaper reading electorate and because they were able to exert a dominant influence on the media in general. We are not arguing for or against the contention that the conservative press was decisive in winning the election, our data and analysis is not designed to answer that question.

However, there are two other issues of considerable importance that our investigation of the literature and our own data can throw light upon. The first is the effect of a change in editorial policy on the political dimension within a newspaper readership's culture of understanding. The second is the phenomenon of 'moral panic', a term which can be used to describe a situation where newspapers produce a rapid and large collective change in public opinion.

We will examine the effects of editorial change in the recent case of the *Today* newspaper and we will examine the case for describing the movement of public opinion on the issue of taxation in the period before the 1992 election, as a 'moral panic'.

The Case of the *Today* Newspaper

The relationship between the *Today* newspaper and its readers has never been a close, successful, stable relationship. During its nine year existence it struggled to maintain a readership of between 500,000 and 600,000 and had frequent

Figure 5-6:   Today *readers (Linton 1995, Table 5.12)*

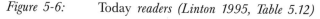
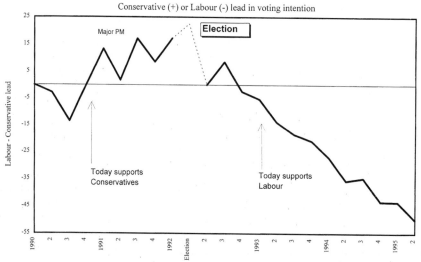

changes of ownership and editor. Nevertheless the changes of policy it underwent have almost certainly had an impact on the concerns and understandings of its readers. Linton's data with respect to its readers political views are quite striking. In the next chapter we will present data which demonstrates a similar relationship with respect to its changing policies of reporting the environment.

Today's readers displayed a pro-Labour lead averaging 4 points during the first 11 months of 1990. John Major's election to leadership of the Conservative Party occurred at approximately the same time as *Today* announced its support for the Conservative Party. The swing to the Conservatives during this period was the second largest of the newspapers in our sample. In the post-election period in 1992 *Today* changed its affiliation and supported Labour. Since this change *Today* has experienced the largest swing to Labour among its readers of any national newspaper.

Table 5-14:   Swing to Labour among national newspapers since the fourth quarter 1992 to second quarter 1995 (Linton 1995)

Today	24%
Independent	20%
Mail	15%
Telegraph	14%
Sun	14%
Times	13%
Star	11%
Express	9%
Guardian	6%
Mirror	6%

Clearly there are many factors at work here, one of which is the general and massive reversal of conservative party fortunes as newspapers that worked hard to ensure a conservative victory have become critical of John Major's leadership. Nevertheless the changes in *Today*'s readership sample are larger than others and they are associated with changes in the papers editorial policy that were greater than all others. The large swings in the *Mail*, *Telegraph* and *Sun* readerships reflect a general disillusionment with the government and specific criticisms of John Major's leadership. Unlike *Today*, however, these newspapers still supported conservatism, albeit a different variety from John Major. As Charles Moore put it:

> The *Daily Telegraph* is Tory. That means when the Conservative government forgets its Toryism trouble starts. There is trouble at present. It's a painful period, though also an interesting one, because we don't want a Labour government, but we cannot pretend we're very joyful about the Conservatives. (*Guardian*, 13/5/96)

It is probable that *Today*'s change of policy not only caught the mood of the time, it provided a service to Labour voters in the mid-market tabloid section of the press that had not been provided since the demise of the *Daily Herald*. The closure of *Today* in November 1995 halted this potential for building a 'left-wing' culture of understanding in this section of the press.

Moral Panics

The phenomenon of moral panics have been written about at some length (see Stuart Hall *et al*, 1978). We will use the term to describe a sudden, large change in public opinion occasioned by the reporting of events in a way that make people newly or freshly aware of something that they have been used to seeing in a less threatening way. It is in effect the sudden increase in salience of a phenomena which becomes newly threatening. In its purist form a moral panic is initiated by a phenomena that is in reality no more or even less threatening than it has been in the past: it is merely seen or believed to have become a greater threat.

When the national press is made up of a wide variety of newspapers expressing a spread of possible explanations and ways of interpreting the news there is the potential for a genuinely exploratory public debate. However, when the great majority of the press act together by highlighting an issue putting forward a single interpretation and suggesting great danger in not adopting a particular course of action, the effect can be a large systematic shift in public opinion. (Fan) There is evidence that the 1992 Election was characterised by one such event, the issue of taxation.

The election arguments ranged between two broad scenarios. Labour put forward arguments about the running down of the public services and a programme of tax adjustments which they claimed would benefit the majority and improve public services. The Conservatives defended their record on the public services and insisted that Labour would massively increase taxation. After John Smith produced a Labour budget on 16 March 1992 the Conservative supporting papers mounted an increasingly high profile attack on Labour's taxation policy. During this campaign they gradually supplanted the original budget estimates with figures derived from Conservative Central Office (Linton 1995). These eventually demonstrated that even the lowly paid would pay hundreds of pounds in extra income tax. Headlines express the vehemence of the attack across the range of right wing papers:

'Labour 'hoax' on tax cuts' (*Sun*, April 6)

'Smith's sting will hit 6 in 10 households' (*Daily Express*, April 6)

'Lamont tots up Labour's incredible shopping list' (*Daily Mail*, March 23)

The effects of this substantial out pouring of articles, reports and editorials on public opinion are picked up in the MORI Omnibus Poll prior to the election. Unfortunately the poll was not carried out in the 2 weeks closest to the election when the taxation issue became even more intense. However, a special General Election Poll was carried out by MORI for *The Times* during March and the first week of April. Of the five polls conducted during this period three included the same question about most important issues as used in the Omnibus polls. Using these three data points we can construct the following graph which illustrates the change in salience of the issue of taxation:

Graph 5.1 shows a remarkable increase in salience during March but returns to pre campaign levels by the end of April, after the election. This general rise needs to be analysed to see to what extent non readers of newspapers were also affected and whether the readers of right wing papers were affected

Graph 5.1: Taxation as a 'most important' issue

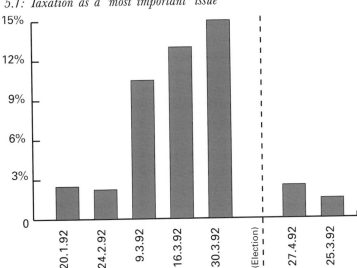

most. For example. the Conservative message on taxation was also covered by television and a substantial bill board campaign so we would expect non-readers to be quite strongly affected. This is illustrated by the next table in which the three polls for March 1992 are averaged and ranked.

Table 5.15: Taxation as a 'most important' issue: analysed by newspaper readership (March 1992)

Times	20.1%
Daily Mail	20.1%
Daily Telegraph	19.3%
Daily Express	15.7%
Star	15.0%
Sun	13.5%
Independent	12.8%
None	11.4%
Today	10.8%
Daily Mirror	9.9%
Guardian	7.5%
Daily Record	7.1%

The differential effect is marked. It is highly likely that these concerns increased during April before the election as an increasing amount of attention was given to taxation by the press. Despite the limited coverage of the data, it is clear that the conservative newspapers that gave greatest emphasis to the tax issue have created a concern over and above the concern expressed by non-readers ranging from 2.0 per cent of readers in the *Sun* to 8.8 per cent of readers in *The Times.* The reverse or dampening effect of the labour newspapers is 1.4 per cent for the *Mirror* to 4.3 per cent for the *Daily Record. Today* is an interesting case. Once again it is ineffective in shaping the views of its readers in its chosen direction; support for conservative myths and deriding labour myths. The *Mirror* is also weak in its relative effect compared with the *Daily Record*, which appears much closer to its readers on a number of issues during this period.

The *Sun* and *Star* are also interesting cases. Their readers are mostly in low paid occupations and were very unlikely to be adversely affected by the Labour Party's tax proposals. It was noticeable that it tackled the problem by utilising general threats which were specifically linked to Kinnock who was pilloried on a massive scale. For example on March 31st the *Sun* published an article under the headline 'It's the Nightmare on Kinnock Street' parodying the cult movie 'Nightmare on Elm Street'. The article described the conservative version of the costs of labour programmes, as if they were uncontested, with predictions of soaring taxes, mortgages and inflation. The examples which they derived from the conservative election literature were especially focused on their readership: 'What breadwinners with two children will pay in EXTRA TAX'. Their list included, a car assembly worker, a nurse, an electrician, and, curiously, a crane driver.

The answers to these kinds of allegations were given prominence in the Labour papers so that on April 7th The *Mirror* published an article under the headline: 'We've no Hidden Taxes, pledges Neil'. The report presents 'confident Neil Kinnock' alongside supportive statements, 'He came out fighting to counter Tory smears that he had a secret agenda of extremist policies backed by massive tax increases' and by quoting 'The Labour Party has never in office applied such policies and will never do so while I am the leader'.

The Labour Party was clearly on the defence over this issue. However, an important dimension in the debate, in addition to the effectiveness of the press coverage in resonating with the cultures of understanding of readers, is the simple number of the various messages being received in the general population. Fan's work indicates that the overall movements of opinion within a large population will be dependent on the number of messages, or infons. Since the conservative messages were being received by potential voters in the ratio of 2.6:1 the effectiveness advantage demonstrated in the table above was multiplied by a factor of 2.6 in relation to its overall effect in the population. In addition it is highly likely that 'effectiveness' and a large imbalance in readership is linked. The general context of the debate being determined by the line taken by the large majority of newspapers.

The tax issue therefore demonstrates some of the characteristics of a 'moral panic'. It arose suddenly and disappeared as suddenly when its usefulness to the dominant group of players had disappeared. It was created by a victory of one myth over another, a highly contested issue over which there could be no resolution. The outcome depended entirely on the skills and weights of the contending players in manipulating the cultures of understanding of their readers. It is not possible to judge the outcome in terms of who was most misled. It is, however, important to note that the understandings created during this debate had to be dealt with in subsequent debates when the conservative government started to increase taxation in the post election period. Newspaper editors of right wing newspapers then had the difficult task of judging how far they could excuse these rises and how far by doing so they risked

3 4 3 4 2 2 3 2 ...

loosing the trust of their readers. The issue became one of the reasons for the Conservative Government loosing the support of some of its press during the mid term period.

The Counter Argument

Despite the argument and evidence presented here some experienced commentators who have looked carefully at similar evidence over a number of years and have concluded that newspapers have very little effect. Part of the answer to this lack of agreement lies in the kind of evidence that was available, before large scale analysis became possible. Both sides could quote examples that aptly illustrated their contention. The second part of the answer lies in the lack of a theoretical framework for the debate and the narrow exclusive circles in which the debate was conducted. Neither side asked deeper questions about the nature of understanding derived from the media or the interplay between its long term and short term effects. Neither side looked more deeply into the issue of cultures, why they exist, what function they perform and how they are created and maintained. When these questions are considered, the old dichotomy between yes they do affect, no they merely reflect, disappears.

Kellner (1995) uses two examples to justify his position: the 1945 campaign launched by Beaverbrook through the *Daily Express*, to vilify the Labour Party and the 1924 campaign by the *Daily Mail* based on the forged Zinoviev letter. In the first case the Labour Party won the election so 'nobody had the gall to suggest that the *Express* lost Labour votes', in the second case Labour lost the election so the blame was put on the *Daily Mail* campaign despite the fact that the Labour vote increased. Using our approach to the question of press influence it is impossible to say whether or not the *Express* or *Mail* campaigns gained votes for the Conservatives. Clearly the first post-war election was held in fairly unusual circumstances. If the *Express* badly misjudged the changing cultures of understanding of its readers it is very likely that the campaign had a minimal effect. On the other hand the campaign could have reduced the scale of Labour's victory and kept in place certain suspicions and doubts that could be built on in the succeeding years. We simply do not know. The data presented in Figure 5-3 shows that the conservative newspapers held a lead of 17 per cent in terms of overall of readership so that although the *Express* was, according to Kellner the largest circulation newspaper, it did not by itself have the power to influence the majority of the electorate or create the feeling that there was a press consensus about the accusations of 'Gestapo' methods raised by the *Express*. Discussion of examples of this kind cannot resolve the issue of press influence.

The second part of Kellner's argument rests heavily on John Curtice and Holli Semetko's article 'Does it matter what the papers say?' Their work was part of larger study of the 1992 election carried out by a team of social scientists, based on the British Election Study (BES). This academic study of elections has been carried out every election since 1964. The 1992 election result surprised most people. Pre-election polls had forecast a Labour victory, in the event the conservatives scored a substantial victory. As we have seen the Conservative press had mounted a high profile and sustained anti Labour campaign which many commentators then blamed on (or praised for) the conservative press for producing a late swing to win the election. The BES casts considerable doubt on this interpretation. The late swing is revealed to be real but small, between 1 and 2 per cent. In addition its absence would not have ensured a Labour victory. On the other hand, without it the conservative majority would have been reduced and this would have probably caused the conservatives to seek an election before the end of their 5 year term. A not insignificant outcome.

Curtice and Semetko's contribution to this study was to analyse the content of a sample of newspapers and relate this to an analysis of the effects of individual newspapers or group of newspapers on the voting intentions of their readers. Their findings are in their own words 'perverse'. They found that between the pre election survey in March/April and the post-election survey conservative tabloids were associated with reduced support among their readers for the Conservative Party (by 3 per cent) and the Labour tabloids were associated with reduced support for the Labour party (by 4 per cent). These results are not statistically significant but in order to understand the uncertain nature of these results we must look at their methodology.

In the period before the election and again immediately after the election they carried out telephone surveys of a sub-sample of the original random sample created for the 1987 election. The history of this sample and the result of shifting to a telephone survey is central to understanding the 'perverseness' of this result.

Table 5.16: Samples used by Curtice and Semetko

1987	Original Random Sample 3,826 (363 refused reinterview)
1991	Telephone Sample 1,631
March 1991	1,323 Interviews were obtained
April 1991	1,203 2nd Interviews were obtained

The panel was therefore reduced to 31 per cent of its original size by the end of the study. The selective effects of drop out and the move to a telephone survey will have removed any realistic claim for the maintenance of a representative sample. It is likely that those people dropped from the sample were over representative of lower social class, people who were less well informed and less certain of their political allegiance. The very people that Zaller indicates are most likely to be influenced by the media. It is difficult to investigate the sample from data given in the text but, based on sales data, it would appear to under-represent *Sun* readers by over 30 per cent. The depletion of the original sample, the small cell size of the table and the evidence that the methodology has systematically depleted the sample of people most sensitive to press influence[2] is sufficient reason for not giving too much weight to this result.

Later in the same article they measure change between the 1987 and 1992 post-election surveys. Here they find some substantial evidence for the longer term effects of newspapers on their readers.

2   An additional drawback of a panel survey relating to election voting patterns is that it necessary excludes all voters who have become eligible since the panel was established i.e. all voters in the age group between 18 and 23 years old. This is also a systematic distortion which it could be argued would militate against finding the effects that were being investigated.

Table 5.17: Newspaper readership and vote change 1987-1992 (from Curtice and Semetko 1994)

Reader Group	Conservative %	Labour %	N
Consistent Conservative tabloid	+2	+4	280
Consistent Labour tabloid	–3	+6	123
Consistent Conservative quality	+6	+4	90
New Conservative tabloid	+9	+5	141
New Labour tabloid	–5	+17	84
Former Conservative tabloid	–4	+7	133
Former Labour tabloid	+3	–5	65
Consistent none/other	–1	+5	523

Note: in order to maintain cell size this table combines the effects of 'successful' and 'unsuccessful' papers in generic groups. This is likely to mask the effects of individual newspapers.

Those readers who read a Labour tabloid throughout this period decreased their level of support for Conservatives by 3 per cent and increased their level of support for Labour by 6 per cent. Those who took up reading a Labour tabloid during this period decreased their support for the Conservatives by 5 per cent and increased the support for Labour by 17 per cent.

While the results displayed in this table are in the main a substantial piece of evidence supporting the notion of cultures of understanding, there are some results which are puzzling. Readers who read Conservative tabloids throughout this periods increased their support for the Conservatives by 2 per cent but also increased their support for Labour by 4 per cent.

Less worrying but still surprising is the result that the consistent readers of Conservative quality papers increased their support for conservatives by 6 per cent and their support for Labour by 4 per cent. These changes must amount to a net increase in the Labour vote among people who read conservative newspapers throughout this period. How is this to be explained?

The explanation stems from a second criticism of Curtice and Semetko's analysis that derives from the simplifying assumptions made in their study. They argue that in order to measure the effects of newspapers on their audiences it is sufficient to select two arbitrary points in time (T1 and T2) and relate the changes that occur in readership behaviour (voting intentions or reported voting behaviour) to the newspapers that they read. This is a powerful and widely used methodology but it is subject to important limitations. There are circumstances in which choosing some time periods for T1 and T2 will give a highly misleading indication of the relationship between newspapers and their readers and the effects of newspapers on their readers. It is our contention that by choosing the election of 1987 as T1 and the election of 1992 as T2 for some of their analysis, they have chosen inappropriate time periods between which to seek for effects. Knowledge relating to the intervening period is essential in order to interpret their results. Let us assume the following scenarios.

The T1 in question is just before or after a general election in which the right wing press has made an exceptional effort to influence as many voters as possible to vote Conservative. Let us suppose that in the period before the election this has been successful and that sufficient voters have changed their mind and voted conservative to ensure victory. This, according to Fan, Zaller and others will have been accomplished by dominating the media with their messages and prevailing on the least well informed and the undecided to vote conservative. After this election the flow of pro-Conservative articles (or infons) is replaced by news about the new government; the honeymoon period. For a short period the voters who changed their minds and brought about a Conservative victory can bask in the glow of satisfaction of having helped to achieve a Conservative victory.

However in the succeeding months this glow disappears and the news of tax increases, job losses, public service cuts and growing personal insecurity reverses the effects of the glossy promises of a secure and prosperous future. This happens despite all the best efforts of right wing papers to explain away the unpalatable items of news and stress the temporary nature of difficulties. In fact during this period some conservative papers may well join the criticism of the government in order to maintain credibility and the trust of their readers i.e. follow the trend of opinion rather than lead it.

If the relative performance of individual newspapers was measured during this period the result could be startling. It would show that readers of some right wing newspaper had changed their minds and in greater numbers than readers of left wing papers (see Table 5-17). This result would not enable anyone to claim that reading a right wing paper caused people to vote Labour. On the contrary it might well be the case that without the dominance of the right-wing paper the Government would have experienced more and massive haemorrhaging of support, leaving them with little chance of re-election.

In the run up to the next election the process is re-enacted: right-wing papers begin the task of undermining public confidence in left wing politicians and policies and they stress the dangers of throwing away the progress that has been made. This process could begin more than a year before the election and be bolstered by a new leader, the jettisoning of unpopular policies and the promise of better things to come. Once again the undecided, the least well informed start to reconsider and change their voting intentions.

If just before or just after the election these intentions are again measured and compared with the result at T1 a number of results is possible. Let us suppose on this occasion they have achieved a spectacular turnaround from the position 12 months previously and once again achieved a conservative victory. However, on this occasion their final high point is not quite as high as it was at T1. In these circumstances, if researchers measure the differences between T1 and T2 and relate them to individual newspapers or categories of newspaper there could be a result in which reading a conservative newspaper was associated with a lesser likelihood of voting Conservative.

This would not mean that this relationship was a casual one. Quite the opposite. It could mean that the changes brought about by the conservative press had once more aided the election of a Conservative Government but that the size of the changes produced had been slightly less on the second occasion.

This scenario is supported by much of the evidence presented in this chapter. We believe that the understanding of the cyclical nature of public opinion;

the understanding of the nature of the relationship between newspapers and their readerships through concepts like cultures of understanding and the availability of alternative and more appropriate data bases,[3] enables us to reinterpret the significance of the Curtice and Semetko data.

It is clear that Kellner is wrong to present this study as 'authoritative' and proceed to make statements like 'so it matters not one jot whether the *Sun* and the *Daily Mail* start saying nice things about the Tories at the next election. That will be far too late' or that their present criticism of the government will contribute 'a smidgen to Labour's lead, but no more'. Curtice and Semetko's article is a carefully constructed piece of research but it is limited by its methodology, and the results should be interpreted with these limitations in mind.

Conclusion

This chapter has reviewed the evidence for the existence of diffuse cultural entities, which we have called cultures of understanding, that are associated with newspaper readerships within the UK. By introducing this concept we hope to have moved the debate about the effectiveness of newspaper in changing public opinion away from the sterile dichotomy which has been the focus of concern far too long. It is not a question of whether newspapers publish what they believe their readers want to hear or whether newspapers lead their readers into beliefs that they would not otherwise hold. In other words shape public opinion. Within the framework of cultures of understanding it becomes clear that newspapers do both and most importantly it is essential to do both if they wish on the one had to continue to survive in a competitive market and on the other to have some influence. This influence generates respect from politicians and activists who see the newspaper as a vehicle for influencing the public and it helps generate and cement a relationship with their readers who see the paper as being able to influence powerful people and to some limited extent represent and speak for them in national and political arenas.

So by saying what they anticipate their readers want to hear they generate a relationship which ensures sales and influence. The question then becomes: How do they influence if they follow rather than lead? We have examined some examples of this influence in this chapter and will be examining one important example in the following chapters. News, as Lippman points out, is a flow of highly simplified accounts of a selection of events through which newspapers represent what is going on in a highly complex and exceedingly complicated world. Even within this highly simplified world of news reports, the number and complexity of events is beyond any one persons capacity to interpret, understand and remember. The selection and interpretation of events is carried out at a number of levels. Herman and Chomsky (1995) demonstrate clearly the importance of the national level when they demon-

---

3   The MORI Omnibus Poll is a monthly quota sample of about 2000. It suffers from not being a random sample and like many opinion polls has been criticised for over-estimating the Labour vote prior to the 1992 election. This failure of quota samples to accurately predict the outcome of an election is disturbing for politicians but it does not impinge heavily on the use that we have made of the poll data. We have focussed on change so that the effects of small systematic errors in the data base are minimised.

strate the overall bias of the US press in selecting interpreting and publishing foreign news stories about 'communists' or 'friendly nations'. A second level, most highly developed within the UK, is the individual national newspaper which can result in the same event being interpreted in a dramatically opposed way by individual newspapers. These fairly typical examples illustrate the divergence during the 1992 election period.

Sun March 17 'Labour Squeeze on the Triers'

> Millions of hardworking Britons trying to get on will be clobbered if Labour wins the election. Middle-income earners like policemen, teachers, nurses and skilled manual workers will all be hit by a massive tax rises unveiled yesterday in the party's "Shadow Budget"...

Mirror March 16 '9 out of 10 better off under Labour'.

> A Tax and Benefits package to make 9 out of 10 Britons better off is to be unveiled today by Shadow Chancellor John Smith. He is confident that the deal will 'trump' pledges made to the low-paid by Tory ministers ...

We are not suggesting that these conflicting reports are immediately believed and internalised by regular readers of these newspapers. On the contrary many readers of the *Express* or the *Mirror* or the *Sun* buy it in spite of its political views and believe that they can made judgement unaffected by its bias. They trust themselves and feel secure in their relationship with the paper as something they know and find amusing, reassuring, stimulating etc. Many in fact succeed in doing this. However, all the evidence now points to a relatively small but important minority who, according to Zaller, will be those who are least knowledgeable and least certain in their political views who will call upon their most recent experiences and the most readily available information when called upon to make a judgement. It is this group who will be most affected by the flow of information, humour and opinion from their newspaper. The picture that emerges is of a natural flux with a fairly large number of people changing their minds from one poll to the next (Worcester, 1995). However, the flow of information from national newspapers ensures a weighted balance of news items in favour of the Conservative Party. From 1990 to the 1992 election period this ensured substantial swings in opinion in favour of the Conservatives.

In this chapter we have presented substantial evidence for the existence of diffuse cultures of understanding within the UK population which are associated with specific newspapers. Some of these cultures are relatively strong and are characterised by having a close relationship with the newspaper that maintains and shapes them. Others are relatively fragile, are subject to loss and characterised by a weak relationship with their readers. For example, Sue Douglas on her recent appointment as Editor of the *Sunday Express* said 'We have an image problem ... I inherited a paper with all the credibility of a flea.' (Greenslade, *Guardian* 12/8/96).

The evidence from the MORI Omnibus Poll strongly supports the argument for the existence of these cultures and the pattern that emerges fits closely with these subjective views of the industry. The notion of cultures of understanding also explains why newspapers are sometimes described as reflecting the views of their readers and sometimes as shaping them. In order to develop trust they need to give expression to the values, world views and valued symbols of their readers. They fulfil the important function of making their readers feel part of a larger grouping, part of an important strand of UK public opinion and culture. In order to exert influence, newspaper build up trust in some public figures and denigrate others, they selectively report and interpret some items of news and suppress others.

We now turn to a new topic in this discussion, environment and development, in order to investigate these processes at work and the extent of their influences on the readers of particular newspapers.

6 Environment and Development Issues:
Press representation and the public response

Press interest in the environment

Our review of research on the effectiveness of the press in shaping public opinion leaves us with a clear balance of evidence in favour of the press having a major influence. It is in the nature of the role of the press that it does not usually exert this influence independently of other major institutions. Items of news are usually generated by other institutions, government, political parties, companies, NGOs foreign governments, celebrities etc. These institutions release news about themselves or events in which they are involved in ways which are highly controlled. The routines of news collection have been revealed as very stable, very institutionalised and in most cases giving very little insight into aspects of an event that powerful or favoured players wish to hide (Fishman 1980; Ericson 1987)

Nevertheless there are occasions when the usual constraints are thrown aside. This can occur for example when an insider leaks details to the press which reveals that the official line of denial is in fact a lie or highly coloured version of the facts. One celebrated case of this kind was, of course, the Watergate exposure which resulted directly in the resignation of President Nixon. There are many other cases from revelations about Charles and Di and in the tabloid press to the Al Fayed saga involving cash for questions and six ministerial resignations (*Guardian* 12 December 1996). These provide us with a reminder that despite the intimate links between government, party and other powerful institutions and the press, the press has an important degree of independence of action.

Quite recently this power has been exercised in its own defence against the Conservative Government. Angered by what it saw as unwarranted intrusion into the private lives of public figures, including the royal family and prominent politicians, the Conservative Government threatened reforms which would curb press powers and expose them to retaliatory legal action. The then Home Secretary, David Mellor made his much quoted remark about the press drinking at the 'last chance saloon' during this period. The subsequent stream of revelations about Conservative MPs and ministers, during the 'back to basics' campaign of the Conservative Government was hardly coincidental. The quiet side-tracking of the movement to reform the press and to protect privacy is an as yet unresearched indication of the extent of press power in its relationship with government and party.

Between these extremes of routine reliance on institutional handouts which reflect institutional truth and the independent exercise of press power through unwelcome revelation and unremitting press campaigning and harassment there are many other areas of news which do not fit into either category. In the remaining chapters we focus on one such area, the environment and development. Within this book we use the concept of development in its broadest sense. In our view it is sensible to include what has been called the economic development of Third World countries with any kind of major development within the old industrial or newly industrialising countries. The reasons for this are straightforward. The development of new roads, or industries or housing has an impact on the environment wherever it occurs. Conversely the major concerns about our deteriorating environment almost always stem from past developments of industrial and agricultural development or urban living. In other words the twin concepts of environment and development encapsulate the interface between our society and its natural environment. It is very difficult in our view to make an argument for separating them. This has not always been the case in the media presentation of the news described by these concepts.

The environment has emerged as an important issue warranting press coverage and in some cases specialist correspondents, in the last two to three decades. The publication of Rachel Carson's book 'Silent Spring' in 1962 has often been cited as the first successful, popular publication which established a link between the use of agricultural pesticides (DDT etc.) and the destruction of animal and plant life. Certainly, early studies of press coverage have mapped the rise of the environment during the late 1960s and early 1970s (Brookes *et al* 1976, Sandbach 1980). However, studies in the UK have been sparse. Within the USA studies (De Weese, 1976, Hornbeck 1974, Minton and Brady 1970, Funkhauser, 1973) show a similar but more dramatic rise in the amount of press coverage of environment issues during 1968 and 1969. Press interest peaked in 1972 at the time of the UN Conference on the Environment. (Stockholm)

Sandbach (1980) reports a falling away of interest in the UK during the mid-1970s but there is little empirical data for the late 1970s and the early 1980s. Hansen (1991) in a careful review of the literature records a decline in the mid 1980s followed by a dramatic increase during the late 1980s and early 90s. It is apparent that the issue of the environment follows the cyclical course of many other major news areas, with major discoveries or new dangers giving rise to high levels of publishing and public concern alternating with periods of low levels of press interest. However, each cycle of press activity introduces new concepts and concerns and new levels of understanding into the public arena. In the late 1980s the issues that dominated the news about the environment were the greenhouse effect and global warming and the destruction of the ozone layer by CFCs but there were also many scare stories about other toxic chemicals.

The environment is therefore a relatively new areas of concern and interest for newspapers. It has completed two cycles of high press coverage but it is currently at a very low level. However, each of these cycles was characterised by different developments and the second cycle changed the nature of the debate almost beyond recognition.

During the first cycle (late 60s and early 70s) environmental issues were first recognised by the press as a major category of news. Brookes *et al* (1976) and Lowe and Morrison (1984) point out that there was a growing tendency to see individual or separate problems, for example, traffic problems or pollution incidents, as part of a single larger problem; the environment. The environment became a broad and definable area of public concern, which was recognisable in the same way that disparate events are recognised as relevant to the 'economy' or 'education'. In addition to this development some analysts have pointed to an unusually rapid assimilation and growth of environmental concerns among media professionals.

Lowe and Morrison (1984) argued that environmental issues possess a number of intrinsic characteristics that recommended them to media professionals. One of these was that they did not lead to accusations of political bias. Environmental issues deployed powerful cultural symbols, for example, the countryside, which they argued embodied strong moral and emotive appeals. These could be pitted against evil, for example, speculators or pollution, in simple conflict situations. Thus they enabled social criticism of industrial society without using established political positions that constrain the reporting of economic or political news items.[1] Lowe and Morrison also point out that many journalists have themselves been campaigners on environmental issues and that newspaper have joined with campaigning organisations to promote awareness of environmental issues. This close alignment of some journalists with environmental issues was aided by the actions of environmental groups who often designed their campaigns so that they appealed to news reporters in their search for news. They therefore saw the media as having an established and structured sympathy to environmental issues that would continue to ensure a favourable coverage.

Hansen's (1990) research lends weight to this analysis. Although his work is specifically concerned with science and the mass media, his findings have relevance to the present discussion. In a study which identified who initiated the contacts between the media and scientists he found that the media initiated over 50 per cent of the contacts, and favoured 'stable sources', that is those receiving a large number of consultations. Hansen argues that his evidence shows that the media is an important site of agenda building and mediation, and his findings underline the importance of Lowe and Morrison's analysis. The sympathetic attitude of some media professionals was an important element in ensuring media coverage of the environment. They possessed both the motivation and the necessary amount of professional autonomy to ensure and sustain press coverage of important environmental issues.

There is little doubt that the first cycle of high levels of press interest in the environment was influenced by the factors described by Lowe and Morrison. It is also true that the first part of the second cycle, beginning in 1988 was deeply influenced by them. By 1990 Alison Love was able to write:

> As we enter the 1990s surely one of the most crucial issues will be the communication of environmental affairs. Television, press and radio

---

1   This relative freedom from established political positions would enable us to study an area of social life as it became transformed by the press to accord with existing political and value positions.

hold an enormous responsibility in ensuring that these issues are com-
municated accurately, clearly and in such a way as to sustain the already
growing mass interest in the quality of the environment. (Love 1990)

Love's research, based on interviews with journalists who covered environmental issues, was carried out between 1988 and 1990 at the height of a new
set of concerns about the environment. Evidence in support of the greenhouse
effect and global warming was being reported in a growing number of articles.
During the summer of 1988 there had been the threat of the toxic waste cargo
carried by the Karin B and a mysterious epidemic in the North Sea had killed
large numbers of seals. Opinion polls reflected the public's concern over these
issues and the *Daily Mail* had run a successful 'Save our Seals' campaign.
Alison Love argues that these events were among those that led Mrs Thatcher
to recognise the popular concern with the environment.

In September 1988 Mrs Thatcher delivered her 'green' speech to the Royal
Society and precipitated a shift in the press's institutional response to environmental issues.

Before Mrs Thatcher's speech most of the serious newspapers had their
own Environmental Correspondents ... Since then virtually all of the
mid-market and popular newspapers have appointed Environmental
Correspondents. (Love 1990)

Mrs Thatcher was soon joined by the Queen, Prince Charles, and other establishment figures in legitimating concern for the environment. As a result a
number of environmental issues moved higher up the agenda of news editors,
making a new ease of entry for environmental issues into the popular press.
Love's analysis made it clear that as new environmental problems were understood and as other key social institutions responded to those problems, the
press, which had played an important part in bringing these problems to
public awareness, underwent internal adjustments that made it more receptive
to environmental issues. This was a very optimistic scenario, a virtuous spiral
only partially clouded by her less favourable analysis of possible future developments.

She anticipated that the lower threshold for the acceptance of stories about
environmental issues was likely to lead to a lower quality of environmental
reporting. In addition, the 'show business' and commercial approach to environmental issues, which was already noticeable in the 1980s, was likely to
become more widespread. Finally, although a political, in-depth analysis of
environmental issues was likely to be favoured by some media professionals,
the Government's plans to deregulate broadcasting were likely to create a context in which funds for serious documentaries became scarce.

Despite the possibility of the undesirable developments which Love
described, the scenario that emerged from the three analyses described above
can be interpreted as substantially optimistic. It can be summarised as follows:
from early days the press possessed a 'built in' autonomy and receptivity with
respect to environmental issues. Its response to environmental problems has
been one of the factors that has led other public institutions to react positively
to environmental challenges. This escalation of concern and sensitivity would
seem to bode well for the future. It implies that the press will report impending

environmental disasters like the failure of rains, crop failure and famine and will be responsible for sustaining 'the already growing mass interest in the quality of the environment' (Love, 1990).

We will argue that this picture is overly optimistic. It is sustained in part by using a narrow definition of environment issues and by creating an artificial separation between environment and development. We take the view that so-called 'environment' and 'development' issues are in fact different aspects of the single complex relationship between human society and the natural environment.

The separation of environment and development issues has had the effect of removing human agency from the problems that seem to stem from the environment and of feeding the myth of 'good' versus 'evil' described by Lowe and Morrison. While environment problems could be held at this level of debate they had in effect a free ride. Unknown or distant causes could be denounced and there was no price to pay. As the debate has matured it has become apparent that the problems are more complex and involve 'us' as well as 'them'. The destruction of the tropical rainforests involves poverty, exploitation, international debt and the demand for tropical hardwoods from Western nations. The problem of global warming involves the vast consumption of fossil fuels by Western nations for heating, transport and manufacture. There are no easy solutions to these problems. However, within the period of the second cycle there was a declared, clear and growing consensus among development NGOs and environment charities that very large transfers of resources of all kinds would be required from the rich nations to the poor nations. Right wing newspapers have sought to prevent this development within the environment debate entering the cultures of understanding of their readers. As Redclift (1987) points out, '... it is necessary to demythologise the view that environmental management is free from political bias. Political conflict is at the very centre of the environment 'problem', at the centre of attempts to devise solutions to it.'

It is therefore apparent that the optimistic view, that the press would continue to give a full coverage to environment issues was erroneous. It was based on research of a restricted period during an upsurge in the press coverage cycle and at a particular stage in the development of the environment debate. As the environment became a more contentious political concern and lost some of its popularity much of the 'autonomy' ascribed to journalists within many newspapers was lost. The responsibility was given to more senior colleagues and the new environment correspondent posts within the tabloid press, described by Love, were abolished. Other issues moved to the foreground of public concern.

In the first part of this chapter we will demonstrate two of our major claims within this analysis. First we will show that there is a common cyclical pattern in news presentation that is shared by all newspapers. It should not be assumed that this cycle represents a 'real' reflection of the state of the environment because it can be the case that important and pressing environmental issues are substantially under-reported at times across all newspapers. Secondly we will demonstrate that despite this common element in news presentation there are substantial and consistent differences in the amount of environment news that reaches the readers of different newspapers. This selection represents the activity of editorial bias. There is the expected differentiation between the quality and tabloid press but there is also a difference within them which at times reflects political motives in the selection of news. We will argue that even at an early stage in the second cycle of press interest in the environment, environmental issues were so packaged by each newspaper as not to challenge or upset the world views and opinions being nurtured by that newspaper.

In the second part of this chapter we will begin our examination of the effects of this pattern of news coverage. Does it produce patterns of understanding and concern within newspaper readerships that are reflected in patterns of news publishing? Or do readers make up their own minds using other flows of information from the media to achieve an independent assessment of the situation? The argument of this book is that there is an interdependence between these two apparent extremes: newspapers are sufficiently geared to their readers' cultures of understanding to make themselves an acceptable and influential source of news. At the same time they are capable of producing tangible and measurable effects on the cultures of understanding of their readers.

Methodology

The method used in this section of the chapter has been made possible by the electronic storage of newspaper text. We have made use of computer searches to count all the articles that contain selected key words. We argue that the frequency with which a newspaper publishes articles containing references to a particular topic is an indication of editorial policy and the importance attached to that topic. There are many issues that impinge on this assumption which could be used to question its validity, ranging from technical questions about the way that searches are carried out to broader questions of meaning and reliability. We have written at length on these issues in a previous publication (Lacey and Longman 1993) and some are dealt with in later chapters by elaborating the computer methodology and by making detailed comparisons. In this chapter we will only address one, the issue of 'noise'. We have raised this issue because it does affect the way that the statistics presented here are viewed. In summary, however, we would point out that we have investigated a large number of potentially damaging objections to this simple methodology and have found that none of them materially affect the results presented here. The essential skill in using this methodology rests in the appropriate choice of key words. Some key words are associated with so many other topics other than the one under investigation (i.e. noise) that they are useless. A good example would be the word 'green'. However, if this keyword is then specified as 'green party' or 'green politics' it becomes a relatively noise free keyword.

The searches were carried out using the *Financial Times* FT Profile Business Information Service. At the time when the research was originally carried out the number of newspaper texts sorted electronically was restricted. The only tabloid thus stored was the *Today* newspaper. Some others had only recently been added to the list so that the time span for their analysis was too short. The list of papers selected for the first stage of the research was therefore, *Guardian, The Times, Daily Telegraph* and *Today*.

The choice of key words is not arbitrary although neither is it extremely precise. We have chosen clusters of key words which recall articles on a wide variety of topics within the areas of the environment and development.

Table 6.1: Keywords used in searches

Group 1: Environment issues	Group 2: Development issues
ecolog*	starv*
greenhouse effect	famine
global warming	hunger
PCB*	maln*
Dieldrin	sudan*

Note: Keywords suffixed with an asterisk are truncated words: all words in the text which begin with the same character string are matched.

'ECOLOG*' (ecology, ecologist etc.) was chosen for the reason that this term has become much more frequent in news articles especially during the 1980s. At the same time it is not a very 'noisy' term and so it is a good general indicator of the coverage of environmental issues (eg habitat, conservation, pollution).

The terms 'GREENHOUSE EFFECT' and 'GLOBAL WARMING' provide a selection of articles dealing with this specific area of concern. Scientific reports (eg IPCC, 1990) have suggested that this environmental issue is a global problem that will affect almost all regions and habitats; potentially the most wide spread and destructive of all environmental hazards that will affect the earth during the 21st century.

'PCB*' (polychlorinated biphenyls) is a much more specific term which refers to a cluster of chemical substances, once thought to be inert and harmless but which are know known to be an extremely dangerous hazard which could also affect human beings. There is very little 'noise' associated with this keyword.

Similarly 'DIELDRIN' is a highly specific key word with little 'noise' and also denotes an extreme environmental hazard, a toxic and persistent chlorinated hydrocarbon more lethal than DDT, used as a pesticide and it also accumulates in food chains. These two quite specific key words represent issues at the centre of the debate concerning the global environment and the quality of food supplies to an increasingly hungry world population.

'FAMINE', 'HUNGER', and 'STARV*' were chosen to investigate coverage of some of the outcomes of environmental disaster. 'FAMINE' has been used as the main indicator both because it lies between the other two key words in frequency and also because it refers to a specific type of event which is linked to politically sensitive issues about the distribution of relief aid and the economic interface between rich and poor nations.

'MALN*' (malnutrition, malnourished etc.) was chosen to search for articles that showed a deeper, more analytical concern with the problems of poorer nations. Malnutrition is a structural, ever present problem in many countries and kills more people than famines. It has been called 'the silent hunger' (Bennett, 1987). A scan of article titles produced by this search shows a concern for the social causes and consequences of persistent under-nourishment and chronic illness. This is a more specialised key word and is much less frequent.

Finally, 'SUDAN' was chosen to provide a specific example of a geographical location where a major famine was recently reported. Although in itself this key word produces a fair amount of 'noise' when it is cross referenced with the other key words in this group very specific data are produced.

The results of the searches

It is important to stress our assumption that the frequency count of articles containing key words is an important indication of the coverage that each newspaper gives to these issues and therefore the degree to which it has informed its readers about these issues. We make no claim at this stage about the content, or quality of coverage which we will analyse later. Nor do we provide any evidence of the emphasis (eg position of article and size of headline) or picture coverage that each newspaper gives to these items.

The data are used in two ways. In the first method the results of the key word searches are compared and contrasted. This can reveal important structural features of press coverage, illustrated for example by Table 6.2 and Table 6.3. The second method involves combining the results of key word searches to produce a set of articles containing two or more key words. This method is illustrated by the analysis of the coverage of the Sudan famine. These examples show how the data can reveal general features of press coverage which taken together with other kinds of evidence (eg. historical events, participant accounts) help to corroborate the view that we have little reason to interpret the press relationship with the environment as consistent with the optimistic scenario described earlier.

In Table 6.2 and Table 6.3 the total article counts for each key word given for the four newspapers. Percentages indicate each newspaper's share of the total number of articles for each key word.

Table 6.2: Total number of articles containing the key words in Group 1 for the period January 1987–April 1991 (4 years 4 months)

	Ecolog*		Greenhouse Effect		Global Warming		PCB*		Dieldrin	
	No	%	No	%	No	%	No	%	No	%
Guardian	1544	45	504	29	436	31	89	34	11	37
Times	965	28	431	25	392	30	80	31	7	23
Daily Telegraph	664	19	524	31	348	25	55	21	10	33
Today	275	8	253	15	144	10	38	15	2	7
Total	3448	100	1712	100	1320	100	262	100	30	100

Table 6.3: Total number of articles containing the key words in Group 2 for the period January 1987–April 1991 (4 years 4 months).

	Starv*		Hunger		Famin*		Maln*		Sudan*	
	No	%	No	%	No	%	No	%	No	%
Guardian	1443	34	1040	39	613	36	184	35	442	31
Times	1170	27	833	31	554	32	182	35	469	33
Daily Telegraph	850	20	498	19	335	20	119	23	414	29
Today	827	19	280	11	212	12	37	7	84	6
Total	4290	100	2651	100	1714	100	522	100	1409	100

Taken together the results in the tables largely support the reasons for choosing the wide range of key words. 'STARV*' produced by far the largest number of articles but was the least differentiated whereas 'MALN*' produced the smallest number of articles in the second grouping and a high degree of differentiation. By contrast 'ECOLOG*' was less 'noisy' but produced a large number of articles, and was highly differentiated.

It is immediately clear that the ranking of the four newspapers is very consistent. In all cases but 'GREENHOUSE EFFECT' and 'SUDAN*' (this key word on its own is not in fact a good indicator) the *Guardian* was consistently the leader in coverage share. *Today* was always the back runner and the *Daily Telegraph* was usually a poor third on key words in the second group. *The Times* was close behind the *Guardian* on most key words and it was interesting that these two newspapers take an equal share of the coverage of malnutrition.

These tables provide additional evidence for one of the findings that emerges from Lowe and Morrison's interviews:

> ...the most significant outlet for all [environmental] groups was nevertheless seen as the national press, with the *Guardian* the most prominent, *The Times* second, and the *Daily Telegraph* third. (1991)

The *Guardian* was clearly devoting proportionately more of its available printing space to articles which contained references to these issues. The tables indicate that despite the varied nature of the key words there was a highly stable ranking in the amount of coverage that these newspapers gave to these issues.

Represented graphically the monthly article counts produce an interesting picture. The time series graphs that follow reveal distinctive patterns in the movement and structure of environmental coverage. First, our general indicator ECOLOG* is represented in two graphs below. The *Guardian* and *Today* are selected to illustrate the two extreme cases.

Graph 6.1: Article count for ECOLOG* (January 1987–April 1991)

Graph 6.1a: Guardian

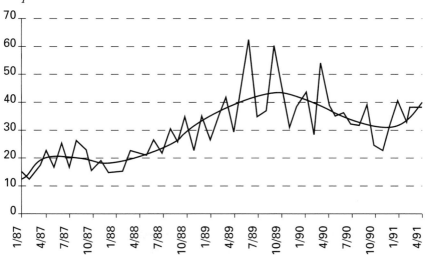

Graph 6.1b: Today

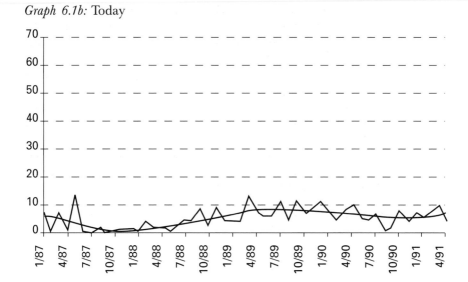

The *Guardian* profile demonstrates three distinct phases in the number of articles published per month:

1 January 1987–May 1988: This seventeen month period shows a relatively stable number of articles appearing each month.

2 May 1988–June 1989: During this year there was a sharp increase in the number of articles published per month from around 20 to a peak of 62.

3 June 1989–April 1991: In this 22 month period there is a gradual decline from the peak to less than 40 articles per month.

The other broadsheet daily newspapers all show a similarly shaped curve with a period of relative stability followed by an increase and a decline. The peaks are not so pronounced and the decline is not so steep. However, all three newspapers demonstrate a peaking of interest between mid-1980 and mid-1990 and a subsequent decline and a slight indication of an upturn in the number of articles mentioning ecology and related topics. *Today*, the only tabloid, rarely publishes ten articles per month which contain this key word. The whole period from June 1987 to May 1988 is marked by only 15 articles in all (1.25 articles/month) but then the norm returns to between 5 and 10.

These graphs illustrate very clearly the undulating nature of news coverage. Moreover, in this example the peaks and troughs in the coverage of the four selected newspapers roughly correspond. The graphs are consistent with the notion of the 'issue attention cycle' proposed by Anthony Downs (1972). He describes five stages: the pre-problem stage; alarmed discovery and euphoric enthusiasm; realising the cost of significant progress; gradual decline of intense public interest; and the post-problem stage. However, his analysis attempts to show that the cycle results almost entirely from public interest and that it is the '…American public that manages the news…'

In this chapter we argue that while there is evidence of a cyclical element in news coverage with peaks and troughs, the full analysis of the reasons for this phenomenon is still to be achieved. The causes are complex and one factor that we hope to demonstrate can influence press coverage of events is the existence of different newspaper practices that promote or exclude some events from individual newspapers.

The keyword 'ECOLOG*' was chosen to pick up a wide variety of articles relating to the environment. The rise and fall of the graph therefore represents the general rise and fall of newspaper coverage of environment issues as a whole. It is interesting to compare this general indicator with the time series graph of a specific issue.

In the next set of graphs a cyclical element is again evident. These graphs represent the combined set of articles which contain a reference to 'GREENHOUSE EFFECT', or 'GLOBAL WARMING':

Graph 6.2: Article count for GREENHOUSE EFFECT or GLOBAL WARMING (January, 1987-April, 1991)

Graph 6.2a: Guardian

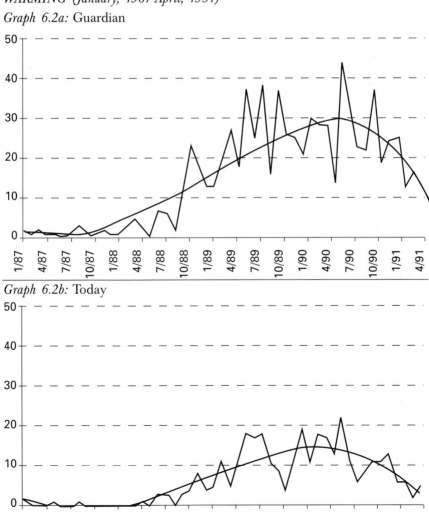

Graph 6.2b: Today

These graphs illustrate a different profile of newspaper coverage. Articles mentioning these key words are relatively rare until mid-1988. The *Guardian* is the first newspaper to publish an article describing the greenhouse effect. It is also the first to publish more than 5 articles per month in June, 1988. Today achieves this level five months later in November, 1988. However, the steep rise and peaking occurs very clearly in all newspapers as does the marked decline.

Restricting the analysis to what appears to be a single issue has the effect of demonstrating the cycle of news coverage in a more clear-cut manner. However, it is important to realise that even a 'single issue' is made up of many parts or sub-issues which interlock and have their own distinctive profile.

An interesting finding emerges when the graphs representing the distribution of articles which contain one of these key words are plotted separately. The *Guardian* and *Today* span the range and illustrate a pattern common to all four newspapers. (See graphs 6.3a and 6.3b below.)

The initial steep rise in the number of articles published (June, 1988 to September, 1988) is almost solely due to articles referring to the Greenhouse Effect. The steep rise in articles mentioning Global Warming occurs later in 1988 or early 1989. The graphs for all the newspapers are similar in two ways. They all demonstrate a rise and fall in coverage and also that the coverage of the greenhouse effect precedes the coverage of global warming in each case. There is therefore a close similarity between newspapers in the overall pattern of coverage as well as a similarity in the internal structure of that coverage. It is difficult to account for the discreteness of these distributions without further research into the content of the articles. However, it is likely that any one of these 'sub-issues' is itself made up of a set of sub, 'sub-issues' which editors explore or block from their particular paper.

Graph 6.3: Separate plots of articles for GREENHOUSE EFFECT and GLOBAL WARMING (January 1987-April, 1991)

Graph 6.3a: Guardian

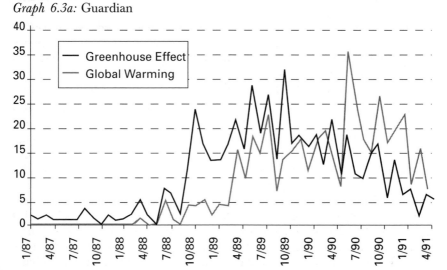

Graph 6.3b: Today

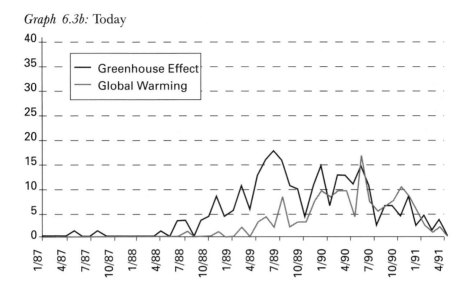

The twin pressures of inter-newspaper competition and the need to communicate with a particular culture of understanding are two of the factors which determine how quickly an issue is taken up, how long an issue runs and how far desk editors encourage or block new avenues or angles, based on the central issue. Despite the gravity of the predictions which followed the acceptance of the Greenhouse Effect/Global Warming hypothesis by IPCC, for example, the destruction of major food producing habitats and the flooding of major population centres in Bangladesh, the UK and Holland, the number of articles written on these topics declines rapidly in the Autumn of 1990 and the Spring of 1991. By May 1991 press interest has waned and other events have become 'news'.

The cyclical pattern of news construction and destruction could hardly be demonstrated on a more critical case. The underlying causes of global warming have not gone away. Carbon dioxide, methane, NOx, and CFCs are still being produced on a scale likely to produce the effects predicted by IPCC. Even the international efforts to find solutions to this problem have produced little press interest in a problem of immense significance. In our view this raises questions about the adequacy of press coverage, the level of public debate and the level of intelligence of the collective cultures within our society.

To demonstrate that the press' coverage of environmental issues has a cyclical element is not necessarily to agree with Richardson (1977) and Gregory (1972) that media coverage derives from an essentially transient concern with the environment or with Downs (1972) that it will inevitably decline. Clearly the cyclical nature of press interest has been demonstrated in this instance but the future is open to change and the possibility of reform. The understanding that the public develops about its relationship with the environment will depend not only on what science reports become available, what international conferences are held, what natural calamities occur and how pressure groups and interested professionals conduct themselves, but also on how powerful institutions, including the press, decide to conduct that debate.

It is important to decide if the institutional structure of the press and the way that the market for news is structured enables a virtuous circle of intelligence and understanding to develop or if there is inevitably a downward spiral of partial information and avoidance leading to a diminished understanding, declining intelligence and mistrust. In other words, the cyclical nature of press coverage renders particular issues vulnerable to being squeezed out of the public debate. If the factors that generate public understanding are themselves better understood it is possible that a more interactive and accountable press could result.

Solesbury's 1976 article provides us with several useful insights into this process by introducing the concept of 'agenda' and examining the factors that affect how situations become political issues. Solesbury is concerned with the agenda of public debate as an agenda for prospective action. The agenda is limited in capacity and there is fierce competition for a place. He defines three tests that an issue must pass through before it is capable of attracting the resources that would lead to action being taken. The tests are whether the 'situation' is worthy of attention (ie it becomes an issue); whether it is defined as legitimate, in terms of some dominant value system and whether it can invoke action.

The ideas of limited space and competition are useful and are elaborated by Hilgartner and Bosk (1988) who shift the focus of analysis from the issue to the political and social context in which it exists. They remind us that social problems exist in relation to other social problems; that they evolve within arenas that have a finite carrying capacity; and that they compete with other social problems for space and attention. They go on to describe some of the characteristics of arenas, in particular that they have gatekeepers who exist at various levels and can decide 'what's news' (Gans, 1979). Therefore they have some control over the flow of messages to audiences (White 1964; Gieber 1964). These gatekeepers, who are not listed but presumably include proprietors, editors and reporters, can act in the interests of powerful groups who wish to control the public debate and élites who '…may actively oppose some problem definitions, relegating some issues to a politically enforced neglect' (Hilgartner and Bosk, 1988).

Abraham *et al* (1990) take one aspect of this analysis even further and use the term 'deception' to underline the fact that the non-appearance or disappearance of an issue from public debate (the agenda) does not necessarily mean that the underlying problem has been solved. It often requires substantial effort by well-informed people to demonstrate a deception and keep the issues alive within the arena of public debate. The experience of some campaigning organisations, for example Greenpeace, has shown that a carefully organised and spectacular event can capture press interest. Nevertheless not all causes can be dramatised in this way. Hansen (1991) has shown that environmental organisations appear as primary definers of environment news in only 6 per cent of news items.

It has been argued that 'waves' or moral panics are more influenced by supply side factors within the news production process, in particular those associated with the bureaucratically structured procedures of organisations which provide sources of news (Fishman, 1980; Ericson *et al* 1987 and 1989). Unfortunately, none of these studies refers to the areas of environment or development news production. Instead they concentrate on the reporting of legal issues and criminal justice where powerful and entrenched organisational procedures already exist for providing material to the news production process. In addition the studies by Ericson *et al* refer to the Canadian situation where it appears that the de-politicisation of the press has proceeded further than in the UK (1989 p.172). We would not wish to prejudge the importance of news production factors in determining the extent and quality of the coverage of environment and development issues. In this chapter we use the term 'gatekeeper' to refer to some of these influences which are internal to the press without at this stage attempting to describe them in detail. There will be other external factors that interact and produce as yet unmapped patterns of influence.

We argue that the process of defining issues as news needs to be well understood and monitored if it is to be prevented from being the prerogative of a small élite. Widespread public reaction to the manipulation of news coverage is one way of ensuring that the power of gatekeepers is constrained and that newspapers serve the long-term interests of their readers by providing a free flow of news, encouraging openness and informed democratic participation. The Ethiopian and Sudan famines are two examples where the power of gatekeepers can be demonstrated. The first example has been brought to light by 'insiders' writing about their experience. The second example can be demonstrated by analysing data from FT Profile.

Press coverage of famine: gatekeepers at work

The story of the Ethiopian famine is now well documented (Abraham *et al*, 1990). The story of an impending disaster had been carried in the quality press at the beginning of 1984 yet it was not until October that the story broke through into television and subsequently into the popular press. The catalyst for this was the audience response to *Seeds of Despair*, a documentary by Central Television. Philo and Lamb (1990) describe the resistance of various gatekeepers to this film. Joe Angotti recounted that his early attempts met with lack of interest from the NBC news office, 'everyone has seen the pictures and the swollen bellies before'. Once the famine had developed and the disaster had reached catastrophic proportions the BBC treated it as a major issue. Even at this point when the BBC offered to The *Sun* a full set of pictures, the response was: 'We're not actually interested in famine'. Five days later, when the story had broken, The *Sun* ran a two-inch headline on: 'RACE TO SAVE THE BABIES' (Philo and Lamb, 1990).

In this case the resistance of the gatekeepers was overcome by the rush of public interest, the willingness of the public to donate money and the public's desire for the government to relieve the famine:

> In November 1984 the *Observer* broke the story that despite the British Government's rhetorical support for assistance to Ethiopia it was planning to cut its overseas budget... there was a backbench revolt in the British Parliament and it is a testament to the power of the moment that the proposal to cut aid was voted down. (Philo and Lamb, 1990)

It is hypothesised that these moments when 'gatekeepers' and governments are overcome by a public response are unpopular with both 'gatekeepers' and government élites. It follows that they will attempt to minimise the risk of this loss of control by attempting to reassert their control over the public agenda and by suppressing the reporting of these kinds of events. An opportunity to study the end results of this process presents itself in the press treatment of the build up of the Sudan famine (of 1991).

The next sequence of graphs shows the distribution of 'FAMINE' in the coverage of the four newspapers:

Graph 6.4: Articles containing key word FAMINE (Jan 87-Apr 91)

Graph 6.4a: Guardian

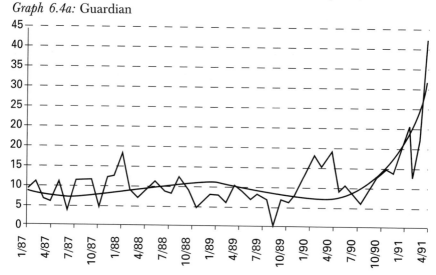

Graph 6.4b: Times

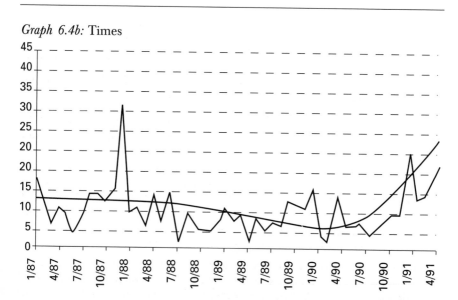

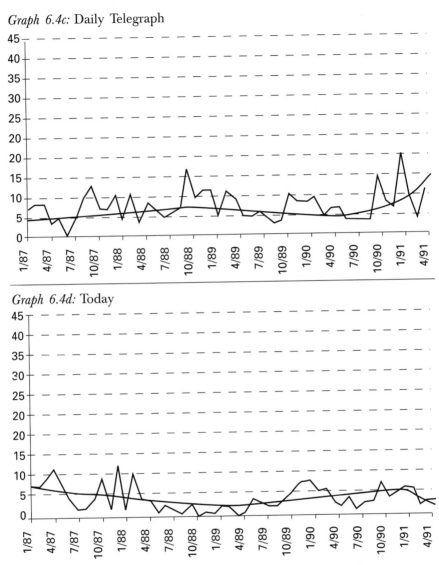

Graph 6.4c: Daily Telegraph

Graph 6.4d: Today

The time series graphs for *The Times* and the *Guardian* show a very similar amount of coverage over time. After a decline in the coverage of famine from late 1988 to mid-1989 both papers show a response to the news coming out of Sudan and Ethiopia of the developing conditions for a new and potentially disastrous famine. By October and November, 1989 both papers were carrying increasing numbers of these stories. When the graphs for the *Telegraph* and *Today* are compared with the *Guardian* and *The Times* a marked difference emerges. The upturn in the number of stories carried by the *Telegraph* is small and the number carried by Today newspaper shows no increase.

It would appear that in comparison with the coverage of the greenhouse effect the treatment of famine shows a marked differentiation in the period of emerging famine in the Sudan (from Autumn, 1990). It is important to look for the reasons for this difference in coverage and why the Sudan famine should have been treated as 'news' by some editors and omitted or played down by others. These reasons are political in nature because donor countries are reluctant to supply aid to:

1   countries that will not admit to famine;

2   countries that have ideologically unacceptable governments;

3   countries that interfere with the distribution of aid in ways that discriminate against some groups;

4   countries that are pursuing unpopular foreign policies, i.e. that are unpopular with the governments of donor countries.

The Sudan drought of 1990 and resulting famine of 1991 was a critical case. It possessed all the above characteristics. There was evidence that donor countries, in particular the USA and UK, withheld or delayed aid in order to force the Sudanese government to modify certain of its policies. The evidence that pressure was used to obtain policy changes with respect to Aid distribution and administration was well established. The contention that Aid was withheld from famine victims, ensuring unnecessary starvation, was of course hotly contested, as was any suggestion that Aid was withheld to punish the Sudanese regime for supporting the Iraqi government's invasion of Kuwait. Nevertheless these accusations were made and this ensured that news relating to the drought and resulting famine was potentially embarrassing to the Conservative government. It is therefore important to investigate how these events were covered by the newspapers in our panel.

The next set of graphs and tables provides a more exact illustration of the differentiation on the issue. They represent the number of articles per month from January 1987 to April 1991 containing a reference to both 'SUDAN*' and FAMINE (January, 1987 – April 1991)

Graph 6.5: Articles with key words SUDAN* and FAMINE (January, 1987 – April, 1991)

Graph 6.5a: Guardian

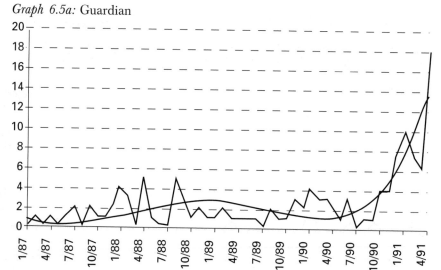

Graph 6.5b: Times

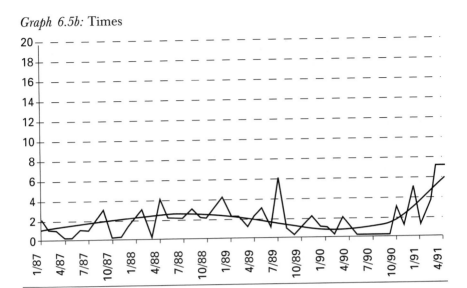

Graph 6.5c: Daily Telegraph

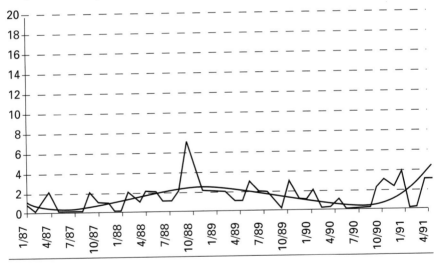

Graph 6.5d: Today

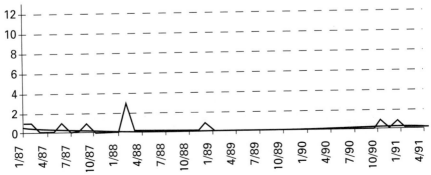

These graphs particularly highlight the extreme difference in the rate of response to the crisis. The *Guardian* responds rapidly and in volume whereas *Today* shows no reaction at all! Overall the share of the coverage for the comparison period is equally extreme:

Table 6.4: Number of articles that contained 'SUDAN' and 'FAMINE' January 1987 – April 1991)

	No	%age
Guardian	127	42
Times	94	31
Daily Telegraph	74	24
Today	10	3
	305	100

The *Guardian* ('left of centre') is responsible for 42 per cent of the total coverage by these newspapers. At the other end of the scale *Today* (right wing tabloid) provides its readers with ten articles (3 per cent of coverage) over a 52 month period.

The distribution over time of these articles during this period is also important. Sudan has had famines before. In this case we are particularly interested in the famine that was forecast in the summer of 1990. The press coverage of this famine is calculated for the period October 1990 – April 1991 (7 months).

Table 6.5: Number of articles containing 'SUDAN' and 'FAMINE' – October 1990 – April 1991

	No	%age
Guardian	57	56
Times	27	27
Daily Telegraph	15	15
Today	2	2
	101	100

Table 6.5 demonstrates that the press coverage of the most recent famine is more starkly differentiated than the earlier already highly differentiated coverage. The *Guardian* is now responsible for 56 per cent of the coverage during this period while Today newspaper sinks to an almost imperceptible 2 per cent. Within the table the differences between the *Guardian, The Times* and the *Daily Telegraph* also increase.

This increased differentiation within the recent period of high politicisation of the issue supports the conclusion that press coverage will differentiate as environmental issues become politicised. In this case, news that could be embarrassing to the government is omitted by the papers most sympathetic to the government. The evidence is consistent with the concept of the 'gatekeeper' mechanism and the power of élites to shape the agenda for debate, but it does not tell us much about the extent of politically motivated bias in determining the press coverage of environmental issues. It tells us even less about the content and quality of that coverage. Both these issues are dealt with later in the book.

It is important to emphasise that this degree of differentiation is not simply of the order that would be expected in newspapers that give different emphasis to environmental issues. Table 6.6 illustrates this point. In the first group the degree of differentiation is most marked in the case of ECOLOG* which is a more specialised key word expected to produce substantial differentiation. This degree of differentiation (8–45 per cent, a factor of 5.6) is very similar to that produced by the most specialised term in Group 2, i.e. 'MALN*. This records a similar order of differentiation (7–35 per cent, a factor of 5). Neither of these key words produce a differentiation of coverage that compares with the Sudan famine which records a differentiation factor of 14.

Table 6.6: Differentiation of coverage share for all key words (Unless indicated Guardian is high, Today is low)

Key word	Low	High	Factor	Except
ECOLOG*	8	45	5.6	
GR EFFECT	15	31	2.1	DTL – hi
GL WARMING	10	30	3.0	
PCB*	15	34	2.3	
DIELDRIN	7	37	5.3	
STARV*	19	34	1.8	
HUNGER	11	39	3.5	
FAMINE	12	36	3.0	
MALN*	7	35	5.0	
SUDAN*	6	33	5.2	TMS – hi
SUDAN* + STARV*	5	45	9.0	
SUDAN* + HUNGER	4	50	12.5	
SUDAN* + FAMINE	3	42	14.0	

Note: (i) This table shows coverage share for two further combinations SUDAN* + HUNGER and SUDAN* + STARV*;
(ii) Table based on results in Table 6.2 and Table 6.3

These results demonstrate quite clearly that although there is an established order of differentiation with respect to relatively non-politicised environmental issues the degree of differentiation is much less.

The public response

The data and analysis presented in this chapter have demonstrated some important characteristic of the UK press coverage of environment and development issues.

1 It has illustrated the cyclical nature of press coverage and pointed out that the peaks and troughs of this coverage has little direct connection with the underlying environment problems that we face.

2 It has raised questions about the adequacy of this coverage in relation to finding solutions within an embattled democracy confronted with substantial long-term environmental problems.

3 It has raised questions about the role of the 'gatekeepers' who select the issues that will or will not become part of the culture of understanding of their readers.

However, even if the news conveyed by the press is subject to shared cycles and patterns of differentiation it remains to be shown how influential this is in determining how readers of that news develop views and understanding of the events portrayed.

In the final part of this chapter, we will investigate if the volume of news (cycles) influences the major concerns felt by the population at large. In order to measure public opinion we will draw on the MORI Omnibus Poll, in particular the answers to the question 'What would you say is the/ are other important issues facing Britain today?' The answers are coded into a fairly stable framework of 25 major issues. Since November 1988, when the issue of pollution/environment was first introduced into the coding frame there have only been a few changes, for example when the issue of the poll tax/local government was introduced in April 1989. The poll is very sensitive to changes in public opinion because it only measures those issues at the top of an individual's concerns. In this respect it resembles the notion of the public arena in which the topics that can be accommodated at any one time are restricted. The graph illustrated below traces the record of public concern for pollution/environment as measured by the poll between November 1988 and January 1994.

Graph 6.6: Percentage of respondents recording the Environment/Pollution as a major issue facing Britain today.

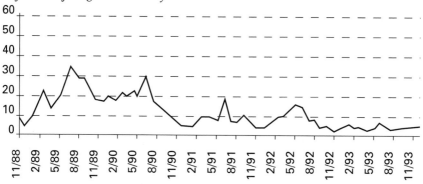

Clearly the interpretation of fluctuations in this poll is a complex matter. Interpretation must take into account events and news items on a broad front, not merely what is happening within the news areas of the environment and development. The major external factors will be news about competing events and issues and even seasonal effects which can affect the public's susceptibility to news. News about other competing issues, for example a great increase in concern for defence/foreign affairs during the Gulf War or increased concern for the rise in unemployment, is likely to diminish relatively the concern for other issues, like pollution/environment.

The combined index

In order to develop an index of press output on environment issues we have combined the results of keyword searches for four of the environment issues described in the first part of this chapter: global warming, greenhouse effect, ozone layer and ecolog*. Since ecolog* picks out articles which use any of a number of derivative terms, it picks out a wide variety of articles on a wide range of topics on the environment. It is a reliable index, not subject to much contamination or 'noise'. The other three terms are self-explanatory. They pick out articles on some of the major environment issues of the last seven to eight years. They provide a supplement to ecolog* in the construction of an index of highly salient environment issues.

A combined index of the articles containing these key words for all the quality newspapers produces a simplified picture of the news flows received by the British public on some of the major issues within the environment debate. The index contains a total of 13,000 articles from a total available newspaper output of 1,596,338 (less than 1 per cent of published articles) in the period November 1988 to January 1994. The graph below illustrates the index in a time series graph.

Graph 6.7: Combined Index

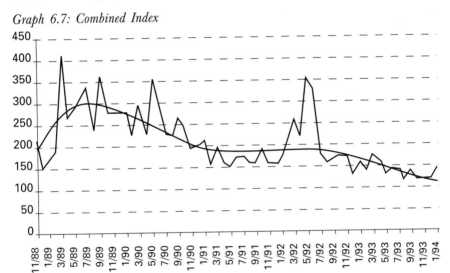

The combined index shows a decline in the number of articles published on the selected topics since the peak of 420 articles per month in March 1989 to a trough of 120.

Public opinion and press output compared: the poll and the index

When the combined index of press publication and the MORI poll of public opinion/concern about the environment are compared the close relationship between the two time series graphs is at once apparent.

This close relationship is confirmed by the correlation coefficient of 0.79 which is significant at the .001 level. Public concern about the environment appears to follow closely the reporting of environment issues in the press, although we must not at this stage forget that the combined index is likely to reflect news about the environment that appears in all media output including television. Therefore we can assume that when public concern about the environment rises steeply the news reaching the public via the media is largely responsible. Exceptional events might be the direct widespread personal experience of freak weather conditions or perhaps a seasonal susceptibility to news about the environment.[2]

Graph 6.8: Combined Index compared with MORI measure of environmental concern

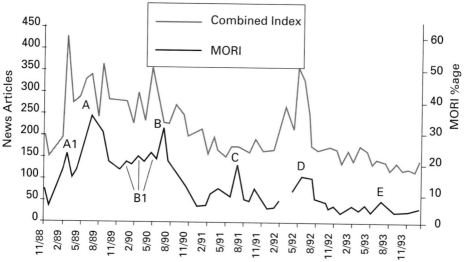

The early peak A1 at 22 per cent in March 89 coincides with a substantial number of articles about the greenhouse effect, including the threat of rising sea levels. The peak in July 89 (A at 35 per cent) follows an outpouring of news in June (311 articles) and coincides with a second peak in July (330 articles) which continues the bad news about ozone and includes a wide range or articles from algae in the Adriatic to straw burning and the return of the seal virus.

Public concern then declines from July '89 to Dec '89. In early 1990 it is maintained on a high plateau between 18 per cent and 20 per cent. Interestingly each mini peak on the plateau B1 is correlated with a peak of publishing. In July 1990 the public's concern undergoes a sudden increase to 30 per cent. This could be associated with news items in the high level of publishing in May and June and/or the seasonal susceptibility hypothesised earlier. Certainly a wide range of issues emerged in July 1990 from river defences, kittiwakes dying in the North Sea to a CFC gas leak and river defences (sea level rises), but no single issue is easily diagnosed as a cause of the increased concern. However, by July 1990 articles throwing doubt on the greenhouse effect as a cause of climate change theories had begun to gain prominence and a steep decline in concern continues until February 1991.

This decline in concern about the environment is also associated with increased concern about other issues. Graph 6.9 gives some examples: a large

2   It is clear that peak C in public concern (June–July 1991) is not matched by a peak in the combined index. This peak in fact coincided with freak weather conditions.

temporary change in the level of concern about defence issues, rising concern about unemployment and to a lesser extend increased concern about law and order. The steep decline in public concern about the environment from July 1990 to February 1991 was therefore associated not only with the emergence of doubt about global warming, but also the onset of the Iraq-Kuwait conflict (reflected in increased concern about defence) and, to a lesser extent, an increased concern about unemployment. It was perhaps a case of environment issues weakening and being squeezed out relative to these other concerns.

Graph 6.9: Selected MORI measures of concern compared.

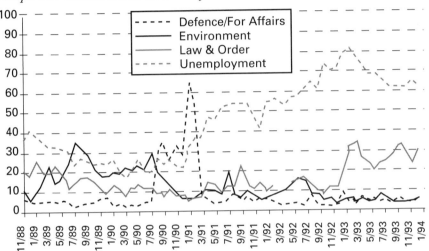

During 1991 public concern for the environment again peaked in July (18 per cent) and declined to a new low for this period at 4 per cent in December 1991. The subsequent build up of articles in press in the period before the Earth Summit is associated with a gradual rise in public concern, peaking in June 1992, the month of the Earth Summit, with a high of 15 per cent. In the build up to the Summit, Today and the four broadsheet newspapers published a total of nearly 700 articles that referred to the Summit and the Combined Index (see Graph 6-7) shows a peak of 350 articles per month. However, compared with other peaks of publishing the public response is relatively muted, a peak of 15 per cent compared with 35 per cent in July 89, even though the level of publishing activity is comparable.

Although the closeness of the relationship between the number of articles published on key environment topics and public concern is a remarkable finding, it should not be assumed that this demonstrates the unfettered power of the media to influence public opinion. It is the media's function to inform the public about important events and discoveries. Few would argue that the implications of the destruction of the ozone layer or global warming do not fall into that category of news. We argue that the power exercised by individual newspapers rests in the amount of coverage, factors such as the prominence that they give to that coverage and the interpretation that they put upon the events. They also rely on the reservoirs of trust and influence built up within the cultures of understanding that they have nurtured over the years to influence the understandings that their readers develop. In order to investigate the effectiveness of these weapons we have chosen to research more deeply into a specific event, the Earth Summit held in Rio de Janeiro in June 1992.

7 The Reporting of the Earth Summit

The Earth Summit and its precursors

The United Nations Conference on Environment and Development (UNCED, *aka* the Earth Summit) was initiated in 1989 following a UN warning about 'the serious degradation of the global life-support systems' and 'ecological catastrophe' with the intention that it should:

> 'elaborate strategies and measures to halt and reverse the effects of environmental degradation in the context of strengthened national and international efforts to promote sustainable and environmentally sound development in all countries.' (IIED 1991)

Under the directorship of Maurice Strong this aim was interpreted as an implementation of the recommendations of the World Commission on Environment and in particular that environment issues should occupy a central place in policy making. In Maurice Strong's view this would be achieved by six elements: a statement of principles; agreement on specific legal measures on issues such as biological diversity and atmospheric damage; Agenda 21 (a framework for specific action to be taken by individual nations and communities), the provision of new financial resources, technology transfer, and finally, institutional reforms aimed at facilitating the implementation of these proposals.

The Earth Summit event itself was simply the public, media oriented finale to a long process of preparatory meetings and discussions where for the basis achieving the aims of UNCED was to be formulated. Even within the Earth Summit itself, the 'real' Summit consisted of only two days in which heads of state would gather to enact ceremonial signings and issue statements of intent with respect to the various agreements. However, this is to oversimplify the wide range of participants and the huge effort of negotiation that it represented. There were four preparatory stages during which many conflicts and disagreements between nations on issues of fundamental principle emerged, especially differences of perspective between North and South on issues such as climate change, forests, and finance, particularly on the issue of the establishment of a Global Environmental Facility through which funds would be channelled.

An important shift of emphasis occurred in UNCED with the involvement of non-governmental organisations (NGOs) which won the right to participate

in the preparatory phases of UNCED. It is important to note that the involvement of these groups (which included industrial interests) reflected a change in
the culture of such events from earlier conferences. UNCED enshrined the
principle that governments alone cannot deliver sustainable development.
NGO participation was not accepted very easily by all participating nations
but this part of the preparatory process 'secured the principle that NGOs with
their close contact with issues 'on the ground', their wide public support, and
their ability through awareness-raising to influence public behaviour towards
supporting environmental measures, have a key and legitimate role to play...'
(IIED 1991)

Sustainable development

The move towards linking environment and development had been proceeding for some time. UNCED's immediate precursor was the 1987 Brundtland
Commission (the World Commission on Environment and Development)
whose report 'Our Common Future' (1987) argued that the development of
both North and South was unsustainable. Earlier reports and conferences (e.g.
Club of Rome 1972; UNESCO 'Man and the Biosphere' 1971; UN Conference
on the Human Environment, Stockholm 1972) raised the debate about negative
effects of economic growth. This debate was sympathetically received by some
in developed countries but in undeveloped nations growth continued to be
seen as a prerequisite for conserving resources (Redclift and Benton 1994).

The 1980 World Conservation Strategy (IUCN), the 1982 Global 2000
Report and the Brandt Commission 1987, helped to establish the link between
environmental issues and economic development, but the problem continued
to be seen in terms of scarcity with too many consumers placing an unacceptable burden on a declining resource base. The Brandt Commission suggested
that absolute limits to fossil fuels posed the biggest threat to environment and
development. The World Conservation Strategy effectively coined the term
'sustainable development' but tended to separate economic development
from environmental impact. (Redclift and Benton 1994).

Caring for the Earth (IUCN 1990) viewed economic development as a
problem in achieving environmental objectives. During the 1990's damage to
the atmosphere (e.g. ozone holes in the ozone layer) and the threat of climate
change created new a sense of urgency within the industrialised countries.
Unlike the 1970s when scarcity was seen to be a major concern, profiligacy was
now seen to be an urgent policy issue.

Differences of interest and view at the Earth Summit

Until the Earth Summit no basis for international agreements existed on many
contentious issues. The environmental concerns of the North were only partially shared by South, where concerns about water supplies, sanitation, soil
erosion, depletion of wood supplies, etc., prevailed. The South also became
more vociferous about its debt burden which was an outcome of international
finance policies that visibly do not help poor and ordinary people.

The need to change the North's view of growth and the competing claims
of local communities and international interests in the conservation or

depletion of natural resources thus dominated the Earth Summit negotiations. The hegemony of the North remained the overriding issue in such issues as conservation of forests and biodiversity. The need to provide proper rewards and compensations for adopting conservation programmes were not clearly addressed (e.g. Malaysia and India opposed the idea of a binding statement on forest principles). None of the solutions offered (non-profit gene banks; private money from North to pay for national scientific institutes for the South; host government exploitation of resources using foreign companies) really dealt with the problems of creating incentives to conserve biodiversity and other environmental resources. For example, it was argued, most natural resources are in the South, but most biotechnology is in the North. This raises the fundamental issue of sovereignty over the primary resources.

Moreover the issue of greatest concern to the developed world – population – was scarcely discussed. Agreements on deforestation and population growth have dominated the debate in the North – but many developing countries believe that population control can only begin when economic growth has raised living standards. Before Rio they requested that population be omitted from the debate on the link between poverty and environmental depletion.

The significance of the Earth Summit

Because of the enormous scale of UNCED and the involvement of over 100 heads of state the Earth Summit was in itself an important event. Nevertheless it was hoped that the significance and back room politicking, the wide range of conference sessions, involving a great variety of organisations and peoples, the parallel strands of the Summit, and the central signing ceremonies would produce substantial progress. With so many heads of state making speeches the attention of the world's media was attracted on an unprecedented scale. This in turn could place environment and development issues on a central global agenda and communicate this fact to all the peoples of the world. The use of this high profile strategy was intended to pressure the heads of nation states to make radical, public moves towards solving the mounting problems of environment and development.

This strategy depended to a great extent on the global media. Without a full exposure of these problems the various national publics would not be able to exert any pressure on their own leaders. The reporting of the summit by the media was therefore an important element in its success or failure. This strategy made our investigation of the UK press coverage relevant to understanding the success and/or failure of the Summit and it also provided us with the opportunity to investigate the press and its treatment of a pre-planned event.

As we have seen in earlier chapters it was unlikely that the aims and objectives of the Earth Summit would be reported in the UK press in a straightforward manner. In general we anticipated that the event would be generally supported by the left-leaning press but more negatively represented by the right-wing press. Reporting of the Earth Summit would be coloured and interpreted by means of selection and emphasis. Selection involved ignoring certain aspects of the event or, if reported, at all given a certain emphasis or interpretation. An event such as the Earth Summit, by its nature, was bound to be an event surrounded by contention and disagreement as well as consensus irrespective of the particular positions adopted by certain newspapers.

However, as the argument of this book makes clear, even this aspect of the Summit could not be expected to be straightforwardly reported. The fact of disagreement among nations was itself an opportunity for interpretation according to the preferred world-view of individual newspapers. Readers would be largely dependent on their newspapers for detailed interpretation about the significance and meaning of the event. Through the use of selective emphasis, expressed directly in the use or misuse of terminology and concepts as well as choice of topics, cultures of understanding about these underlying conflicts would be sustained, manipulated and reconstructed.

Validating the Research Design

To explore the differential treatment of the Summit we selected a sample of newspapers to represent the spread of opinion offered in the British press. We adopted a simple framework to classify our sample into a two-dimensional model (see Figure 7.1), using an audience-dimension, which classifies newspapers according to the general social position of the readership, and a political-dimension that classifies newspapers according to their predominant political stance.

The audience dimension arises from the highly differentiated readerships illustrated in Chapter 5. The clearly demonstrated association of readerships with social class also introduces a literacy element to this dimension. These literacy qualities are reflected in the style, presentation and content of newspapers, which are designed to appeal to different reading habits and tastes. No direct comparisons between newspapers can be made without bearing this dimension in mind.

The political dimension is essentially dictated by the controlling proprietor and his/her relationship with the editor. As we have seen in Chapter 2 it is, for example, a historical matter that the diversity of political positions in the UK press has almost vanished, There is now no significant independent radical press and the UK press is now almost entirely controlled by capitalist organisations espousing right-wing, conservative politics (Curran and Seaton 1988).

Nevertheless there are still some important differences within the press that can be used to construct this dimension. Elements of the centre-left press remain in being. Among the quality press there is the *Guardian*, a newspaper owned and managed by a trust, and a tabloid, the *Daily Mirror*, not totally undermined by its past owners. In addition, the newer Independent retains some of its reputation for autonomy. In the middle-market section of the press, appealing literally to the middle classes, there is no example of a left-oriented newspaper. This section is dominated by papers such as the *Daily Mail* and the *Daily Express*. However at the time of the Summit, *Today* was more committed to environment issues than its more conservative rivals.

At an early stage the *Financial Times*, which had unexpectedly decided to support the Labour Party in the 1992 election, was dropped from the sample because we were unable to obtain a workable readership sample. In addition the *Express* and the *Star* were dropped because they duplicated the *Mail* and the *Sun* which were retained as stronger newspapers, much more likely to generate large enough readership samples.

Figure 7.1: Model of UK Press Differentiation

Characteristics of Readership:	Broadsheet/Quality	Tabloid/Popular	
	(high literacy)	(low literacy)	
Political Dimension	Middle Class	Middle Class	Working Class
Centre Left	Guardian		Daily Mirror
Independent	Independent		
	(Financial Times)	Today	
Right Wing	The Times	Express	Sun
	Telegraph	Mail	Star

Our previous research had generated a number of expectations with respect to press coverage of the Summit. We expected the coverage or number and length of articles to diminish horizontally as a function of the literacy/class characteristics of the various readerships. We expected the coverage or number of articles (but not necessarily length) to diminish from top to bottom of the framework as a function of the newspapers dedication to environment and development issues. Finally, we expected a critical or oppositional element to the Earth Summit within the coverage to increase vertically from top to bottom in the framework as a function of the political affiliation of each newspaper. This relates to the fact that right wing newspaper's would find themselves against the overt recognition that the future economic development of the world and the fate of its major natural systems are inextricably intertwined. Bringing them together effectively politicises both environment and development issues and opens the door for discussions about who is responsible for major pollution problems, who should pay, and whether the poorer nations of the South are able to develop their declining economies for the benefit of their own people while coping with a huge burden of debt. The co-ordinated, interventionist and regulatory policies seen as necessary by UNEP and the conference organisers were clearly at odds with the open market, free trade, and less regulation, traditionally advocated by the UK right-wing press.

The first step in validating what had become in effect a prediction about the way the UK press would cover the Earth Summit was to collect all the copies of the eight newspapers in our sample and familiarise ourselves with the coverage as it developed during the months of May and June 1992. The text of five of these newspapers were available electronically via the FT Profile but three of the tabloids in our sample (*Daily Mail, Daily Mirror* and the *Sun*) were not available in this form and so were coded and analysed initially by hand.

Our first subjective assessment of press coverage seemed to bear out our predictions but we needed to develop more objective indicators and then to proceed to an in-depth descriptive analysis of the coverage. Our approach had to be divided between those newspapers stored on FT profile and those which we would need to analyse by hand. In effect we carried out two analyses, the broadsheet newspapers using FT profile and the tabloids using traditional hand methods. In the case of Today we used both methods so that we could compare results. An early step was to identify and store in the computer all of the articles in all of the newspapers that mentioned the Earth Summit. The result of these searches clearly validates the patterned response to the Summit that we anticipated.

Figure 7.2: Number of Articles containing the keyword 'earth summit'
1 May 92–30 June 92

Characteristics of Readership:	Broadsheet/Quality (high literacy)	Tabloid/Popular (low literacy)	
	Literate Middle Class	Middle Class	Working Class
Characteristics of the organisation			
Centre Left or Independent	*Guardian* 241		*Daily Mirror* 20
	Independent 193 *Financial Times* 191	*Today* 38	
Right Wing	*The Times* 174 *Telegraph* 155	*Mail* 25	*Sun* 8

There are two points of note that we did not predict. The first is the relatively low differentiation within the quality press between the largest number of articles and the lowest (1:1.55). The second is the enormous gap in the amount of coverage between the popular and quality press. The whole of the popular press represented in this study published 91 articles referring to the Earth Summit; compared with the least prolific of the quality press which published 155. This disparity constitutes an important issue in itself given that between them the *Daily Mirror*, the *Daily Mail*, *Today*, and the *Sun* are estimated to reach a readership of over 25 million people whereas the five quality newspapers only reach about 6 million readers (Central Statistical Office, 1993).

The prediction about length of article was also borne out. The articles in the middle class tabloids were approximately 60 per cent of the length of articles in the quality press, while the articles in the popular tabloids were about 60 per cent of the length of articles in the mid-market tabloids. There was no clear relationship between length of articles and the vertical dimension.

This analysis vindicates our crudest assumptions about the way the British press would represent the Earth Summit to its readers. The volume of news reaching the audiences of the various newspapers was highly differentiated. *Sun* readers were presented with less than two words of reported matter on the Summit for every 100 words printed in the *Guardian*. However, by itself this differentiation does not inform us about the position taken by the newspapers towards the Summit, nor does it tell us how the news was received by readers. We will proceed with a first level analysis of the news presented by the tabloid press.

The tabloid coverage

Our initial analysis of tabloid coverage had been limited by our lack of computer access to these newspapers as a whole. In order to overcome this difficulty we scanned all the articles referring to the Earth Summit. Our first analysis was then to note the occurrence of two key words that summarised the main purposes of the Summit: 'sustainable development' and 'biodiversity'. In this case our choice of key words was influenced by the weight placed on them within the literature generated by the Earth Summit. The terms are in effect 'lexical items' (Halliday, 1966), or as Fairclough (1992) describes the process of creating lexical items,

> Creating lexical items brings particular perspectives on domains of experience into wider theoretical, scientific, cultural or ideological purview ... it guarantees new culturally important categories. (191)

We coupled this selection of key words with a coding exercise in which we classified each of the articles in the tabloid press according to its support or hostility to the Summit.

The key word search was important because it measured the extent to which newspapers had both understood and been prepared to pass on their understanding of the purpose of the Summit to their readers. These concepts are central to environmentalist concerns. Sustainable development encapsulates the notion of responsible development in which the effects of that development are measured and held against the possibility of it continuing into the future without depleting resources or damaging the environment through pollution. Biodiversity encapsulates the notion of the wide and interconnected web of plant and animal species that is currently being attacked and narrowed by the kinds of unsustainable activity that are presently essential to our life styles. The rate of species destruction is disputed but the fact that is proceeding at a fast and damaging rate is generally agreed. Biodiversity is therefore a 'green' concept that environmentalists would wish to be widely understood; part of our understanding of the natural world.

When newspapers wish to make a particularly indelible mark on their readers and deeply affect their understanding of events or influence their opinion of personalities they frequently introduce a term or label which acts as a marker to that understanding. Terms like 'mugging' which highlights violent street crime, 'looney left councils' which directed unfavourable attention to labour controlled councils, and more recently 'hypocrisy' and 'sleaze' which have been used to deride Labour and Conservative 'myths' of competence and integrity, are examples of negative labelling. Newspapers are sensitive to their role in shaping cultures of understanding through introducing new concepts and vocabulary. Certain words introduce ideas that some newspapers are reluctant to see gain widespread understanding.

During the two months of May and June 1992 when reporting of the Summit was at its heaviest no tabloid newspaper in our sample used the term 'sustainable development'. In addition we found that Today, despite its erstwhile policy of promoting green issues (*Guardian* 25/3/91) never used the term in the whole of its existence as a newspaper. It is of course possible for these issues to be raised using other words and phrases, but by not using this particular key word, or by using qualifying words and phrases, a newspaper appears to be taking a decision to advance the public debate along preferred lines.

For example, the *Daily Mail* also did not use the term 'sustainable development' but on one occasion it did use the phrase 'sustainable Third World development' thus subtly shifting the framework of understanding about sustainable development away from the idea that it is an appropriate aim for industrial nations or in particular the UK. Interestingly the term 'biodiversity' was used by the tabloid press but only 14 times in the whole of its coverage of the Summit, again indicating that concepts with an environmental focus are less unpopular with the tabloids than development concepts.

The detailed analysis of the content of the tabloid press is presented in this chapter in two forms; (i) an analysis of the degree to which the articles published in the four selected tabloids were supportive, balanced or critical of the Summit and its aims; (ii) as a summary of the particular descriptions and selected themes used to present the issues by each newspaper. The aim is to present a condensed, analysed overview of the coverage of the Summit by the tabloid press. Then by presenting descriptions of the coverage to give a deeper insight into the tactics of news presentation used by each paper. All the 91 articles published by the four selected tabloid newspapers were read and coded using a five point scale:

Very Critical (VC)	Includes articles in which the criticism was basically an attempt to trivialise or ridicule the conference or the people attending or the issues being discussed as well as extreme forms of more rational kinds of argument.
Critical (C)	Includes all those articles which were mainly or on balance critical but were reasonable and within bounds of normal argument.
Straight reporting or balanced articles (B)	Articles which include both sides of an argument. Sometimes this category includes very critical statements made by important actors when these are simply reported. If, however, these statements were highlighted or used to develop a critical stance towards the Summit the article would be coded as Critical.
Supportive (S)	Includes those articles that spelled out the purposes of the Summit and indicated the importance of these issues and the hope that the Summit could make some progress towards solving them, i.e. mild support.
Very supportive articles (VS)	These articles indicated strong support for the Summit etc.

The result of this coding produced the following distribution of articles for each newspaper.

Figure 7.3: Number of Articles Critical or Supportive of the Earth Summit published by the 'Popular' Press

	VC	C	B	S	VS	N
Today	–	5	20	9	1	35
Mail	4	8	15	–	–	27
Mirror	–	4	9	5	–	18
Sun	3	2	5	–	–	10

In this table the Mail *is the more rightwing of the* Today/Mail *pairing and the* Sun *is the more rightwing of the* Mirror/Sun *pairing. The totals for each newspaper vary slightly from Figure 7.2 because some articles were dropped (low relevance) and some added (high relevance but did not use 'Earth summit' – see Chapter 8)*

The table illustrates that not only did the right wing press report less about the Earth Summit but what was reported was far more likely to be critical or hostile. Critical articles account for 50 per cent of the *Sun's* meagre coverage and 44 per cent of the *Mail's* slightly more generous coverage. Neither paper produced articles that were supportive of the Earth Summit compared with *Today* and the *Daily Mirror* where, in spite of the low priority given to the Earth Summit, there was some effort to promote a supportive line.

This association between critical articles and the more right wing press, clearly bears out our prediction of the tactics that would be used by sections of the press. However, at this point we should remind ourselves that the table represents only a sample of newspapers, and does not reflect the number of readers reached by each newspaper. The combined sales of the *Mail* and the *Sun* in June 1992 were 5,230,000 compared with 3,340,000 for the *Mirror* and *Today*. If the full range of right wing tabloids is brought into the reckoning then the imbalance becomes even more pronounced, 7,600,000 compared with 4,090,000 . The great majority of newspaper readers in the UK will have been getting a critical or trivialised version of events at the Earth Summit, from their newspaper.

We recognise that the coding of articles in the manner presented in the above table represents an attempt to be objective but still contains many subjective judgements on the part of the coders. We therefore present a fairly full description of the themes and arguments presented by each newspaper so that the reader can explore the reasons for these judgements. In addition we present in an appendix the full list of the headlines of articles coded in the table.

Themes and presentation within the tabloid press: building cultures of understanding

The debate over whether the press follows public opinion or whether public opinion is formed by the powerful influence of the press has often been bedevilled by the implicit use of simple 'either-or' models used on narrowly defined themes, issues and events. The result has been a somewhat contradictory range of studies with some researchers claiming powerful effects for the press and others that the press follows powerful movements in public opinion (Hansen ed (1993)).

The Earth Summit was an international event organised by the UN which was intended to project a powerful message to a global population. The world stage was intended to be both a lure to world leaders and a constraint. Pressuring them to agree to international measures and to finance expensive programmes or to risk appearing in a negative light and attract damaging publicity. However, the images from the Summit received by the worlds population would depend on the world's press and television and the tactics used by world leaders to attract maximum good publicity without jeopardising their political position at home.

The analysis that we have presented thus far has attempted to show that newspapers both follow and lead and closely tailor their approach to their readerships. Even when they follow public opinion they seek to influence, gain control and interpret events in line with the understandings that they feel that they have established with their readerships.

It will be important to notice in the descriptions that follow how each newspaper associates the Summit with particular images and concerns. In almost every case these have already been established within the culture of understanding of their readers over a long period of time.

The analysis that follows treats, for the purposes of analysis, all the articles which mention the Earth Summit published in an individual newspaper as a single text. The analysis will describe in brief the major themes chosen for prominence within each newspaper and present the associated images and associations, in other words the attempts to establish cultural resonance with established cultures of understanding.

Daily Mail

In the period before the Earth Summit the *Mail* published ten articles which mentioned the Earth Summit and which established most of the major lines of argument. These can be summarised in condensed form as follows:

1   The major issue facing the world is population, therefore birth control is the most important issue facing the Earth Summit.
2   The Earth Summit will probably fail because family planning will be off the agenda due to pressure from Roman Catholics.
3   Wealth creation is the answer to over-population. Improved living standards will limit family size.
4   Criticism and trivialisation of the Summit itself.
5   Criticism of ecology and green philosophies; only real science can save the world.
6   The Earth Summit will probably fail because of self-interest on the part of participating nations.
7   The Third World has no special claim – they are motivated by greed – their claims will be resisted.
8   John Major has worked hard for success and has far-sighted and far-reaching proposals and has intervened with President Bush.
9   President Bush is portrayed as the potential wrecker of the conference for his refusal to sign the treaty to protect the world's animals and plants.

The population issue was introduced by the front page headline 'Human Time-bomb'. The article which followed was based on a recently published

UN Report. It presented a frightening picture of 'spiralling numbers', 'swamped resources', rife poverty', 'mass migration' and a 'rush of immigration to the industrialised nations' which will be 'uncontrollable'. 'The EC countries are already under pressure from a tide of immigrants from the South' (30 April 1992). In a later issue, where readers were told 'Wealth creation limits procreation', they were also told that the tide of illegal immigrants had reached the UK, 'Asian gangs supplying illegal immigrants as slave labour to farmers...' and 'Slavemasters hunted...' (19 May 1992).

Criticism and trivialisation of the Summit is a recurring theme. In a major article (30 May 1992) which is headlined 'Is this the way to save the world?' two contrasting images were presented, a picture of a crying, starving child and a picture of 'the glamour of Copacabana Beach'. 'Luxury hotels and glittering restaurants' that line the 'golden beaches' will, we were told, have 'the greatest bonanza ever'. However, while the starving child image was used to discredit the glitz and 'razzmatazz' of the conference it was not used to argue for more aid or a better deal for Third World countries; quite the contrary. The Third World, readers were told, has no particular claim to 'righteousness'. Their claims exhibit 'simple greed'. They once used strategies which flirted with the Soviet bloc. Now that this no longer works 'the environment has been seized as a handy new lever', ... 'Debt for Nature'. Who will pay the 'staggering $70 billion a year' that their demands cost?

Criticism and trivialisation was developed even further on the day of the official Summit opening. In a page 8 article of 28 column inches the Summit is described in the following terms, 'having already generated enough column inches to account for a small rainforest'; 'the swirling fog of word pollution'; 'a great mushroom cloud of recrimination and evangelistic blathering'; 'the Rio Rave-up'. At the same time the official opening is described on Page 10 in 8½ column inches under the heading 'Fight for Earth starts in silence' (4 June 1992).

Images associated with 'greens' and green philosophies are similarly negative and threatening. 'Ecology has become a substitution for religion and Marxism'. Scientists distrust 'the ecological mystique', 'the ecology extremists will be in Rio' ... 'to challenge the moderation that will come from the world leaders'. Phrases like 'eco-fervour', 'dedicated Greenies', 'eco-evangelists' and whinging 'health freaks' cement the image of greens. Against this '... Science can save the World' and 'Major's mission to rescue Earth Summit – from collapse' produce contrasting images for *Mail* readers.

There are, of course, ambiguous and potentially confusing messages in this collection of articles. For instance, John Major is portrayed as sensible and caring and set on rescuing the Summit from President Bush's unwillingness to sign the Biodiversity Treaty or even attend. Yet the conference itself is portrayed as a Tower of Babel, an occasion of fruitless politicking in 'smoke free rooms'. So there is a danger that John Major could be associated with a failure. This is possibly one reason why the event quickly disappeared into the middle pages.

This analysis is selective, but it portrays major themes and illustrates the way that the *Mail* has carefully chosen the items of news and presented them in ways that associate the conference with images of threat, danger, extremism, greed and fruitless politicking in which only John Major is trustworthy. The most surprising feature of this coverage is that most of it occurred *before the Summit* had begun and before the *Mail* correspondents had arrived in Rio. On the day the Summit opened the *Mail*'s front page was dominated by the headline 'Lead us out of trouble, Mr Major' and a large picture of Joan Collins, who had had a tiff with her male escort at the Derby. In the subsequent period news was dominated by the matrimonial problems of Prince Charles and Princess Diana. The selective relegation of the Summit news to the inner pages of the paper can be measured by the average page score:

Figure 7-4:   *Position of Critical and Balanced articles in the* Daily Mail *May 92–Jun 92*

n=27	Very Critical/Critical	Balanced
Position (average page number)	7.3	11.5
Length (average column inches of articles)	12.6	4.9

Critical articles were almost three times the length of 'balanced' articles.

This relegation of the 'balanced' or 'news' articles amounted to trivialisation when on 8 June the Summit was reported in 9 column inches on page 15 underneath a much longer story headlined 'Cub turns detective and finds sleeping fugitive'.

The degree to which the *Daily Mail* was prepared to pursue marginal or contextual issues to damage the image of tribal peoples and the need to preserve their habitats can be gauged from the coverage it gave to the case of Paulimbo Paiakan. In a page 6 article on 12th June the *Mail* devoted 57 column inches of space with 24 column inches of text to an Amazon Indian leader, reported as befriended by Sting and signed up by Anita Roddick, who had been accused of raping a fifteen year old girl who was teaching his daughter Portuguese. This was the largest single article published by the *Mail* devoted to any issue connected even indirectly to the Summit. The prominence given to this event illustrates the values behind the selection of articles representing or colouring the Summit.

The *Mail*'s conclusion on the Earth Summit is almost inevitable: an 'unseemly wrangle' between 'advanced and developing countries'. One of its final sentences on the subject is derogatory to all concerned: 'The Summit had given the Third World the opportunity to dust off old and discredited demands for development aid and present them all over again as bills for conserving the environment' (13 June).

The outcomes of the Summit in terms of explaining what the agreements might mean or the plans for future conferences to pursue agreements on climate, population, forests, fisheries etc. were not mentioned.

Today

Today's coverage of the Earth Summit contrasts with that of the *Mail* in a number of respects. It is certainly more supportive of the Summit and more concerned to report the wide range of issues being dealt with. On the other hand, it did not give the Summit much prominence, for example it never reached the front page, and the newspaper did not engage in the process of building a strong positive culture of understanding.

The coverage began on the 19 May with an article indicating that Prince Charles' support for the major aims of the Summit could bring him into open conflict with George Bush and the Prime Minister who he accused of 'dragging their feet on pollution, the ozone layer and rainforest'. In contrast to the *Daily Mail* the population issue was not stressed and far from suggesting that it was being excluded from the agenda, Today lists it as one of the '10 Green Issues they'll discuss'.

1 Global Warming	6 Population – the birth explosion
2 Protecting species	7 Boosting the power of the UN
3 Disappearing forests	8 Deserts
4 Cash for poor countries	9 Oceans
5 Sharing Green technology	10 The future – The Rio Declaration

Today did not give great prominence to John Major's role and John Smith is given a small mention. On the other hand, the editorial makes clear *Today*'s support for the Summit and its aims 'nothing like the Earth Summit has ever happened before'; 'They will discuss such massive issues as global warming...'; 'Why are they (Bush and Michael Howard) so reticent?'.... 'Unless ministers are prepared to put their money where their mouths are...'; 'For all our sakes this Summit must not be a waste of time'. *Today* maintained this line up to the Summit and produced a double page centre spread on 'Timebomb Earth' which included a series of coloured graphs, diagrams and photographs highlighting a wide range of environment and development issues from hydro-electric schemes to endangered species and lead pollution. This generally supportive stance was continued on 11 June with a feature on '30 species they saved for us all'. While on the 12 June it reports 'Green Treaties may mean nothing ... without American support and cash'.

The critical dimension of *Today*'s coverage was therefore targeted on the major powers and their unwillingness to pay rather than the Summit itself and the Third World. On 13 June this critical dimension became stronger with an editorial headlined 'Selling our future short' and a clear statement 'The delegates needed to agree on a package that would secure £37 billion. They also gave prominence to the Labour Party's criticism, reported on Page 2 'Hot air is the last thing the planet needs at the moment, but that is all Mr Major has to offer'.

Today's coverage of the Summit contrasts with that of the *Daily Mail*. However, its support does not project the same conviction as the *Mail*'s opposition. The debate was superficial and proceeds without examining the complexity of many of the issues. *Today* also failed to explain the outcomes and future conferences.

The *Sun*

The whole coverage of the Earth Summit by the *Sun* newspaper was contained in eight articles and 43 column inches of print. Despite its brevity and lack of substance it contained a remarkably clear message. The Summit was a complete waste of time. It achieved maximum impact by pouring ridicule on the Summit, its aims, the people attending and its outcomes. The amount of information about the Summit was kept to a minimum. The main points made by the *Sun* closely resembled those made in the *Mail*. The differences were in the brevity, the selection of an even smaller number of issues, and the strength of criticism directed at the Summit.

The coverage of the Summit did not begin until 2 June, two days before the opening. In an article headlined 'PM warns on Earth Summit', it was reported that the Summit could 'collapse' if Third World countries asked for too much money. Mr Major is described as using his 'influence to persuade other world leaders to attend'. On the next day, however, the *Sun*'s editorial described the Summit as a 'Doze-Zone':

'The hot air rising from the Earth conference in Rio is the greatest threat to the environment in years. All the freaks known to man are gathering. Those who believe the earth is getting *too hot* ... Those who believe the earth is *cooling down* ... The Flat Earth Society will be there too ...They only want us to pump in an extra £70 billion. .... they denounce the ecological danger done by industry. ... Rio could seriously damage your health'. (*Sun*, 3 June 1992)

The coverage ends on the 15 June, as it began, with a editorial attack entitled 'Farce in Rio': 'Was there ever such a waste of natural resources as the Earth Conference.... let's hope the Rio beano is but definitely the last.' The coverage was consistent in reporting bad news and gave space to 'Body Shop Indian is Rapist''; the story about the Caipo Indian leader who allegedly raped a Portuguese woman. Only the Ken Livingstone column produced an alternative view with a 4 column-inch insertion on 'The Earth Summit at Rio is vital for the health of our children', in which he listed some of the major environment and development issues and criticised Bush and Major. Generally however news items from the Summit are briefly reported with little salience and sometimes placed alongside items that are themselves ridiculous asides, for example Ronnie Biggs offering delegates advice on 'how to avoid thieves'.

The attack on the Summit and on almost all those who show any concern for the environment and development is uncompromising, uninformed by any complications; it is simple and direct. The major tool in building a culture of (mis)understanding is humour. There are fewer sinister symbols and associations than in the *Mail*. It is an attempt to build a culture of avoidance, relieving the individual of any responsibility for understanding any of the problems faced by society and being faced up to or avoided by the Earth Summit.

The *Daily Mirror*

The *Daily Mirror*'s coverage of the Summit fits almost exactly into the predicted pattern in terms of quantity and quality. The 18 articles that it published which mention the Summit give a total of 97 column inches of print; more than twice the coverage provided by the *Sun* but less than half the column inches in the *Mail*.

The first mention of the Summit occurred on 11 May with a very short, very straight report on a pre-Summit agreement global warming. Bush is mentioned as watering down the cuts in emissions.

The first major article introducing the coverage occurred on 3 June under the headline, 'What on earth can they do?'. The *Mirror* sets out fourteen questions, for example, 'who called the Earth Summit?' 'What are its aims?' 'What could happen if they are not achieved?'. The report gives balanced answers to each question. The *Mirror* also gave some prominence to the Labour Party's criticism of the Conservative policy. 'Aid blast at Tories' occurred in the same issue (3 June). As the coverage developed during the Conference, criticism of John Major became more and more prominent. In this respect the *Mirror* differed markedly from the *Sun* and the *Mail.*

It is interesting to compare the *Mirror*'s coverage with the *Mail*'s and note some of the major differences (the different treatment of the political parties has already been noted). There were not prominent critical pieces in the *Mirror*, while the *Mail* gave prominence to four. There was one long informative article in the *Mirror* against a number of short informative pieces in the *Mail.* The *Mirror* concentrated on global warming and the protection of species, there was no corresponding xenophobic coverage of population and migration. The *Mirror* selected the plight of Rio's street children as its main contextual issue and therefore created a sympathetic context for aid and the support of the Summit. As we have seen the *Mail* covered in detail the Paulimbo Paiakan rape case and produced a much less sympathetic context.

In parallel to the coverage of the Earth Summit the *Daily Mirror* ran a mini-campaign on the nuclear reprocessing plant at Sellafield. The reprocessing plant was linked to nuclear waste pumped into the North Sea and child leukaemia. This highly emotional and high profile campaign featured the death of 'Jessica' a child leukaemia victim and a series of highly publicised events staged by the pop group UB40 against Sellafield. This series of 19 articles was more prominent and designed to have more impact than the Earth Summit reports. However, the two sets of articles overlapped at a number of points and the issue of nuclear pollution must be considered alongside the *Mirror*'s treatment of the Earth Summit. We will include this campaign when we consider the readership's response to the Summit.

The *Mirror*'s support of the Summit was illustrated in its 'Win Earthrise' competition and some relatively weak supportive statements in some articles. For example, 'Can it therefore be fair to expect the poorer nations to shoulder the entire bill for our wastefulness?'. However, compared with the forthright opposition to the major purposes of the Summit by the *Mail* and the *Sun*, the *Mirror* support was weak and lacked any kind of depth or conviction. It also failed to adequately report conference outcomes or point out the future agenda.

The Broadsheet Coverage

The number of articles which referred to the Earth Summit published in the quality press between 30th April and 30th June 1992, was very large; 763 in the four newspapers that we included in our sample. With this number of articles it was not possible, given our resources, to use the same methodology that we employed with the 91 shorter articles published in the tabloid press. However, by using keyword searches on the FT Profile database we were able to investigate the same issues using a computer-based methodology.

The batch of key words chosen for this task included two that related to the well established public discussion of climate change, 'global warming' and 'ozone layer', and two that referred to the central issues within the Earth Summit agenda, 'sustainable development' and 'biodiversity'. The term Earth Summit was also included as a general indicator of coverage of the Summit. Since these searches were computer based we were able to carry them out over much longer time periods than the 2 months surrounding the Summit. We were therefore able to trace changes in the usage or acceptability of those terms.

Figure 7.5: Ratio of Articles in Quality Press containing selected key words: Oct 88 – Mar 93

	Lowest	Highest	Ratio of diff
Ozone Layer	359 (Tel)	519 (Gdn)	1:1.45
Global Warming	440 (Tel)	717 (Gdn)	1:1.63
Earth Summit	210 (Tel)	395 (Gdn)	1:1.88
Sust Development	57 (Tel)	181 (Gdn)	1:3.18
Biodiversity	24 (Tel)	86 (Gdn)	1:3.58

The results bear out our expectations. The left of centre newspapers give more coverage to all environment issues in this period. Well established issues like the ozone layer and global warming show relatively low levels of differentiation compared with the Earth Summit and the more sensitive issues of sustainable development and biodiversity are the most differentiated. However, the increases in differentiation (ratios of 1:1.45 to 1:3.58) are relatively small, showing that the right wing broadsheets were prepared to give even the most sensitive issues a substantial coverage. It will now be necessary to see if levels of differentiation increased at the time of the Summit or decreased.

The following graphs of the occurrence of these key words in the *Guardian* and the *Daily Telegraph* show how they have been introduced into the debate in a 'quality' centre left newspaper compared with a 'quality' right wing newspaper. The graphs are presented on the longer time line.

Figure 7.6: Graph of key word 'biodiversity' Oct 88-Mar 93

Figure 7.6a: Guardian

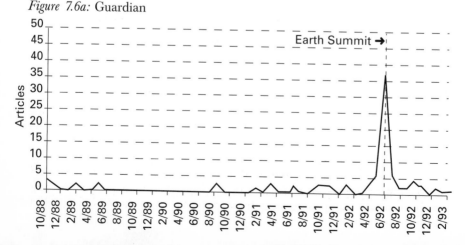

Figure 7.6b: Daily Telegraph

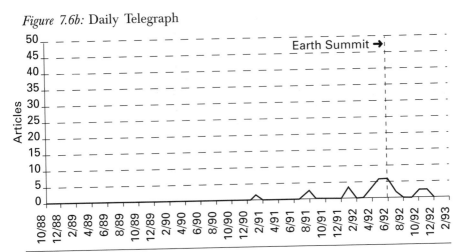

Figure 7.7: Graph of keyword 'sustainable development' Oct 88-Mar 93

Figure 7.7a: Guardian

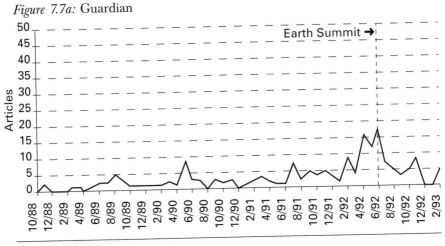

Figure 7.7b: Daily Telegraph

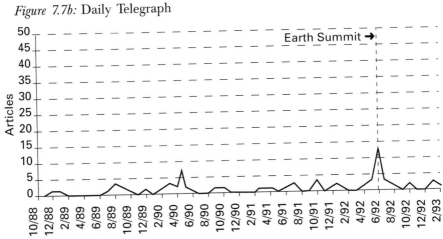

It is clear that the Earth Summit was closely associated with an increased use of these terms in both newspapers. However, while the *Guardian* introduced both these terms gradually in the period before the Summit (particularly sustainable development) the *Daily Telegraph* trailed behind with rather less coverage. Since the purposes of the Summit were less in sympathy with right wing ideologies we would expect (from our predictions) that these terms would find less exposure and would be less part of the 'education drive' of right wing newspapers. This is illustrated in Figure 7.5 by the fact that the frequency of articles referring to these topics are more highly differentiated. However, at the time of the Summit itself in June 1992 while the differentiation with respect to biodiversity was maintained, the term sustainable development became less differentiated and entered into more common use at the *Daily Telegraph*. The index of differentiation slipped from 3.18 to 1.5.

Clearly there were internal shifts in the editorial culture of the newspapers as they developed their coverage of the Summit. Evidence for this comes from a series of interviews with correspondents which we conducted shortly after the Summit. Correspondents were asked how they saw the effect, if any, of the Earth Summit on any aspect of the coverage of environment and development issues. One correspondent of a right wing broadsheet replied: 'It means that I can get the words 'sustainable development' into copy without a sub-editor rewriting it, that's an important statement really ...'. This correspondent had experienced some easement of 'gatekeeping' processes with respect to reporting on this particular aspect of the Earth Summit. The evidence for increased differentiation of press coverage among the quality press is therefore relatively weak.

Guardian coverage

Providing the most substantial coverage of all the broadsheet papers the *Guardian* adopts an overtly critical line. It gives emphasis to the linkage between environment and development. Although the *Daily Telegraph* also gives some emphasis to this aspect of the Earth Summit, the Guardian returns to it frequently, reiterated for example in a guest article by Vaclav Havel (4 June). Articles are long and detailed on every aspect of the Earth Summit, including the Global Forum, the historical background, the agenda, and the positions adopted by key groups such as the US and Europe during the preliminary negotiations leading up to Rio.

The *Guardian* raises concerns about moral leadership and argues that Europe should take the lead for there is virtue in a unilateral approach. The environment is too important for national self-interest to prevail, for example the UK's argument that EC proposals for a 'carbon tax' will have a major impact on the coal industry: '..the EC should try to cajole its own members to go it alone and give the movement towards an integrated Europe the moral dimension it badly needs.' (14 May)

On the population issue the *Guardian*, in sympathy with most other papers, regrets that pressure has kept it off the Earth Summit agenda. However, it is more critical of the Roman Catholic Church which should confine itself to dealing with its own members and not try to interfere with the agenda. It is naïve to think that population can be tackled without contraception and the Catholic Church should seriously reinterpret its doctrines in the light of changing circumstances.

Population should be on the ES agenda because it is as serious as, but more immediate than, global warming. The UN Population Fund report shows how serious the situation is. Education is vital – it demonstrably leads to reduction in population growth. Chalker is on strong ground when she challenges the Roman Catholic Church at the Earth Summit, but this would be stronger if the UK devoted more than 1 per cent of its aid budget to family planning.

The *Guardian* is very critical of Bush and the US position, describing him as paranoid and showing an amazing disregard for world opinion. Moreover, the *Guardian* is explicitly left of centre in its criticism of Bush's posture: 'The view that Rio represents an ambush by the South on the North is either geopolitically naive or a diplomatic alibi for failure. The imbalance of power and influence between the two hemispheres rules out any such possibility.' (1 June)

There is a need for N-S co-operation, particularly over biodiversity, but this is not in sight. Referring to the 'third decade of a series of developmental and environmental binges' the *Guardian* points to a failure of 'modernity' not socialism, and the economic models that the North promotes. 'The Earth Summit will see divergent objectives. The North wishes to talk about the environment while the South wants to talk first about development. A new world outlook has to begin with the inter-connection of these goals. Tragically, there is no reason to believe that it will start in Rio.'(1 June)

The *Guardian* was the only newspaper to raise the issue of Third World debt in a substantial way and link it to the problems of the environment and development. In Victoria Brittain's hard-hitting article (15 May 1992) the links are made explicit:

> In the last decade debt has emerged as the main cause of hunger and misery in the world, and 1000 children are estimated to die every day from its effects. Over this period the poorest have grown even poorer, while banks and public institutions have received 1.3 trillion dollars from debtor nations.

She points out that during 1985 when many people in Britain thought that Live Aid was solving the problems of poverty and hunger 'the hungriest African countries gave twice as much money to the developed world as we gave to them.' She makes the link with the environment quite explicit.

> The Philippines' debt payment is 6 million dollars a day. To pay interest the country has cut down its rainforests, dug up coral reefs, replaced agriculture with industry, and squeezed its poor beyond endurance.

The readers of tabloid newspapers and some other broadsheets would have to develop their understanding of Third World debt problems and the attendant problems of the world's environment without the benefit of such information.

As for outcomes the *Guardian* takes the view that although 'most of the elements of a positive alternative already feature in the language of the Rio Declaration and Agenda 21' (15 June) the opposite scenario is also plausible – a global 'eco-shock' early in the next century and a global crisis. The Earth

Summit is in the decade of final choice. Rio needs to lead to fast action, co-operation, and funds, but none of these will materialise. A commitment to 0.7 per cent of GDP would result in a real net transfer on a scale not yet considered. 'That would mean a decision on priorities whereby the developed world postponed current benefit for a global few in order to prevent future suffering for the whole world. This may not seem practical politics, but it is the only way to practical survival' (15 June)

The *Independent*

The Earth Summit is given considerable coverage by the *Independent* with many long and detailed articles. Explanations of the Earth Summit agenda and its historical context are good and highly informative. The Independent's overall position is that although it is probably true that expectations are too high, the event is vitally important. Small steps are steps nevertheless: '...the Summit will be useful if it contributes to incremental change, raises consciousness and sets standards against which progress can be measured.' (29 May 1992). The *Independent* regards the Earth Summit as worthwhile even if it has only modest outcomes. It supports what it describes as John Major's position that the Earth Summit is not about outcomes but about consciousness-raising. 'To be cast down by Rio's shortcomings would be as irrational as to have expected it to achieve miracles. The Earth Summit leaves the world better-informed if not necessarily wiser.' Any outcomes that do emerge from the Summit will provide 'yardsticks' against which to measure progress. Those, like Bush, who stand opposed to many of its aims may find themselves the victims of these outcomes as electors come to find his position untenable. 'The central paradox of Rio is that both prosperity and poverty can severely damage the health of the environment.' (13 June 1992).

It is critical of the US, describing the US performance at Rio as 'crassly inept'. Bush is arrogant and insensitive to the fact that many other nations who are willing to sign up to the climate convention and the biodiversity convention are also likely to be affected in the same way as the US yet are willing to sign. Bush has shown a sad lack of leadership. At times a doubtful note is raised about the nature of the political process. For example, a long article on 6 June questions the state of consensus referring to the failure of the G7 Summit to construct an agenda before it meets. 'Is the system of Western summitry breaking down?' On the Earth Summit the lack of consensus achieved by the various pre-summit preparatory negotiations are well described with the US position dominating the coverage.

Coverage is relatively low-key on population, and gives little coverage to Carey's speech or the general debate about population and birth control. Japan is profiled quite extensively, even qualifying for a leading article explaining Japan's attempt to participate as a world power, which is critical of its environmental record in relation to the virtuous posture it is said to be adopting.

In a leading article about the Biodiversity Convention, the Independent explains that it is about halting the mass destruction of species, not about saving every species for its own sake. The Global Environmental Facility is a good idea but care is needed over funding. It is better not to proceed if suitable arrangements cannot be made. 'There would be a risk of paralysis, but that would be preferable to a misuse of funds.' (2 June 1992).

The *Independent* also contains the standard 'jokes' about the ES contributing to deforestation. On 3 June the Finance page writes that '...it is worth reflecting on how many forests have perished to provide the raw material for legislation covering banking and investment activities in the world's leading economies ... ' and argues for the cessation of off-shore financial status. On 6 June an article from the Law section notes that 'it has taken a whole rainforest to provide the bumf for the Earth Summit jamboree...'.

On climate control the *Independent* is clear that something needs to be done but that proposals such as those put forward by the EC are not the right answer. A solution to pollution through taxation will not work. 'Intended to make the EC look good at the Earth Summit the tax is more likely to make it seem hypocritical and feeble. All in all a less than historic day for the environment' (14 May 1992). Elsewhere the carbon tax is described as a hasty measure.

The *Independent* is informative and provides a high rate of coverage throughout the Summit. It maintains detailed coverage to include the final outcomes and agreements. It's position is that although the outcomes of the Earth Summit are now deemed to be a failure by environmentalist lobbies there are important successes, principally that no hasty action has been agreed! 'The fact is that the Rio conference has been mainly about money, and how to persuade the advanced countries to transfer funds.' But there has been too much concentration on global warming and biodiversity, with little attention given to issues such as population, poverty, and 'genuine' local, regional and global environmental problems (15 June).

Daily Telegraph

The *Daily Telegraph*'s coverage is similarly detailed and provides good information about the historical background and the context of the problems addressed by the Earth Summit. The Global Forum, hardly mentioned in the tabloids, receives a good deal of favourable attention in the *Telegraph* and a long and detailed article on NGOs provides good background and a historical view of their changed importance in the context of the Earth Summit. The Earth Summit is treated as a serious event which deals with issues of great importance. It also helps to draw out the links between environment and development and in at least one statement in an article by Charles Clover, the Environment Correspondent, this is made explicit:

> The idea that environmental protection must be linked with development might be a somewhat dry thought, largely of academic interest in London; in Rio, amid the stinking favelas and the street children, it strikes you with visceral force. (Charles Clover, 3 June)

The *Telegraph* espouses an essentially 'free trade' position on the solutions to the problems of North-South divide which are caused by overconsumption in the North and population and poverty in the South:

> What is needed most is trade, not aid. The best way to help the South – and by extension to ensure the long-term future of the rainforests and the species therein – is for the North to open up its markets. (2 June)

Free trade, with little state regulation, is the key to dealing with environment and development because market forces will determine that industry and trade clean up their act. Poverty and environmental degradation are at their worst in those countries where people are ruled by oppressive and corrupt governments. Funding for Earth Summit initiatives should be tied to greater accountability on the part of such governments, although and unfortunately, corruption will not to be dealt with directly at the Summit.

Corruption is the unspeakable issue at the Earth Summit, 'politically incorrect'. The anxiety that many share is the 'blank cheque syndrome'. In the view of Northern nations (mainly Britain and the US are reported) many of the agreements to be made contain funding arrangements (e.g. the financial clause of the Biodiversity Convention) which are too much in favour of the South where governments tend to be unaccountable for their use of the money. Third World nations are attempting a kind of blackmail 'pay up or we will cut down our forests' but the donor countries need to stand firm against the unaccountability of the proposed funding. John Major should be tougher and ask questions about how aid already given has been used. Coverage is upbeat on Major who is portrayed as calm and rational, even statesmanlike in his efforts to persuade Bush to change his position on the Biodiversity Convention, and he is expected to be unmoved by emotional arguments at the Summit.

Population issues, birth control, and poverty are treated neutrally in relation to the Roman Catholic position on contraception. Two leading articles are devoted to Carey's speeches and his visit to Rome. The *Telegraph* distances itself from the particular issues of the Roman Catholic position on birth control taking the view that the 'ills of poverty' have more to do with political systems under which people live. The emphasis is given to approaches which put family planning in the context of health and education programmes.

The reader is provided with good information on the purposes of the Summit. In two articles on 26 May and 3 June we are given a useful summary of what the conference is aiming to achieve. 'Two set pieces', the Climate Convention and the Biodiversity Convention, and Agenda21, a 'mop-up operation' for everything else (population, aid etc.). However, Agenda21 is also described as one of the 'unresolved issues' at the Summit (along with forests).

Overall the Summit is thought to be successful although simultaneously some prominence is given to the view that its outcomes are just as the starting point of a long process involving yet further negotiations. Although no firm agreement on forests was achieved, even here the Summit managed to agree a set of principles on which to base further talks in the future. John Major and Michael Howard are quoted several times as saying that this is the beginning of a process not an end, and that on the various conventions that have been agreed we cannot expect big changes too soon, for most of the conventions and other agreements will require further negotiation.

Conclusions

The press coverage of the Earth Summit described and analysed in this chapter largely bears out most of our predictions. It also demonstrates the enormous difference between the broadsheet and tabloid press in the amount and quality of coverage. The degree to which tabloid editors shaped the reporting of the Summit to fit existing lines of argument developed by the newspaper. Differences in perspective and argument certainly existed within the broadsheet press but within a much more generally informative framework of news that could be used to further the readers' own understanding of the Summit.

The *Guardian*'s coverage of the effects of debt illustrates a difference. The readers of the other newspapers were protected from this information. Unless they obtained the information from other sources there were not as able to integrate the role of Third World debt into their understanding of poverty and exploitation of the environment. They remained in relative ignorance.

From our interviews and detailed reading of articles it would appear that the quality of news coverage and the autonomy and professional standing of environment correspondents within the broadsheet press largely overcame marked editorial bias of the kind that the tabloid press exhibited. As Paul Brown, Environment Correspondent of the *Guardian* put it:

> ... [the] environmnet is more mainstream than it was in every sense of the word, partly because Rio has had an educational effect, like I can now say 'biodiversity' to someone on the newsdesk and they are not allowed to look blank because it is a word that has been around and so they are expected to know what biodiversity means. (Interview, Summer 1992).

Within the tabloids there were no specialist environment correspondents with professional standing who could approach the task with deep insight and prepare reports that demanded respect from sub editors. Instead within the tabloids the coverage was accomplished using a rag-tag group of 'diplomatic' and 'political' correspondents along with 'special' correspondents some of whom did not attend the Summit. One special correspondent who did attend the Summit for a right wing tabloid complained that although over 10,000 words of 'bloody good' copy on the Summit had been filed, often staying up late at night and ploughing through masses of documents, hardly any of it was published. Instead the paper carried stories from other correspondents who treated it from a political and diplomatic point of view.

In the next chapter we examine some of the effects of this highly differentiated coverage on the understanding of the Summit developed by the readers and non-readers of national daily newspapers.

8 Evidence of Newspaper Influence on Cultures of Understanding

The research design

The study of the press coverage of the Earth Summit has borne out our prediction that the newspapers making up the UK press would interpret this event rather differently and vary widely in the amount of coverage and the understandings offered to their readers. In this chapter we grasp the issue of readership response. Do these facts about differences in newspaper coverage matter or do readers simply use newspapers to make up their own minds independently of the interpretation of the news by the newspaper they read?

This is a very difficult question to answer decisively. It would be futile to simply ask respondents how much they are influenced by their newspaper. Most of us do not know. We do not usually monitor the sources of the information that we receive on a day to day basis. Even if we do, it would be very difficult to say how a particular article, report of an event or picture has changed the way in which we think about issues, personalities or situations. Research based on an individual's perception or interpretation of news would be extremely detailed, time consuming and would depend on a series of very intensive interviews over fairly long periods of time. Such a study has yet to be carried out.

Our approach was based on the idea developed within this book, that cultures of understanding are sustained and developed by individual newspapers. In the case of new, important events like the Earth Summit individuals will be in general dependent on three sources: a newspaper, the television or the radio. As Lowe and Morrison (1984) pointed out there was no deep, political experience of environmental issues, unlike say trade union affairs where opinion might already be hardened by long exposure to messages within cultures of understanding. Our method would therefore depend on measuring differences that emerged between readership groups (as in Chapter 5) and relating these differences to the differences in newspaper coverage. In order to pursue this comparison in detail we will limit our analysis to the coverage of environment and development events, in particular the Earth Summit. In this case, however, we will be able to argue much more strongly for a newspaper's role in influencing its readers because of the relative newness of the phenomenon and the lack of well established partisan (i.e. differentiated) attitudes and perspectives. The research design can be portrayed in diagrammatic terms and contrasted with the design used by most North American researchers.

Research design used by North American researchers

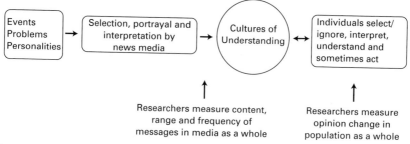

Research design used in this research

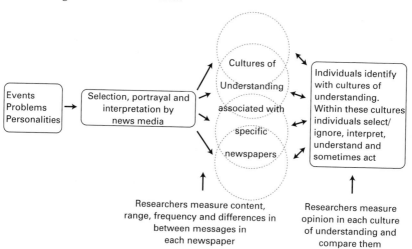

We present this latter design as a substantial improvement on the former, especially in the UK context. The North American studies treat the media as an undifferentiated whole. This means that they cannot comment on the influence wielded by individual newspapers or even in most cases different sections of the media. This issue is most damaging for Page and Shapiro's idea of a rational public. In order to establish the rationality of the whole public, as opposed to individuals, they assume that '... the public as a whole, so long as the errors are randomly distributed, will make use of all available information and choose the appropriate policies.' (p26)

We will be able to show, using our model, that news is not randomly distributed. In fact the opposite is true. However, the improved model remains a considerable simplification of reality. There are many important and influential aspects of the social world that are omitted, not least the fact that existing cultures of understanding affect events, the definition of problems and the selection, portrayal and interpretation of events. This happens because newspapers are part of the social world and newspapers serve existing patterns of belief and understanding as well as shape them. Nevertheless, by carefully recording the differences between newspapers in their treatment of the news we will be able to trace evidence of these differences within their audiences. It will then be for individual readers to judge for themselves how likely these differences were to have emerged by themselves, independent of newspaper influence.

Data gathering methods

We present data gathered by two independent methods, the Mass Observation Archive at Sussex University and the MORI Omnibus Opinion Poll.

The Mass Observation Archive undertakes two or three data gathering exercises a year based on an established panel of respondents. The instrument used for data gathering is known as a Directive. This usually consists of a list of open-ended questions rather than a questionnaire. The respondent is invited to write on the proposed topic, directed by the questions. This mode of response allows for a wide range of responses from a few pages to 50 pages or more. The open-ended nature of a Directive generates a committed response but one that can weave its own path through the questions that are asked. Responses can sometimes be quite idiosyncratic but in most cases the responses are carefully thought out and reflect the opinions and belief of the respondent in a highly personal and considered way. We reproduce a copy of the directive in Appendix B.

Over 700 MOA Directives were sent out during the Earth Summit in June 1992. The Directives were therefore received towards the end of the conference or after the Earth Summit had ended. The entire return of 411 usable Directives was coded for general indicators using a traditional coding frame. This exercise quickly revealed a high degree of skew in the original panel. It was skewed in favour of the elderly, women, professionals and retired people. More importantly from our point of view the panel did not represent a cross section of newspaper readers.[1]

We had anticipated some of the atypical characteristics of the panel because it consisted of self selected individuals who volunteered to write at length on matters of importance affecting the general population. We had anticipated that they would be highly literate (middle class) with some leisure time (retired) and that we would have to use the samples in a comparative design. The fact that the panel would not reflect the population at large was not a major concern. We had planned to select sub-samples of respondants who reported that they read only one national newspaper to represent the culture of understanding of each newspaper. These sub-samples of one-newspaper readers would all be skewed in the same direction by the same set of factors and therefore we would be comparing sub-samples with similar characteristics.

We were able to stick fairly strictly to the rules we set ourselves in selecting one-newspaper readership samples but the lack of representation of some newspaper readerships meant that we were only able to achieve sub-samples of 10 or more individuals for five newspapers. Fortunately we were also able to achieve what we regarded as a useful sample of respondents who did not read any national daily paper on a regular basis, the no-newspaper or non-

---

1   The skew in the sample is partly a product of the way the panel has been recruited. In the past methods for recruiting panellists have included articles or letters published in selected newspapers thus resulting in a skewed readership profile.

reader sample. This group as in our previous analysis of MORI data, represents an important bench mark. They can be regarded as relatively free from the influence of a particular national newspaper, although not free from the collective influence of local and regional newspapers or the rest of the media.

The rules set up to select the sub-samples were intended to reduce the imbalance in gender, age etc. The results presented below show that despite the problems of readership we were able to do this to a modest degree.

Table 8.1: Major characteristics of one- and no-newspaper sub-samples compared with total panel

	% Male	% Female	% 60+	% Prof/Man	% Retired	% SE Region
Panel Total (n=411)	29	71	57	51	50	42
Sub-samples (n=107)	41	59	54	61	47	40

The only dimension in which there is not a reduction in skew is the occupational dimension. Unfortunately in correcting the gender imbalance we were sometimes increasing the number of respondents in the professional/managerial category. The breakdown of these dimensions into one-newspaper groups is given in an appendix and the following table shows the size of the 'one newspaper' sub-samples.

Table 8.2: Size of one- and no-newspaper sub-samples compared with total panel

Newspapers	Total Panel	Sub-Samples	%
Guardian	97	27	25.2
Daily Telegraph	65	24	22.4
Independent	46	14	13.1
Daily Mail	37	17	15.9
None	28	14	13.1
Times	19	–	–
Daily Mirror	18	11	10.3
Express	17	–	
Other	14	–	
Today	8	–	
Sun	5	–	
European	4	–	
Financial Times	2	–	
Star	2	–	
	362		
Local/Regional	153		
	515	107	

Total n= 411 (NB the total panel includes a large number of multiple readerships)

The Times was omitted because of the very small number of male respondents, the *Express* was omitted because of the small number of one newspaper readers. In all the included newspapers it was possible to achieve a one newspaper readership of more than 10. Although we had included the *Sun* and *Today* newspapers for their coverage of the Earth Summit it was not possible to select one-newspaper sub-samples for the *Sun* and *Today* newspapers from the MOA Directive responses.

Discussion of directives

Feelings towards the environment and knowledge that the Summit was taking place were at a surprisingly high level across all newspaper sub-samples. For example, 96 per cent of the sub-sample respondents felt that there were substantial environmental and developmental problems in the world. Also 93 per cent knew about the Earth Summit before receiving the Directive. These percentages were only marginally different from the full panel where they were 93 per cent and 91 per cent respectively. The difference is entirely due to a slightly higher non-response rate in the full panel. The similarity in the results of the two samples is such that only the sub-samples will be reported here and unless otherwise stated, it can be assumed that both samples give a broadly similar result.

By contrast, the question asking respondents whether or not they took a 'close interest' in the Summit, split the respondents into three almost equal parts.

Table 8.3: Respondents' 'interest' in the Summit

Close Interest	Some Interest	No Interest	Non Response
25%	39%	34%	2%

When the 'one newspaper' groups of respondents are examined for their level of interest in the Summit, there are some interesting differences. By constructing a simple index of interest ('Yes' scores=2, 'Some' scores=1) it is possible to compare the amount of interest expressed by each of the one newspaper samples.

Table 8.4: Index of interest in the Summit for each one-newspaper sample

Newspaper	Points	Newspaper	Points
Independent	114	*Daily Mirror*	91
No-Newspaper	107	*Daily Telegraph*	83
Guardian	93	*Daily Mail*	65

The main surprise demonstrated in this table is the relatively high level of interest expressed by no-newspaper respondents. This result is replicated in the full panel where the no-newspaper group score is marginally higher than both the *Guardian* and the *Independent*. One interpretation of this result is that reading a newspaper could have the effect of damping interest in the Summit. Our descriptions of the coverage of the Earth Summit in Chapter 7 make clear the extent to which negative features of the Summit were given maximum coverage. In addition the failure to give prominence to the positive outcomes of the Summit, either the agreements or plans for future conferences, make this damping effect a plausible explanation. Certainly the readerships of the newspapers with the most negative coverage record the lowest level of interest. The results of the full sample bear out this result with the additional piece of evidence that the level of interest of *Express* readers was slightly below that of the *Daily Mail* group of readers.

The analysis of the Directives indicates that within our sample the press was a slightly more important source of information about the Summit than television: 73 per cent rated the press as a main source compared with 63 per cent for television and 27 per cent for radio. This was true for all the readership groups in our sample. In addition the quality press was rated as the most reliable source, and the tabloid press the least reliable, by most people. While this was dramatically true for quality press readers, it was also the case for tabloid readers. Tabloid readers rated television as more reliable than tabloid newspapers!

Respondents also expressed some awareness that the coverage of this event could have been more substantial. Almost three quarters of *Daily Mirror* readers and two thirds of *Daily Mail* readers thought that their newspapers could have been more informative and even among the quality press some 50 per cent of readers thought they could have received more information about the Earth Summit. However, when respondents were asked whether environment and development issues were important enough to influence their choice of newspaper, only a small minority felt this, ranging from about 10 per cent for tabloid papers to over 30 per cent for the *Guardian* readers. As for the available choice of newspapers a rather large minority, 26 per cent, felt that this was not adequate.

It must be recognised that this data is approximate because the varied style of response to a Directive makes it difficult to evaluate precisely the ways in which people interpret a question relating to the above. The issue of choice has to be considered within a given context, not merely the range of papers available at the time, but also a range of other factors, e.g. that a newspaper is read out of habit and tradition more than intent, and so these responses must be treated with the usual caution. Our MOA sample does not represent a random or cross sectional sample of the population. It would therefore be wrong to interpret this finding as reflecting the population as a whole. Nevertheless it is important to see that for this sample of the population, a highly literate, committed and articulate group of people, there was a considerable feeling of discontent about the adequacy of the press coverage of the Summit and the choice of newspapers available.

Methods of analysis

Once the general descriptive analysis[2] of the MOA sample had been completed the more detailed job of matching the newspaper coverage with individual responses could begin. In order to achieve this, all the Directives of the 'one newspaper' samples were typed or scanned into the computer. The text analysis programmes, NUD*IST and TACT were then employed to produce tables and directories. Used in tandem with a statistical package (SPSS) and a spreadsheet programme (MS Excel) we were able to develop research meth-

2   In the analysis presented in this chapter our newspaper articles were collected using a slightly wider key word or search term that captured articles referring to the Earth Summit by other names such as 'Rio Conference', 'Earth Conference', 'or Rio Summit'. The full data for this chapter is as follows:

Newspaper Articles 30th April 1992 – 30th June 1992

Gdn	Ind	Tel	DMl	Tdy	DMr	Sun
272	209	167	30	39	20	12

A further 20 *Daily Mirror* articles were used as part of the analysis presented later in this chapter.

ods for exhaustively and flexibly analysing two very large full-text databases, consisting of all the articles published on the Earth Summit in our sample of newspapers and all the text of the 107 Directives in our one-newspaper and no-newspaper sub-samples of readers.

NUD*IST allowed us to code or mark sections of text that could be recalled and collected together with all other samples of text dealing with the same topic. This meant that, for example, all MOA responses giving reasons for buying the newspaper of choice could be speedily collected together in a single document for further analysis. In addition it was possible to bring together all three line contexts of a specific key word so that coding was facilitated. TACT on the other hand enabled us to construct directories of entire database sub-sets, for example, all two word combinations in the entire set of *Guardian* articles or the MOA Directives of readers of the *Daily Mail*. These directories then enabled us to explore all the qualifiers attached to important key words such as 'population' and to identify the frequency of use of particular qualifiers, for example 'explosion', 'crisis', or 'growth'. This analysis of word association provided us with another level of analysis in which it is possible to identify matches between newspapers and their readers.

Discussion of results

The list of key words used in the first matching exercise was constructed by reading all the newspaper articles and noting the major issues and personalities that appeared in most of the newspapers. It was augmented by adding technical items and less frequently occurring issues and some words were added that reflected some of the concerns expressed by MOA respondents. Finally, the list was further extended by adding words that had particular relevance to the three mini-campaigns in the press that were examined in greater detail. Seventy-seven key words were eventually selected.

The searches were carried out on both the MOA Directives and the newspaper texts. The detailed tables are reproduced in full in an appendix so that it is possible to follow up the results for individual key words. The first table represents the number of newspaper articles and the second presents the number of MOA Directives, in which the key word appears at least once. In addition, to enable comparisons, percentages have been calculated using the total article count or the 'one newspaper' sample size as a base. However, it is important to note the differences between some of these bases (12 to 272) when making comparisons. The broad pattern is clear from Table 8.5 and Table 8.6.

Table 8.5: Summary of individual newspaper coverage.

	GDN	IND	DTL	DML	TDY	DMR	Sun
No. of Summit articles	272	209	167	30	39	20	12
Total no. of key words used	1883	1571	1343	249	219	113	58
Average of key words/article	6.92	7.52	8.04	8.30	5.62	5.65	4.83

Table 8-6: Summary of MOA directive respondents, by newspaper groups

	GDN	IND	DTL	DML	DMR	None
Number of Respondents	27	14	24	17	11	14
Total no. of key words	414	212	328	222	138	143
Ave. no. of key words	15.33	15.14	13.67	13.06	12.55	10.21

In the newspaper samples there are major differences in the frequency of key words between the quality press and tabloid press. These differences are directly reflected in the MOA Directives. This is important because the Directive was not a direct test of memory and the questions did not focus on the use of this vocabulary. Yet in respondents' accounts the use of specific language to describe and discuss the Earth Summit and the issues raised by it follows closely that of their newspaper in important respects.

In order to check the degree of this correspondence between the two tables we carried out a simple matching exercise. This was based quite simply on the coincidence between the highest percentages in each row of the detailed tables for both readers and newspapers. We found that after eliminating the 16 key words that were not used by any MOA respondents, 18 matches occurred out of 61 key words. This represented 30 per cent of cases when the expected percentage of matching cases would be 4 per cent. This degree of match is obviously more than would be expected by chance.

It could be argued that respondents turned to their newspaper or television in the process of replying to the Directive and this might lead us to dismiss this relationship between newspaper texts and Directives as an artefact of the response situation. There are a number of arguments against this. The major argument is that there is no direct evidence of what we might call 'copying' going on. Although key words and phrases are repeated by respondents this does not amount to wholesale replication of newspaper stories and articles when responding to the Directive. People are using what they consider to be their own words. Respondents sometimes write about newspaper stories and television programmes they have read or seen but these are typically used by respondents to support or otherwise express an opinion.

It certainly was the case that the Directive increased the salience of these issues for some respondents but by doing so the Directive was merely activating a process that is an example of the way in which a culture of understanding works. We would argue that by raising and emphasising some issues connected with the Summit and by not reporting others, each newspaper influences its readers' understandings of what is relevant and significant for their concerns about the environment and other issues. It is the need to express these concerns, in their response to the Directive, that leads to much of the similarity of vocabulary between the readership groups and their newspapers.

Words relating to the concern about 'population' or 'debt' are examples of this process of culture maintenance and formation. On the other hand there were new concepts introduced by some newspapers during the reporting of the Summit, for example 'sustainable development', and we will also be examining the significance of this process. The matching patterns therefore reflect a process of culture formation and renewal, albeit diffuse and as yet only vaguely identified.

In addition we cannot assume that the newspapers (or the media generally) are the only source of key words in MOA responses. Much of the vocabulary of environment and development issues is already in everyday use and when respondents are asked to write about the Summit they will bring to bear all their recent and relevant experiences, including the reading of newspapers.

This result therefore reflects what they have learned from newspapers within a range of other relevant sources and influences.

It is important to remember that any effect that we are able to demonstrate will have been achieved despite the moderating influence of television and other media sources. This could be particularly important for tabloid newspaper readers who regard broadcasting as more reliable than their newspapers. The effect of broadcasting could therefore have been to reduce the polarising efforts of the press.

The clear and consistent difference between quality and tabloid readers points to the possibility of a newspaper influence. A further difference, one of the largest differences in Table 8.6, is between readers of newspapers and non-readers. This suggests the interpretation that reading newspapers augments the relevant vocabulary available to respondents. This reader/non-reader difference cannot be explained by the social class origins of non-readers or their interest in the Summit. Non-readers are *more* likely to have a professional or managerial background than the sample of any tabloid paper, and they express *much more* interest.

We will argue that this result has occurred because we have picked many key words from newspapers that the non-readers have, by definition, not read. They therefore exhibit a scatter of concerns not influenced by the selective reporting of any particular newspaper and they do not match as closely with the concerns as represented by the vocabulary selected from those newspapers, as do the associated readership groups. That is, they do not exhibit some of the characteristics that we have identified as a culture of understanding. We now turn to more detailed comparisons within these broad patterns.

Findings – discussion of more detailed newspaper comparisons

The more detailed comparisons of word use were carried out using the two-word directories constructed from news texts and MOA responses. It follows that the tables, from this source, relate to frequency of word use, not the number of respondents or articles using the term (as in the previous tables). This will give rise to higher frequencies in the following tables.

The *Daily Mail* and the *Daily Mirror*

The rationale for comparing the *Daily Mail* and its reader group with the *Daily Mirror* and its reader group is that they provided us with adequate samples of one-newspaper readers from the MOA responses while also being outside the traditional set of quality newspapers. In addition, these two newspapers provided strongly differentiated coverage of the Earth Summit.

The *Mirror* was generally supportive of the Summit's purpose and critical of right-wing politicians who did not undertake to support this purpose, in particular Bush and Major. The *Mirror*, however, also ran a mini-campaign on the dangers of Sellafield B, in parallel with its coverage of the Summit. Thus, although the direct coverage of the Earth Summit was relatively low, the *Mirror* was dealing with related issues, with somewhat greater emphasis. The *Mail* was fundamentally opposed to some of the principal aims of the Summit, in particular North-South aid and funding, and the possible regulation of free enterprise exploitation of natural resources. It also sought to promote Major as the 'sensible' saviour or supporter of the Summit and to pass all opprobrium on to Bush. In particular it highlighted the failure of the Summit to deal with population control and was directly critical of the Vatican.

The key words for this exercise were 'population', 'birth control/rate', immigrant/migrant', 'Pope', 'Catholic' and 'Vatican. The two-word phrases that these searches generated reflected in the *Daily Mail* readers' MOA responses but are relatively muted in the *Daily Mirror* responses.

Daily Mail respondents refer to population growth or increase thirteen times,' overpopulation' thirteen times, and also use adjectives like 'wild', 'explosion' and 'problem'. *Daily Mirror* respondents on the other hand use 'growth' only once, 'over-population' not at all and although they use 'explosion' and 'huge', the range of adjectives associated with 'population' shows much less pre-occupation with 'growth' and 'threat'. Table 8.7 presents the results for the *Daily Mail* and the *Daily Mirror* which are also compared with non-readers.

Table 8.7: News text and MOA directive comparisons derived from two-word directories

Keywords	Daily Mail		Daily Mirror		None
	News articles	MOA (readers)	News articles	MOA (readers)	MOA (readers)
Population	31	40	3	9	24
Over-population	4	13	0	0	2
Contraception	11	3	0	0	0
Birth control/rate	18	12	0	1	1
Immigrant/migrant	4	1	0	0	0
Pope	3	1	0	0	0
Catholic	11	4	1	0	0
Vatican	10	1	0	0	0
TOTAL	92	75	4	10	27
N	30	17	20	11	14
Ratios of use	3.1	4.4	0.2	0.9	1.9

NB: *ratios of use refer to ratios of use by respondents (readers and non-readers) and to ratios of use within the articles that mentioned the Earth Summit*

The *Daily Mail* readers are clearly aware of the population issue. The *Mail's* articles on the Summit use the spectrum of key words that highlight this debate 92 times, compared with the *Daily Mirror's* use of the same set of key words only 4 times. The readers of the *Mail* use these same key words 75 times in describing the Summit and the major environment and development issues facing the world. By contrast the *Daily Mirror* readers use the same terms only 10 times.

When the number of respondents/articles is taken into account by calculating a 'ratio of use' the differences remain large. It is interesting to note that the level of concern about the population issue, shown by *Daily Mirror* readers is smaller than that shown by the no-newspaper sample. It could be argued that the great emphasis placed on the dangers of nuclear re-processing and child leukaemia by the *Mirror* has deflected the *Mirror* readers away from the population issue. We therefore decided to extend our investigation to include this issue. The spectrum of key words used to highlight the nuclear issue were; 'nuclear', radioactive/radiation', 'BNFL', 'leukaemia', 'cancer' and 'Sellafield'.

In this analysis we searched the newspaper articles about the Earth Summit as before but we included those articles that were published at the same time as the Earth Summit articles and discussed nuclear reprocessing. In the case of the *Daily Mirror* this was an additional 20 articles, and none in the *Daily Mail.* Table 8.8 illustrates the results.

Table 8.8: News Text and MOA directive comparisons derived from two-word directories

Keywords	Daily Mail		Daily Mirror			None
	News articles	MOA (readers)	News articles	News articles*	MOA (readers)	MOA (readers)
Nuclear	6	14	7	65	19	8
Radioactive/radiation	2	5	3	34	7	7
BNFL	0	0	0	20	1	0
Leukaemia	0	0	4	20	2	0
Cancer	4	3	4	19	6	7
Sellafield	0	0	6	82	3	0
TOTAL	12	22	24	240	39	22
N	30	17	20	40	11	14
Ratios of use	0.4	1.3	1.2	6.0	3.8	1.6

*This column includes the additional articles from the Daily Mirror *covering the nuclear issue but not directly reporting the Earth Summit*

In this table the positions are reversed. The *Daily Mail* barely mentions the nuclear issue key words; it uses them 12 times. The *Daily Mail* readers are apparently more concerned than their newspaper and use them 22 times. On the other hand the *Daily Mirror* uses these terms 240 times, if both sets of articles are taken into account. The smaller number of *Daily Mirror* readers respond by using them 39 times in their Directives. It is clear that *Daily Mirror* readers show much greater levels of awareness and concern about an issue, raised in a substantial number of articles, by their newspaper than the readers of the *Daily Mail,* whose newspaper hardly raises the issue.

It is worth noticing that the *Daily Mirror* readers record a higher ratio of use on this issue in the context of a general position of using fewer key words (see Table 8.6). In general, *Daily Mirror* readers use 93 per cent of the level of key words used by *Daily Mail* readers. This general difference is likely to reflect class position and levels of literacy as well as exposure to these words during the Summit. Once again the no-newspaper readers hold a position between these two extremes. The next table brings together the ratios of use to summarise these results and illustrate the differences.

Table 8.9: Ratios of use – key words per article or key words per directive

	Population Issue		Nuclear Issue	
	News text	Directive	News text	Directive
Daily Mail	3.1	4.4	0.4	1.3
No-newspaper	–	1.8	–	1.6
Daily Mirror	0.2	0.9	5.2	3.8

A convincing interpretation of these results is that the newspaper texts read by the respondents during, or prior to, the completion of their MOA Directives influenced their understanding of the major issues presented in the context of the Earth Summit. The concerns expressed within these two newspapers clearly became the concerns expressed by some of their readers in their responses to the MOA Directive.

The Quality Press and its Readers

The final issue reported here concerns the Guardian's reporting on Third World debt as a major issue facing the Summit and crippling the economies of many Third World countries. This issue was almost totally ignored by all the tabloids and was given a relatively low profile in the rest of the quality press. The original key word searches illustrate this.

Table 8.10: News articles and MOA directives containing the key word 'Debt'

	Gdn		Ind		Tel		DMI		Tdy		DMr		Sun		None	
	n	%	n	%	n	%	n	%	n	%	n	%	n	%	n	%
News texts	29	11	19	9	13	8	1	3	0	0	0	0	0	0	–	–
Directives	9	33	3	21	3	13	3	18	–	–	1	9	–	–	2	14

In order to expand the number of key words relating to this topic the list was increased to; 'debt/indebted', 'interest rates', 'loans'. Later the additional word 'corruption' was added. The table below presents the results from the two-word directories of the quality newspapers and their readers.

Table 8.11: News text and MOA directive comparisons derived from two word directories

Debt Issue	Guardian		Independent		Daily Telegraph		None
	News	MOA	News	MOA	News	MOA	MOA
Debt/indebted	66	36	37	7	26	6	2
Interest rates	10	4	7	0	2	0	1
Loans	12	7	1	0	2	0	2
Total	88	47	45	7	30	6	5
N	272	27	209	14	167	24	14
Ratio of use	0.32	1.7	0.22	0.5	0.20	0.25	0.36
Corruption	7	4	6	2	19	5	1

The table demonstrates a clear difference in the *Guardian's* coverage of the issue and the rest of the quality newspapers. The MOA Directives show a similar trend with the *Guardian* readers using the terms more frequently. There is also a small difference between the *Independent* and its readers and the *Telegraph* and its readers.

The extent of the difference between the *Guardian* coverage and the other quality papers was revealed by the lists of associated words in the two word directories. Words such as 'high', 'massive', 'debt-ridden', 'debt-stricken', revealed the main emphasis but other associations within the *Guardian's* articles made it clear that the effects of debt were traced into the 'environment' and development issues such 'hunger'. These connections were reflected in the word associations of *Guardian* readers' Directives. They also used words like 'huge', 'crippling', 'appalling', 'burden', 'health', and 'poverty'. The more muted treatment by the Independent was not associated with any of these sentiments in the Independent readers' responses.

In marked contrast, the relatively sparse treatment of debt by the *Daily Telegraph* was associated with some articles that blamed the Third World for their debt and pointed to the dangers for British banks. This argument was put forward by only one MOA respondent, a *Daily Telegraph* reader. Corruption in Third World governments and states was also advanced in some *Daily Telegraph* articles as part of the argument put forward for resisting increases in funding without instituting accountability. It is noticeable that the relatively large exposure to this idea from articles written in the *Telegraph* is echoed by its readers in their Directives (see Table 8.11, bottom row).

It was clear that the campaigning style adopted by the *Guardian*, particularly a major article by Victoria Brittain, struck a chord with *Guardian* readers who subsequently reflected these concerns in their MOA responses. In order to check these observations we coded all the contexts in which 'debt' was mentioned in all the Directives in our 'quality' newspaper samples.

Table 8.12: Key word 'Debt': Articles and responses coded for topics covered and positions adopted

Subjects and Positions Taken	Guardian		Independent		Telegraph		None
	News	MOA	News	MOA	News	MOA	MOA
1 Debt blamed on Third World and problem for British banks.	0	0	0	0	3	1	0
2 Debt mentioned but not specified.	3	0	4	0	2	0	0
3 Debt real problem for Third World.	25	9	14	3	8	2	2
4 Linked with exploitation, terms of trade, S. pays more to N.	16	7	12	0	6	0	–
5 Advocate/discuss Cancellation.	4	3	8	1	5	2	1
6 Linked and Development problems, distortions, cash crops etc.	2	6	1	0	1	0	1
7 Linked and environmental problems	9	5	1	0	0	1	2
8 Linked with poverty, child deaths, hunger.	6	5	0	2	2	0	1
9 Third world demands for cash from 1st World.	1	1	1	0	1	0	0
TOTALS	66	36	41	7	28	6	7
Total specified uses	63	36	37	7	26	6	7
N	272	27	209	14	167	24	14

Table 8.12 demonstrates that the broader implications of Third World debt which are clearly discussed in the *Guardian* articles are picked up by *Guardian* readers and find their way into their responses to the Directives. In this way

the newspaper provides information that strengthens the culture of under-standing of its readers. On the other hand the *Telegraph* approaches the topic with far less enthusiasm and commitment. It introduces arguments about cor-ruption in order to dispel any ideas for a simple solution to what it sees as a complex and intractable problem.

In this section we have illustrated the way in which the content of newspa-per articles is picked up by their readers. In the examples that we have pre-sented ('population', 'nuclear reprocessing' and '3rd World Debt') there is substantial evidence of the direct role that newspapers have in the selection and presentation of news such that it contributes to shaping, strengthening and maintaining the culture of understanding of their readers about these topics. We will pursue this issue within a second case study; the Today newspaper and its vacillating policy on representing environmental issues to its readers.

Today and the Environment

On 25 March 1991 the *Guardian* reported on 'the racy revamping of a newspa-per in trouble' describing the change in editorial policy at the *Today* newspaper. David Montgomery, the editor, is quoted as saying that *Today*'s philosophy is 'one of enterprise, the environment and women's issues' and that this part of the newspaper's change of approach is unaffected. Although there was no subse-quent announcement that any of these special features of the paper had been dropped it became clear that some were slowly allowed to wither away. The MORI Omnibus poll, coupled with our analysis of newspaper content presents us with the opportunity to trace changes in the newspapers' output on environ-mental topics and relate them to changes in the level of concern of its readers.

Today readers and their concern for the environment

The MORI Omnibus poll is conducted on a monthly basis and usually con-structed on a sample of about 2000 respondents who are questionned on a range of topics including their newspaper reading and their assessment of which issues are of most concern. This yields useable newspaper samples which range from about 60 per month for *Today* to 350+ per month for the *Sun*. *The Times* is the most marginally useful with monthly samples ranging from 31 to 61. Others like the *Scotsman* are too small for our purpose. Because the sam-ples for individual newspapers are fairly small we will not put a great deal of trust in the results of individual months. In addition we will look for patterns involving several months at a time and relate these patterns to changes in pub-lishing articles about the environment.

The period of our investigation ranges from January 1990 to December 1992 for which we have 33 months Omnibus poll data. In addition we have added data for March 1992 using adjusted figures. This was the period of the General Election and the Omnibus poll was conducted across a larger sample with five polling points during the election period. The ranking table below records those newspaper readerships that recorded the highest levels of concern about the environment and pollution in this three year period . The three highest levels of concern are recorded for each month and the table records the frequency with which readerships groups report these issues as their greatest concern.

Table 8.13: The number of times each newspaper readership is ranked 1-2-3 in terms of concern for the environment and pollution (January 1990–December 1992 – 34 months)

	1st	2nd	3rd	Unranked
Guardian	19	7	4	4
Independent	7	12	6	9
Times	4	6	3	21
Today	4	4	4	22
Telegraph	–	2	6	26
Express	–	2	2	30
None	–	–	7	28
Daily Mail	–	–	3	31
Daily Mirror	–	–	–	34
Sun	–	–	–	34

The overall pattern displayed in this table is for the most part what might have been expected. The readers of 'quality' newspapers are highest in their concern for the environment. This reflects the class composition of the readership and the much lower amount of coverage given to the environment by the tabloids. However, there is one exception. During this period the table shows that the readership of *Today* outranks the overall levels of concern shown by the *Telegraph* readers. It also shows that on a number of occasions *Today* readers show more concern than *Guardian* readers. We will need to investigate further to see if these high levels of concern shown by *Today* readers are linked to the publishing policy of the newspaper. The varied levels of concern for the environment are illustrated in Graph 8.1 below. The levels of concern shown by *Guardian* readers and no-newspaper readers are compared with *Today* readers.

Graph 8.1: Level of concern about environment compared: Guardian, Today *and no-newspaper readers*

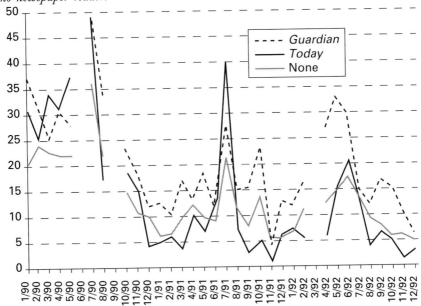

The no-newspaper samples from the MORI Omnibus poll have a social class composition which is very similar to that of the *Today* readership samples. It therefore makes sense to monitor the relative level of concern shown by *Today* readers by comparing them with the no-newspaper samples. It is noticeable that *Today* readers demonstrate their relatively high concern for the environment during two fairly discrete periods. The table below sets out those periods and the relative position of *Today* readers.

Table 8.14: Today *readers compared with No-Newspaper samples for the levels of concern for the Environment and Pollution*

Concern of *Today* Readers	Average Difference	Period	Period
Period of high concern	10.5%	Jan–July 90	7 months
Transition period	1.7%	Aug–Nov 90	4 months
Period of low concern	–3.2%	Dec 90–May 91	6 months
Blip of high concern	11.0%	Jun–July 91	2 months
Return to low concern	–3.8%	Aug 91–Apr 92	9 months
Period of moderate concern	2.0%	May–June 92	2 months
Return to low concern	–2.3%	July–Dec 92	6 months

Note: A positive difference indicates that Today *readers show a higher level of concern than the no-newspaper group*

In order to test if the levels of concern shown by *Today* readers in the first 3 periods of widely fluctuating levels of concern had anything to do with relative levels of publishing about the environment we constructed a combined index. We selected ten of the most important environment issues that have appeared in the news over the last five years. The selection is not exhaustive but attempts to combine a wide range of topics with a general indicator, 'ecolog*'.[3] The topics selected were, 'ozone', 'acid rain', 'PCBs', 'CFCs', 'toxic waste', 'water pollution', 'greenhouse effect', 'global warming', and 'nuclear waste'.

It is not possible to compare the relative level of publishing using the no-newspaper sample so we chose the *Guardian* as the most stable performer of all newspapers; it usually published more articles than any other newspaper on almost all environment topics.

Table 8.15: Relative levels of publishing about the environment: Guardian *and* Today

	1/90–7/90 High Concern	8/90–11/90 Transitional	12/90–6/91 Low Concern
Today average no articles	44	30	14
% of highest monthly average	100	68	32
Guardian average no articles	108	92	78
% of highest monthly average	100	85	81
Today articles as % of *Guardian*	41	32	18

This table demonstrates a change in editorial practice with respect to publishing articles on environment issues. Over the 3 periods defined earlier, the *Today* newspaper shows an absolute and relative decline in the number of

3 This term is a truncated key word. The asterisk is a wild card that will match any endings to the stem thus retrieving 'ecology', 'ecological', etc.

articles published. These three periods correspond to a relative decline in the *Today* readership's concern with the environment of 13.7 per cent!

The match between levels of concern for the environment and pollution issues and the levels of publishing of their daily newspaper provides more evidence of the influence of a newspaper in framing the culture of understanding of its readership. We are not claiming that the overall decline in public interest in the environment during this period was subject to direct manipulation by an interconnected network of editors or proprietors. There were other emerging issues like the Gulf War and unemployment that were bound to cause issues like the environment to recede in importance in the public arena. We are concerned to demonstrate the relative importance of newspaper publishing and the relative concern shown by newspaper readerships.

There was one small but important anomaly that emerged from our analysis which illustrates a related effect. We could not explain the sudden widespread increase in public concern about the environment in the summer of 1991. There appeared to be no substantial increase in levels of publishing recorded by our new combined index, yet public concern expressed in the MORI Omnibus poll rose from 9 per cent in May and June 91 to 20 per cent in July 91. What is more, levels of concern expressed by Today readers rose to 40 per cent, completely out ranking Guardian readers who recorded 28 per cent concerned.

Before admitting defeat on this issue we decided to scan the stored copies of *The Times* for this period in order, record any events that might have given rise to this 'blip' of high concern felt by the population as a whole and *Today* readers in particular. Our scan of *The Times* revealed a period of freak weather. The weather reports included drought, flooding and snow that interfered with sport, in particular Wimbledon and cricket, threats to the strawberry crop, and contradictory consequences such as hose-pipe bans and floods.

However, in order to demonstrate that the relatively high level of concern shown by *Today* readers was linked to reading the newspaper, we would have to demonstrate a relatively high level of publishing by *Today* on those topics. We therefore conducted a series of searches using the key words 'rain', 'flood', 'weather' and 'drought'. The results are recorded in Table 8.16.

Table 8.16: The number of articles in which the key words rain, flood, weather and drought occur in Today *and the* Guardian

	May 91	June 91	July 91
Today Total no. articles	2819	2430	2814
Rain	24	72	53
Flood	29	27	25
Weather	26	71	52
Drought	6	6	2
	85	176	132
Guardian Total no. articles	4002	3734	3982
Rain	67	147	121
Flood	62	53	53
Weather	80	108	112
Drought	23	14	7
	232	322	293
Today Articles as % of *Guardian* articles	36	55	45

The table demonstrates a sharp increase in the level of publishing by *Today*'s editorial team during this period relative to the level within the *Guardian*. A selection of the kinds of issues that were reported are listed in the Appendix. As with the previous analysis of environment topics, a sharp increase in the relative level of publishing is accompanied by a sharp increase in the level of concern shown by *Todays*' readers. Although the experience of freak weather affected the whole population, and all newspaper readerships showed an increase in concern, the relatively heightened concern demonstrated by the *Today* readership is paralleled by the relative differences in newspaper coverage.

Case Studies

We have pursued the analyses of the consequences of newspaper publishing in great detail, using lexical indicators of the vocabulary used by newspapers and the words used by their readers. However we have always done this in terms of groups of people, frequencies of use in collections of articles and comparative levels of concern. The analysis has been at an abstract level, concerned with groups rather than individuals. We now seek out the individuals within the analysis and present example cases reconstructed from their MOA Directive responses which illustrate the way in which newspaper reading interacts with cultures of understanding.

We received over 400 Directives and have included over 100 in our detailed one-newspaper readership analysis. If we were to present cases of even a cross section of the individuals in this panel in any detail it would fill a second book. We have therefore selected our cases within the context of the analysis that we have already presented and we have selected them to illustrate the range of response and some of the points that we have made using the larger samples. We therefore expect these cases to add clarity and detail to the general points already made.

In order to simplify our presentation of cases we have chosen them from two newspapers, one tabloid and one broadsheet. We have chosen the *Daily Mail* as the tabloid. It had a strong line on the Earth Summit. However the amount of coverage was small and it sought to present the Summit as a waste of time. An opportunity for the 3rd World to dust off their 'begging bowls' and attempt to extort money out of rich, developed nations. Only John Major was given a good press and the population issue was used in conjunction with poverty, migration and immigration to cast a shadow of racial danger and crisis and push the blame and responsibility for environment and development problems into Third World countries.

The *Guardian* on the other hand gave the Summit a very full coverage. It was also critical of the Summit but from a different perspective. The strongest criticism was aimed at Western governments who failed to accept their share of the responsibility for many of the world problems, pollution, Third World debt, environmental degradation, etc. and who were seen to be dragging their feet over signing treaties and providing the resources to tackle the problems. John Major and the UK government attracted substantial criticism. However the analysis offered to its readers was very wide, spelling out the connections between for example, Third World debt and poverty and the degradation of important natural resources. The overall picture offered by the *Guardian* was not optimistic and the Earth Summit viewed as a lost opportunity. The three case studies selected illustrate the greater breadth and understanding demonstrated by *Guardian* readers.

The *Daily Mail* Readers

The *Daily Mail* is generally credited with being a successful paper with a close relationship with its readers. In our MOA sub-sample ten of the twelve *Daily Mail* respondents who expressed a view made positive statements about their newspaper. This contrasts, for example, with the *Today* readers where none of the five respondents expressed a positive view. Two referred to 'good' times before Murdoch purchased the paper and the most positive remark relating to the then current situation was 'I read *Today* because mother buys it as a daily paper – I am not too keen on it but it is preferable to the other tabloids that are nothing but Conservative party news sheets.'

We present here, two examples of *Daily Mail* readers who are positive towards their newspaper and one reluctant reader.

Mrs D.R. aged 49, housewife, formerly a book keeper

Mrs D.R. we describe as an individual who is positive about the *Daily Mail* but at the same time sees no alternative to this newspaper even though she realises that the *Daily Mail* is not always giving her all that she needs to inform her understanding. Therefore we describe her as a dependent reader.

Mrs D.R. reads only the *Daily Mail*, no Sunday papers and feels that the *Mail* is 'the best of tabloids'. However, on several occasions she expressed annoyance 'when it descends into trash' but she also feels 'I can't be diving into huge papers like the *Telegraph*, good as that paper is ...' so she remains dependent on the *Daily Mail*. She is very concerned about the environment, 'I feel the situation is becoming very serious and I do worry as to the state the planet will be in for future generations ...' but she is deeply confused about what to do.

She took an interest in the Summit but not 'a close interest'. She points out, 'It seemed to be very difficult to know for certain what the main issues addressed by the conference were'. When confronted with direct questions about the main issues she seems to become aware of her dependence 'I only had two sources of information anyway, the BBC (radio and television) and the *Daily Mail*'. Yet despite her lack of information, her concern comes through, '[The Earth Summit] should have been about pollution, global warming, the destruction of the ozone layer etc. but I don't recall hearing any of these issues mentioned. The only subject I really heard anything about was the problems associated with over population. There was also something about the protection of flora and fauna'. Nevertheless she remarks later, 'I see over-population as an extremely dangerous thing'.

In these last quotations she not only shows her concern and her knowledge of relevant issues but she demonstrates how much her reading of the *Daily Mail* has shaped her understanding of what apparently went on. It should be noted that she does not accurately reflect the *Mail*'s line on the Earth Summit and over-population but she has remembered that over-population was the main issue that the Mail associated with the Summit. The *Daily Mail* actually made population into its main issue and used it to criticise the Earth Summit for failing to tackle what it presented as a fundamental problem. It also laid the blame for this failure firmly with the Vatican and the Catholic Church.

Mrs D.R.'s frustration about her lack of information comes to the fore when she answers the question 'Do you feel that the press and TV could have been more informative?' She answers, 'Most definitely I feel that the TV ignored it apart from the row over President Bush's refusal to sign certain parts of the treaty and John Major's speech about over population. Likewise the *Mail*.' Similarly when asked if there were any major issues that were neglected, she replied 'Because I don't really know what issues were discussed, because TV and papers didn't tell me, I find that a difficult question to answer. I imagine since so many people from all over the world were involved for something like two weeks, they did discuss some important issues, but to go by the media coverage one wouldn't have thought so.'

She continues with her criticism of the media. 'It is extremely difficult to make sensible assessments of what is going on in the world, environmentally, from newspaper and TV stories. They either seem hyped up to sound much more immediate and dangerous to help sell their papers etc., or they are ignored. I often find reports on these things unbelievable.' Mrs D.R.'s concern for the environment is underlined by the detailed account she gives of the individual action she is prepared to take. It ranges from her refusal to buy herself a car and her willingness to cycle to the shops to detailed accounts of her recycling aluminium foil, 'those go to Oxfam who recycle them,' plastic bags, paper, bottles, second hand clothes and rags. Yet she feels that 'the little things we can do are unlikely to make very much difference to things overall.'

This respondent's position is fraught with contradiction and uncertainty. She is convinced that environment and development problems are too big for individual action. 'It is one area where the world could and should unite as it affects us all and therefore I think it should be very much the concern of the U.N.' In addition she feels that 'unless something is done soon the acceleration in the deterioration of the planet will get out of hand.' Despite this understanding she is meticulous in her individual behaviour in terms of recycling, not buying a car and avoiding waste but unable or unwilling to participate in or support collective action. For example, she would not accept a lowering of her standard of living, 'life is pretty good right now,' unless 'the situation became deadly serious ... that's a feeble attitude I know, and terribly selfish.' In addition she would not go as far as changing her newspaper. 'No, environmental issues would not affect my choice of newspaper. I would read the *Mail* anyway unless it went down the same road as the *Sun* and became simply a means of spreading gossip about so called stars and the Royal family, which it's on the verge of doing lately.'

This reader therefore remains blocked and uncertain and dependent on, in her own estimation, inadequate sources of news. In her view, at the end of the Summit the world simply moved on to Yugoslavia, the recession and an escalation in the number of murders. There was no outcome that would affect her life or anyone else's, 'I think it was probably a complete waste of time and money.' In particular, the *Daily Mail* by cutting her off from constructive news about the Summit, the agreements, the allocation of resources, the commitment to further meetings and action, has effectively cut her off from the possibility of understanding the relationship between her own actions and the problems they address. This is not to argue that it would have been enough to strengthen her support and enthusiasm for the U.N. It is to argue that the reporting of the Summit by the *Daily Mail* did not allow for this possibility. It therefore limited her understanding and helped to establish her ignorance about the Summit and its outcomes.

Mrs B.I. aged 50, Nursery Nurse

Some readers do not choose their daily papers and some feel out of sympathy with their daily read. Mrs B.I. is in both positions. Moreover, her attitude towards environment and development issues differs from that taken by the newspapers she has access to. She takes a more critical, activist stance than the *Daily Mail*. Therefore we describe her as a 'blocked idealist' and a 'reluctant reader', someone who is aware of significant problems and possible solutions, whose opinions are not supported by her newspaper, but who has no control over the choice of reading material.

Mrs B.I. reads the *Daily Mail* and *Sunday Express* as well as local papers. She does not choose either paper, they are her husband's choice. She is effectively blocked from choosing her source of news but deals with this situation with a blanket of condemnation of all papers. 'I feel they all, to some degree or other, incline towards their own particular bias, and the frequent sensationalism and virtual manufacturing of news, sickens me.' She prefers TV and the facility for seeing news items or interviews. This she feels gives her the opportunity to draw her own conclusions and formulate her own opinions. She watches BBC News at 6.00pm and 9.00pm and ITV at 10.00pm, in addition BBC's look North and Panorama.

She states that she was aware of the main issues but lists a hotchpotch of issues that roughly correspond to the main agenda of the Earth Summit. Nevertheless they do reveal knowledge of a wide variety of environmental problems: '... decline of the rain forests; pollution of oceans causing destruction of marine life; over fishing; damage to the ozone layer by man-made chemicals, endangering plant and animal life; acid rain and the dumping of toxic waste.' Mrs B.I. is convinced of the seriousness of environment and development problems, e.g. in relation to the threat to other species and natural resources, and she feels that 'it is up to us to try to prevent this happening by reassessing and modifying our behaviour and lifestyles to this end.'

This stance is at odds with the *Mail*'s general attempt to minimise the responsibility of rich, developed nations for these problems. For her, this responsibility is both individual and collective, 'unless these problems are addressed on a grand scale and people and governments take appropriate and determined action, they will continue to exist.' In addition, she takes seriously her own responsibilities (like Mrs D.R.): she recycles paper, glass, plastic and aluminium, she walks and cycles when possible and uses public transport in the city, insulates her home, does not waste electricity or gas and wears sweaters rather than use the central heating, does not use peat, buys ozone-friendly and phosphate-free products and re-uses plastic bags.

She would support a lowering of standards of living across the board if it would help in solving environmental problems but she is pessimistic about this possibility. She returns several times to the dual problem that newspapers and TV will only give space to 'outrageous protest' and 'sensationalism', in which common sense and reason are ignored. This was, she thinks, the main reason for the press and TV ignoring the Earth Summit, that it was not sensational enough and would not 'result in selling newspapers.'

Finally, she confirms the extent to which the press and television have contributed to her lack of knowledge of the Summit, knowledge which might have contributed to breaking down her isolation and enabling her to use her conviction and idealism towards collective action. She remarks that the Directive has 'certainly made me more aware than I would otherwise have been, about how short term its news value has proved to be and how little I know, via press or television, about the long term effects the conference has had or about any action taken by governments as a direct result of the Earth Summit. The outcome is very obscure to me.'

Mrs B.I. is therefore a trapped or blocked idealist, who is isolated in a hostile world. The media (TV and her newspaper) make her aware of the problems, and she has responded by taking precise and far ranging individual action. However, she is blocked from appreciating any 'serious' and 'genuine' effects because she does not hear or read about them. One essential element of sub-culture formation is missing. Those she does read about are sensationalised and (as in the *Daily Mail*) ridiculed. She therefore feels distanced from those forms of collective action that do exist. This ignorance and the strong pessimism about the possibility of collective action, which was pushed very hard by the *Daily Mail,* contributed to Mrs B.I.'s blocked idealism. Her isolation is compounded.

Mrs C.M. aged 65, retired personnel clerk

Some respondents seemed almost completely in tune with their newspapers; happy with their choice and sometimes almost completely reproducing the main lines of argument taken by the newspaper. These respondents can be regarded as core members of the readership. Mrs C.M. is one such person.

Mrs C.M.'s reasons for taking the *Daily Mail* reveal her satisfaction: 'good cover of news. Topical and informative articles by good journalists also crosswords.' and her understanding of the Summit is clearly in line with the major items of news and interpretations published by the *Mail:*

> After reading about the Earth Summit I was left with the impression that it is all down to money. The poor countries can't or won't do what needs to be done without vast amounts of money from the better-off countries. They, in turn, are unwilling to trust the leaders of the poor countries to use the money for its intended purposes. So many countries in Africa for instance, which were fertile and prosperous have become

barren deserts since getting their independence as their civil wars and power-crazed dictators have ruined their economies.

She has other concerns which reflect themes in the *Daily Mail* such as over-population and birth control, 'The Catholic Church could change its ruling on birth control which would help over-population in certain poor countries like South America, but I don't think it is likely to happen as it would mean, eventually, a lot less Catholics.', and fears about immigration, 'Our economy can be affected by what is happening in other countries and there is always the problem of immigrants. More and more seem to want to come and live here, either legally or illegally, and we just can't afford to support all these people much as we may sympathise with their plight.'

Alongside these understandings Mrs C.M. demonstrates a set of commonly held concerns about the environment, patterns of individual action and a deep pessimism about the present basis for collective action and the future. She feels strongly about the environment and in her case this love of nature is deeply linked to her Christianity. 'One only has to consider how wonderful everything in nature is, it could never have all happened just by chance. God created us and our world and in his great love for us be sent his son Jesus to pay the price for our sins and to teach us to love him and to love one another.'

She feels the need to do something within her family. 'We have fruit, vegetables and herbs ...' 'I am a very "water conscious" person and hate to see it wasted ... I save all my waste paper, newspapers, bottles etc. I try to save energy by being careful not to waste electricity. We use lead-free petrol in the car. Other than this I don't know what else I can do.' She is deeply pessimistic about the fate of the environment and the effectiveness of the Summit: 'The destruction of rain forests for instance is ... positively frightening for the future of the earth, yet nothing appears to be going to be done to stop it.'

In common with many respondents she is confused. No clear messages have come from science or government and she mistrusts large companies and the media. 'TV where the latest scientific discovery about the ozone layer for instance, will do its level best to frighten us all to death.' Yet despite this pessimism and mistrust there remains a willingness to make personal sacrifices *if* she could be sure they would be effective: 'I would be prepared to accept a lowering of my standard of living (i.e. pay higher taxes, have metered water) only if I could be assured that such measures would really contribute to a solution of these problems, for the sake of my grandchildren.' Finally, she is also aware of the need for collective action: 'Individuals ... need a lot more guidance in what can be done and more convincing by governments that it must be done. I think legislation on important issues will be necessary ...'

The picture that emerges from this case can be portrayed in a three level structure. A deep layer of belief expressed in concepts like nature, god, creation, ultimate purpose, love etc. A second level, which is in effect an understanding of issues relating to the environment and development and is partly shared with others as a culture of understanding. Finally, a third level of practice and action or support for potential action.

Mrs C.M.'s deep convictions would seem to be compatible with principled individual action, and support for collective action at the national and international level. However, if the real world is pictured as unable to support these actions because of greedy dictators, crises caused by over-population and immigration, useless international organisations and unreliable allies (USA), the possibility of support for national sacrifice and international co-operation is substantially diminished. The possibility of Mrs C.M.'s deep convictions providing her with solutions to the problems that she perceives in the environment, are blocked. She is left with an outlet for these beliefs in her individual actions but remains troubled, confused, and ultimately pessimistic about collective action.

'The Directive has increased my awareness to some extent, but I feel that we are not really doing anything to help the environment or even anything to make people more aware.'

These *Daily Mail* readers were chosen to illustrate the wide range of attachment to their daily newspaper. Despite these differences, however, it is clear that all three respondents are dependent, in different ways, on their newspaper for knowledge and understanding of the events at the Earth Summit.

Mrs D.R. and Mrs C.M. who are most in tune with their newspaper and have positive reasons for reading it, both closely reflect the main lines of argument (overpopulation and dismissing the Summit as a waste of time) developed by the *Daily Mail*. Mrs B.I. who does not reflect these perspectives is nevertheless blocked from developing her understanding of and desire for collective action.

It is remarkable that all these respondents are deeply worried by the evidence of damage to the environment and are seriously committed to individual action (recycling etc.) to help the environment. Yet because the Summit was represented as a wrangle and a waste of time, with only John Major attempting to save it, they were cut off from positive collective action with respect to the Summit (for example, the kind of popular pressure that reversed Government policies at the time of the Ethiopian famine). Instead they are resigned to collective failure and are deeply pessimistic about the future.

Guardian readers

Guardian readers are perhaps even more enthusiastic about their newspaper than *Daily Mail* readers. In our sample a reluctant *Guardian* reader was almost unknown. One respondent wrote: 'I AM A *GUARDIAN* READER' (Need I say more?!)' The reasons for taking the *Guardian* are replete with phrases like 'its philosophy is akin to my own – left wing, not rabid, fairly free thinking on 'religious' matters, educationally and socially aware ...', 'Comprehensive coverage on a wide range of issues with a liberal/leftish (small 'l') bias' and 'I like the breadth of its news coverage and the way it is presented; I like its attitudes (to me slightly left wing) while giving a voice still to many differing views.'

Many readers were prepared to write at length about favourite features, writers and sections. Assessment of its approach ranged from 'objective' to 'left wing' although many inserted 'liberal' or 'progressive' in their descriptions. The *Guardian* clearly supports a left of centre culture of understanding, and it is enthusiastically supported by its readers. When they happen to read outside their chosen newspaper they are often dismayed by what they find. 'the tabloids are really rubbish. I only see them when I am at the barber's.' 'Recently I have seen a few issues of the *Daily Mail*, which shows such prejudice, e.g. against teachers and refugees, as to distort the news. It is very selective and sensational in the items it covers.' One reader goes as far as stating that the heavy political bias in the *Daily Mirror*, *Daily Mail* and *Daily Express* in favour of one party and to 'the deliberate detriment of others' is 'wrong and antidemocratic.'

Guardian readers tend to hold strong opinions, wish to see them debated openly and often pursue these opinions actively. They are more likely to be members of environment or development organisations than any other newspaper readership. However, not all *Guardian* readers took a close interest in the Summit. Some were 'somewhat' interested while others were repelled by it and took 'no interest'. We have therefore chosen to use this dimension to exemplify the range of *Guardian* readers.

Mrs A.R. aged 63, retired infant school teacher

Mrs A.R. is an active reader. She is a member of Oxfam, Greenpeace, Friends of the Earth, Derbyshire Wildlife Trust, WWF, RSPB, RSPCA and the Woodland Trust and therefore situates her reading of the *Guardian* within a wide range of environment and development journals and magazines. She took a close interest in the Summit.

Nevertheless, she is adamant about her need for the *Guardian*. She likes its 'breadth of news', 'the way it is presented ... its attitudes' and 'It covers environmental and 'Third World' topics reasonably widely.' When she first retired she gave up the *Guardian* as an economy measure relying on Radio 4: '... but it didn't work. I found I had voids of knowledge after a few weeks and decided that I was becoming politically illiterate.' She now exchanges her *Guardian*, after she has read it, for her neighbour's local paper and thus makes the necessary saving.

She is, like the three *Daily Mail* readers, sceptical of governments and large organisations (multinationals) but unlike any of the *Daily Mail* readers she feels that she has a clear understanding of the working of these organisations and an informed analysis of the contemporary events relating to the Summit. The *Guardian* made an important contribution to that understanding but throughout the Directive it is clear that Mrs A.R. is actively in control of her understanding of events and the actions that she takes. There is no sense of blockage and confusion, although there is a sense of dismay and even outrage.

Her concern for the environment dates from 1957 'when Windscale blew'. She heard about Strontium 90 in contaminated milk and its links with leukaemia. Her son was eighteen months old and she was pregnant. The fear for her children then lay dormant, 'to flair into life whenever they were ill.' She read books by Barbara Ward, René Dubois and Paul Ehrlich. Within her Directive she mentions or quotes from seven other writers and thinkers from Lewis Carroll, Bishop Montefiore and Gandhi to the reports from the Royal Society (UK) and the US Academy of Sciences. 'The future of our planet is in the balance. Sustainable development can be achieved but only if irreversible degradation of the environment can be halted in time.' She greeted this report as a milestone. At last the causes of her fears and feelings of isolation had been recognised by an important scientific body as a serious threat to our future.

Her independence of thought is demonstrated by her intelligent use of those sources and also by her analysis of the value of the range of sources available to her. Her response contains a well argued case against trusting some sources:

A politician has but one over-riding aim – to be re-elected. Environmental measures are controversial and cost money which means higher prices or higher taxes. That is why at the recent general election the environment was not an issue; the two main parties did not bring it up at all, the Social Democrats did ...

The second reason concerns the power of the business lobby particularly the multinationals, which are so powerful they transcend governments ...

The third reason is ignorance ... It is necessary to have an elementary understanding of ecology ... Sadly most of us do not. [This, in her view, allows the press (tabloids) to devote their space] ... to the private life of the Prince of Wales and his wife.

However, since her analysis of power and government is linked to an intelligent understanding of how major institutions work she is not blocked or rendered passive. She sets out a detailed itinerary of personal action which goes beyond the actions taken by all the *Mail* readers. She recycles and re-uses, she uses a bicycle and environmentally friendly products, she lives as 'organically' as possible and avoids waste. Most noticeably, she supports collective action and acts politically as an individual. 'I think that individual action prods government into action, but it has proved a very slow process.'

She wrote twice to John Major at the time of the Summit, once through the NGO sponsored Tree of Life initiative and once by writing a personal letter. 'In it I asked if he was seriously prepared to go to the Summit and there lecture the developing countries on the need to preserve rainforests while in the UK he failed to preserve SSSIs from road building development. I mentioned particularly, Twyford Down ... for which bit of vandalism we have fallen foul of EC Environmental Impact Assessment Directive. I received an answer to my pledge but not to my letter.'

She found it impossible to answer the question on the most important environmental and developmental questions, the issues are so inter-related. She lists habitat destruction linked to loss of species, pollution linked to climatic change, poverty linked to soil erosion and over population linked to starvation. It is interesting to notice that, unlike some *Daily Mail* readers, over-population is not here linked to migration, immigration and threat. Instead she points to 'greed' as exemplified by the developed world where 'one quarter of the world's population consumes three quarters of the world's resources' and 'two weeks of the world's expenditure on arms could give fresh water supplies to all of the people in the developing world.' In her view it is the rich governments who should take responsibility for this: 'It was the rich nations who encouraged the poor to borrow vast amounts of money. It is they who want the interest repaid through the sale of cash crops which dispossess the small farmer.'

It is clear that Mrs A.R. is not dependant on the *Guardian* but it is nevertheless an important source which helps to sustain her interest, her knowledge and her activism. As she puts it 'knowledge is vital ...'

Finally it is important to point out that Mrs A.R. is prepared to pay for her ideals. 'Why should I expect other people to work for wages which keep them in poverty?' but she challenges the notion that this sacrifice might mean a lower standard of living. 'Standard of living is meaningless to me. Quality of life is what matters, and the two are not the same.'

We have set out the arguments in Mrs A.R.'s response in some detail but we are aware that we have not done complete justice to her detailed and carefully illustrated discussion. Nevertheless it is clear that Mrs A.R. must come close to being an example of Walter Lippman's omnicompetent citizen with the difference that the problems and blockages seen by Lippman as a major obstacle to obtaining sufficient intelligent information are no longer insurmountable. It is possible for Mrs A.R. to find information sources that are adequate and relevant in her efforts to sustain and apply an active philosophy of understanding to the contemporary world. In Mrs A.R.s case, the range of NGO magazines, the *Guardian*, books, television and radio (Radio 4 and the World Service) provide a more than sufficient source.

However, it would be wrong to suggest that the availability of information and the opportunity for positive cultures of understanding is all that is required to ensure that an active reader response to environment and development issues develops. Many other perspectives are possible. One fairly strong strand within the *Guardian* readership group was to see the problems as insurmountable within a deeply corrupt and unreformable world system.

Mr R.C. ex-lecturer

Mr R.C. gave 'half his mind' to following the news about the Earth Summit. He answered the question about whether the Earth Summit changed the way he thought about environment and development issues with, 'No. It hasn't even deepened my cynicism. I saw reports that some of the 'fringe' groups and meetings, were real, but media-Rio was an 'event' rather than an intervention.' However, his cynicism masks an idealism:

> ... I'd find it difficult to live without some ideal of nature as regeneration, and I don't see why Mount Everest should be covered in shit and debris for the sake of macho climbers' ego-trips, I don't see why much uncultured moorland a few miles from here should be owned and fenced off by millionaire parasites who live in London or beyond.

Mr R.C. reads the *Guardian* because of its 'reasonable coverage of public affairs.' He felt that his reading 'gave some detail and at least a limited range of viewpoints' and 'Anything from a British, or particularly an American, government source I would treat as self-serving disinformation.' His pessimism about environment and development issues derives from the collapse of left wing politics. Green politics do not 'address the dialectics of social conflict.':

> The failure of the left means that these problems won't be radically tackled until there is a new set of political alignments. We may expect some piecemeal improvement, perhaps – thanks to pressure groups, to waves

of popular opinion, and perhaps to the 'rational self-interest' of the transnational blocs that make, usually in secret, the ultimate decisions.

This pessimism leads to a similar position on the Summit as that taken by the right wing press, although for very different reasons: 'telling exposures of the Rio circus' where 'there will be more talk than action' and 'I'm angrier than ever, if that's possible, at American string-pulling.' 'Global warming has a status in popular myth and will get batted around' but here the similarities end 'silent emergencies that are killing people every day' are not brought to the publics attention.

Of these two cases Mrs A.R. is one of eight *Guardian* readers who took a 'close interest' in the Summit and Mr R.C. is one of seven *Guardian* readers who took some interest. Our last example is one of the 12 readers who took 'no interest'. However, before examining Mr N.I.'s views in some detail, it is important to point out that those *Guardian* readers who expressed 'no interest' in the Summit often did so from a radical and deeply concerned perspective. It was frequently the case that the Summit appeared to them incapable of preventing the exploitation of the poor. In addition it appeared that the greed of rich Western nations was responsible for the major part of the pollution of the world and the Summit was an attempt to obscure this. Some actually avoided any news or TV programme about the Summit, because they found it too distressing and depressing.

This sub-division of *Guardian* readers gives us an opportunity to find out if taking a close interest i.e. reading the *Guardian* articles closely, gave rise to differences in concern on an issue which the *Guardian* treated very fully, Third World debt.

Table 8.17: Relationship between taking a close interest in the Summit and whether the issue of 'Debt' was taken up in the directives of Guardian *readers*

	Close Interest	Some Interest	No Interest	Total
Debt mentioned	6	1	2	9
Debt not mentioned	2	6	10	18
TOTAL	8	7	12	27

This is a very small sample. The tabulation does, however, give support to the notion that those with a close interest read the *Guardian* more 'closely' and thus brought the issue of 'debt' into focus, thus influencing the way that those respondents answered the Directive.

Mr N.I. aged 35, a writer and carer

Mr N.I. reads the *Guardian*, 'though not especially thoroughly', because, 'it is about the only newspaper I can trust not to be partisan in some way or another. (Though the same can be said for the Independent)' He is a member of Greenpeace and his wife is a member of Friends of the Earth. He knew about the Summit in advance and although 'the *Guardian* ran a series of large articles' he did not read them. He did however watch 'quite a lot of what turned up on TV.'

Mr N.I.'s lack of interest derives from the feeling that 'I do not believe that the powerful western nations will take any effective action to avert disaster, and I do not believe they really want to. The Summit was just a bit of window-dressing to fob off those who say there is a problem.'

Mr N.I. records CO_2 emissions and global warming, ozone destruction and the danger of nuclear accident and contamination as the three most important environmental problems and the exploitation of the poor nations by the rich nations, over population and the belief that industrialisation on the model of the western nations is the only sort of development possible, as the three most important development problems. He feels that 'All these problems, and especially the way they inter-relate, and their historical origins are very poorly treated in the media. Telling the truth cannot be done unless it is recognised that a lot of things in this culture stink: the idea of a free market economy, the idea of economic growth, the idea of exploiting the environment, the idea that there is a particular sort of material 'progress' which must be pursued ... These deeper underlying causes of environmental and developmental problems are generally not recognised, so do not appear in any newspapers.'

Mr N.I. found the question on being prepared to accept a lower standard of living extremely difficult to answer. He cares for his disabled wife and their one luxury, the car, enables them to travel 1000 miles per year. They cannot afford to heat their house, buy new clothes or afford a mobile phone (for safety reasons) so they have few luxuries to give up. However, he believes strongly that rich people and rich nations should help the poor and protect the environment but 'in writing about what I think of it all, it is distressing to face up to my rather overwhelming pessimism about the future.'

Conclusion

In this chapter we have examined evidence from two very different sources; from a MORI nation-wide poll, taken on a monthly basis and from a MOA panel, a one-off Directive on the Earth Summit and press and media coverage of environment and development issues. The MORI poll consists of a relatively simple set of questions asked in an identical form each month demanding relatively simple answers. The MOA Directive consisted of a fairly complex series of questions, which the respondents could consider at their leisure and answer in a complex, lengthy and highly individualistic manner. The MORI poll is superficial but covers the UK with a representative quota sample while the MOA Directive is much deeper but not representative.

We have attempted to maximise the strengths of these contrasting data sets to test the idea that the way newspapers cover events influences the understandings that their readers develop about these events. In other words newspapers support and develop among their readers particular ways of looking at the world and those cultures of understanding are related on the one hand to deeper values and on the other to policy decisions about collective action and also individual action. Cultures of understanding overlap and have common elements but they also diverge and have contrasting elements. It is by focussing on the contrasting elements that we have demonstrated that the different treatment of key events has given rise to different understandings of those events.

In the first part of the chapter we demonstrated with the MOA data that *Daily Mail* readers and *Daily Mirror* readers reflected the particular concerns that their newspapers associated with the Summit; the population crisis and the threat of nuclear pollution from Sellafield, respectively. In the same section we showed that the strong theme of Third World debt developed in the *Guardian* was a strong feature in the returns of *Guardian* readers. Later on we demonstrated that those *Guardian* readers who took a close interest in the Summit were most likely to reflect this concern of Third World debt.

In the second section we were able to show that the fluctuating policy of the *Today* newspaper in its coverage of environment issues, was mirrored by the concern shown by *Today* readers, as demonstrated by the MORI poll. This match between the publication of articles on the environment and the degree of concern shown by the readership even extended to the coverage of the freak weather conditions of the Summer of 1991.

Finally we looked in some detail at individual responses to show the nature of the relationship between reader and newspaper. By selecting carefully we illustrate a variety of relationships and adjustments. Not all readers were enthusiastic readers of their daily papers, not all readers took a deep interest in the Summit, readers were not equally influenced by their newspaper, nor did they respond to it in the same way. Nevertheless it was possible to trace within these cases evidence of this influence in the way that the chosen or received newspaper sustains a particular culture of understanding by suppressing and highlighting certain aspects of an event and relating these to deeper values and fears held by individuals within the culture.

Although we also chose cases where individuals were reluctant readers and/or avoided articles about the Summit we also came across some spectacular cases of an apparently unquestioning assimilation of the most suspect reporting. For example, one of the more bizarre cases was a 39 year old woman, a department store supervisor and *Daily Mail* reader who wrote, 'A whole rainforest of trees must have been cut down to provide the mountain of literature presented to the delegates – what a waste!' This 'belief' had clearly influenced this respondent's understanding of the Summit. It accurately reflects colour pieces written by Keith Waterhouse in the *Daily Mail.* They are characteristically outrageous and flamboyant pieces. One begins, 'The Mother Earth Summit having already generated enough column inches to account for a small rainforest ...' and the other contains, 'The Mother Earth Summit photocopiers turn out 100 million sheets of unrecycled bumph ...' While this kind of 'influence' is not typical it occurs rather more frequently than we had anticipated.

We have therefore attempted to sketch the strengths and weaknesses of the kinds of influence exerted by newspapers, without exaggerating either. They are clearly diffuse entities, cross cut with many differences, apparently held together by the single act of reading the same newspaper. In our research we have focussed on individuals who restrict their reading to one newspaper for reasons of research design, but we must remember that 50 per cent of the Directive respondents read more than one newspaper, thus diminishing the discernible effects of an individual newspaper. In addition approximately 25 per cent do not read a national newspaper regularly and this compares with about 30 per cent in the MORI Omnibus data.

This would seem to further weaken the influence of newspapers on the population as a whole. However, this is not an easy conclusion to draw. We have pointed out in earlier chapters that citizens need to have understandings of complex, often distant, sometimes fast moving events in order to play their role as citizens in a democratic society. As Lippman pointed out, if large numbers of citizens are ignorant of events affecting their own futures and interests then public opinion is a sham and democracy is fatally flawed.

We now turn to a discussion of the evidence that we have presented and ask questions about its significance within a democracy and in a society which, on the best evidence available, is facing an environmental crisis, unprecedented in recent history.

9 Educating the Public

In this chapter we take stock of all the evidence that we have presented and make judgements about its significance for the debate on the press's influence on public opinion and on public cultures of understanding. We follow this with a set of suggestions and recommendations about the future direction of policy and debate. In particular we address the development of the media and the possibility of improving the public's understanding of important issues and events and the level of debate that feeds and sustains public cultures of understanding. In short we will make a link between the media and the intelligence that the public can bring to bear on the growing uncertainties and escalating macro-problems that threaten our environment and the future development of our society.

We began this book by reviewing Walter Lippman's classic but pessimistic analysis of the condition of U.S. democracy based on the myth of an informed public opinion. Lippman was dismayed by the lack of interest and the effort made by the majority of Americans to inform themselves about the major issues of the time and he was daunted by the powerful interests and immense difficulties standing in the way of making complex national and international problems comprehensible in a relatively unbiased manner. However he dismissed any criticism of capitalism and refused to place blame on the press itself. Instead he proposed a new professional cadre of auditors of social institutions who would make reliable information available. He seemed confident that if the right sort of information became available the press would use it to 'more perfectly' present 'an affair ... as news.' He saw this lack of information as the 'primary defect of popular government' and stressed his belief that 'all its other defects can, I believe, be traced to this one'.

In the seventy years since Lippman wrote his deeply perceptive analysis the world has changed. The information that he believed could revitalise democracy is in many respects now available. New professions, new organisations, new electronic media and to some extent new transparency within government itself, makes available much of the information that is required to achieve the levels of objective reporting and up-to-date unbiased information that Lippman could only speculate about. We describe studies published in 1988 by Herman and Chomsky and an analysis of Gulf War reporting by Maggie O'Kane (1995) and Martin Shaw (1996) to show that despite these improvements, the reporting of wars is subject to the same constraints and distortions as it was in the 1920s. Lippman's hypothesis fails and we need to look at the press itself for some of the reasons for this failure.

Our review of the historical evidence on the role of the press is very condensed and by no means complete. Nevertheless the evidence is convincing. The modern structure of the UK press has very little connection with the concern expressed by Lippman for making unbiased information available to a wide public. The Liberal myth, that a free market in ideas will ensure that the best ideas will triumph is exposed as part of the ideological justification for a virtually unregulated, free market capitalist press rather than an accurate statement of its actual function. Curran and Seaton's analysis of the effects of legislation, advertising revenue and the capital requirements for setting up a newspaper, demonstrate a set of factors, other than 'good ideas' or good reporting, that has led to even greater concentration of ownership and control over yet fewer newspapers. By 1988 three proprietors controlled 73 per cent of the total national circulation of daily newspapers and 81 per cent of the national Sunday newspapers and 73 per cent of the press espoused right wing views. This concentration of publishing power has subsequently been linked to transnational media empires which include, film making, magazines, television networks and satellite communication as well as newspapers. Massive cross media subsidies mean that even some of the constraints of the free market can be ignored as some national newspapers reduce their price below their operating costs in order to drive their unsubsidised or less subsidised competitors out of the market. The need to understand more fully the effects of information, packaged and presented by these media giants is more pressing than ever before. It is important to realise that the recent changes in the political spectrum of the UK national press do not diminish this need. On the contrary, they demonstrate the power of proprietors to pursue their political and commercial interests infettered by any constraint.

The debate about the public accountability of these institutions can only begin after the extent of this influence has been demonstrated. If their effect on shaping public understanding is negligible or benign there would be no political will to reform them or make them more open to criticism. If their ability to shape public cultures of understanding is demonstrated to be considerable then the intellectual arguments for reform are in place. Whether it will then be possible to implement the debate is another matter. There will be powerful people, controlling most media outlets, who will deny the intellectual arguments and more importantly deny space to the debate.

In a move to attempt to overcome this denial of space we have developed two strands to our argument. The first concerns the social/environmental context in which the debate is being proposed. We argue that massive changes in society and its relationship with the environment are already underway. The second and main strand involves an assessment of the influence of the press, which goes beyond a narrow interpretation of the empirical issue of whether the press leads or follows public opinion. We argue that in order to build trust, a newspaper needs to support and sustain a pattern of values and beliefs that reflect those of its readership. In order to 'lead' and influence its readership a newspaper needs to select and interpret 'news' so that it fits and influences the culture of understanding of its readership. The influence that a newspaper wields is therefore dependant on the skills of its editors and journalists in bringing about a balance between satisfying reader demands and shaping the news to influence what the readership understands. In our view the reshaping of this debate is as important a contribution to understanding the role of the press as the focused interpretation of empirical data, which makes up the greater part of this book.

The social and environmental context

The context of the debate needs to be examined in order to counter the argument that whatever the faults of the present system it has been adequate in the past and is therefore likely to be adequate in the future. Proponents of the status quo suggest that the dangers of reforming the press are too great and represent an unnecessary risk to press freedom. Our argument is that future uncertainties are unprecedented and the press and other media need to be substantially reformed if the public is to be equipped to deal with them and freedoms are to be preserved.

In Chapter 3 we examined the social and environmental context in the form of the 'doom' or 'boom' debate and attempt to show the inadequacy of a discussion framed in this way. We bring to a reformulation of the controversy Giddens' notion of 'manufactured uncertainty' and argue that while it is futile to definitively predict the future, because the uncertainties are too great, it is also futile to ignore the best evidence available about the nature of that future. In today's world the IPCC constitutes the best source of advice that is available about the future of our global climates. They have recommended a reduction of 60 per cent in CO_2 and other greenhouse gases. The debate about this recommendation and how it could be achieved has almost disappeared from the public arena since the Earth Summit in Rio in 1992. 'Manufactured uncertainty' has clear implications for the future. The orientation to the future should be flexible and experimental; a rational approach based on the best available information, which accumulates knowledge and understandings as carefully designed experiments are completed and affect practice and public opinion. As presently structured the press is incapable of fulfilling this role.

We have introduced two concepts that are intended to provide a basis for this kind of development in relation to the press; cultures of understanding and a new definition of intelligence. The concepts of culture and sub-culture are important because they provide a way of mapping patterns of belief and understanding in a more precise way than in previous research. While it is true that these concepts have been developed in the study of small groups within institutions, we argue that the mechanisms of culture formation can be applied to large diffuse collectivities like newspaper readerships. Newspapers provide a means of communication and therefore the vehicle for developing the common understandings so central to the notion of culture. These cultures are not as constraining or as easily reinforced as small group cultures but of course newspaper readership is an essential part of many institutional cultures and as Silverstone makes clear, like television, it plays an important role in the continuing definition of an individual's identity and community. The concept of a culture of understanding therefore unites psychological and sociological explanations of the modern condition and provides an empirical tool for testing the influence of newspapers. Either these diffuse cultures are very weak and public understanding is determined by events outside their sphere or they are relatively strong. In the latter case it will be possible to map them, describe them empirically and relate their characteristics to the particular version of the news published by particular newspapers.

This new definition of intelligence is a more radical and more controversial break with academic traditions. The notion that intelligence tests do not measure intelligence is not a new idea (Gardner 1968, Gould 1981). Indeed the idea of I.Q. as measuring something akin to intelligence, rather than intelligence itself is central to orthodox psychology. The view put forward here, that intelligence needs to be conceptually and empirically separated from intelligence testing, is rather more radical. The measurement of individual characteristics becomes the measurement of talents, and intelligence as a concept is freed from this meaning to become part of everyones' concerns about themselves and their environment. It follows that in order to be 'intelligent' one needs to be informed, to understand the major problems, uncertainties and issues facing oneself and one's society and be capable of making reasoned and logical judgements about courses of action and their effects (for collectives and individuals). This faculty is not open to precise measurement. It is, however, open to relative judgements based on evidence. For example, definitions of problems that do not take into account all of the relevant issues and interests, solutions that do not make use of all the available evidence and actions which repeatedly fail to solve problems, are evidence of a lack of intelligence.

On the positive side, intelligence can grow as information flows are improved, as more individuals understand the full scope of the problems they face and as solutions are properly evaluated and built into public cultures of understanding. The reformulation of the concepts of intelligence and cultures of understanding is in some respects parallel to the debate about the reformulation of the concept of 'knowledge' within vocational education (see for example Eraut 1994, 1997). In other words the media (including newspapers) can be an important element in developing intelligence. This trio of concepts, uncertainty, intelligence and cultures of understanding form a framework within which it is possible to better understand the significance of the debate about the influence of the media and the press in particular.

The research literature

Our review of research literature dealing with the influence of the press is not intended to be exhaustive. We have selected recent key studies based on substantial research which have made important claims about press influence in the UK and USA. Our selection of key studies allows us to give greater space for each study and include detailed critical appraisal. We realise that there are important differences between the political and media systems in these two countries but feel that if these differences are made clear it strengthens the debate to include a wide range of research.

Page and Shapiro, Fan, and Zaller each in their different ways demonstrate press influence on public opinion. Page and Shapiro show that reputation and trust is an important factor in the public response to news. Fan demonstrates public susceptibility to the volume of news items stressing one aspect of an issue (pro or con, one candidate or the other). Zaller provides a broad theoretical framework for understanding how the public makes up its mind in answering opinion poll questions. In particular he deals with the issue of individual variation within serial polls and shows that those who are least informed are most volatile and most open to influence. Zaller provides a robust explanation of the relative stability of polls, despite this high degree of individual variation. In contrast Page and Shapiro produce the mystical notion of a 'rational public' which is subsequently destroyed by evidence produced in their own book.

The importance of this work, beyond demonstrating the overall importance of media influence, is that it demonstrates the dependence and vulnerability of some sections of the public, particularly those who are least informed and most dependent on interpretation and direction supplied by powerful figures and élites. This review therefore draws attention to the issue of the quality of public cultures of understanding, first raised by Lippman. It also gives substantial support to the view that the press represents an important influence on the quality of these cultures.

The review of British studies is restricted to a comparison of Martin Linton's study of press influence on the outcome of the 1992 election with Curtice and Semetko's alternative interpretation. These studies utilise very different methodologies and while Curtice and Semetko are able to bring to bear a superior technical quality in their research, there are some substantial problems with their research design. In choosing two points in time (just before the elections of 1987 and 1992) Curtice and Semetko are really comparing the extent of press influence at one maxima with another maxima. The design enables them to conclude that the extent of the predominately conservative press' influence on the election was very similar prior to both elections. It does not enable them to make claims about the extent to which the press influenced public opinion in the run up to the 1992 election. Linton's design is quite different. It utilised monthly opinion poll data over a period of 5 years. This technique clearly demonstrates the effects of press reporting of events like John Major taking over the leadership of the conservative party and the substantial but differential effects of newspapers in the run up to the 1992 general election.

Linton's conclusions are supported by a study based on a MORI study (McKie, 1995). McKie points out that swings from one party to another must be seen in the context of the political and social composition of the various readership groups. When this factor is made part of the analysis the extent to which each newspaper delivers a vote that is not in line with 'how [their readers] would have voted if typical of their social class' provides a context for interpreting swings. Mckie concludes that while the evidence for the effectiveness of individual newapapers is mixed the overall pro-Conservative bias prevents elections being held on a 'level playing field'

The overall message in the studies that we reviewed is that the press can have a substantial overall effect on shaping public opinion and from the British studies it would appear that different newspapers can be shown to have different effects.

Factors contributing to the present study

The problems with most of the research that we have reviewed were twofold. Firstly it was strongest in demonstrating the overall effects of news reaching the public. While this is an important finding, it is impossible to differentiate between the effects of television and newspapers within the designs that were used. We were particularly interested in examining the influence of individual newspapers on their readers. Only Linton addressed this issue and emerged with a positive result. However, his focus had been the role of the press in influencing the outcome of an election. We wanted to look at the emergent problems associated with the environment and development. Secondly, none of the studies had been very strong on addressing the issue of the quality of the news and gauging its adequacy in the light of the seriousness of deep seated and emergent problems within society. The North American studies have been strongest on this issue but they had focussed on the extent of factual public knowledge, for example the location of Nicaragua and the names of prominent public officials. They had not linked this knowledge with the quality of news presented by newspapers and the adequacy of the public debate.

The highly differentiated British national press was able to provide us with the perfect test bed for examining the effects of individual newspapers. By choosing environment and development issues and focusing on the Earth Summit, we were choosing areas of great importance and public concern. In addition, we could know in advance that a major event of international importance would occur within the period of our study. Finally, we would be able to use two measures of public response: the MORI monthly Omnibus Poll and a more detailed panel study under the aegis of the Mass Observation Archive at Sussex University. This combination of events and methodologies would give us a window enabling us to look into the effects of newspaper publishing on the public and trace these effects back to the way individual newspapers treated the news about the Summit.

During the late 1980s and 1990s a series of major discoveries and events had made the environment a major public concern. In the European elections the Green Party polled 15 per cent of the votes and mainstream politicians realised that they could no longer ignore the environment. Mrs Thatcher, members of the Royal family and almost every major public figure seemed to be prepared to make a statement about conserving or preserving the environment. The tabloid newspapers appointed environment correspondents and the amount of news reaching the public about the environment peaked in 1989.

At this stage in the public debate the environment was universally portrayed as 'good' and the polluters and users of natural resources as 'the bad'. However, the debate was superficial. The link between consumption and pollution was targeted on relatively few dangerous chemicals and inessential items (aerosols, leaded petrol, waste paper and plastic etc). The links between the environment and development were rarely drawn except in some of the quality press and famines were treated as relatively discrete happenings requiring 'one-off' solutions. Those solutions were themselves sometimes sold like soap powders and became painless if not enjoyable media events. The deeper underlying issues and problems were not reaching the public.

In the run-up to the Earth Summit it became clear that many of the major charities in the environment and development field were disturbed by the superficialities and omissions within the debate and along with many international bodies were determined to link environment and development issues at the core of Earth Summit proceedings. The key concepts of 'sustainable development' and 'biodiversity' represented these twin concerns. They became the carriers of the all important message which carried with it deep and substantial implications in terms of technology transfer, capital transfer and new international regulations for restricting the use and trade in many natural products from timber and animal products to fossil fuels.

It was also apparent at an early stage that this new development within the debate would be deeply unpopular with some Western governments, particularly the USA and the UK. Both of these governments were deeply committed to de-regulation, free market capitalism and open access to foreign markets and resources. Particularly in the case of the USA, there was the demand for easy access to the new raw materials for bio-engineering. It was therefore quite clear, long before the Earth Summit, that the UK national press would be deeply divided on the issues to be debated at the Summit and most probably on the Summit itself. The Summit was therefore almost perfectly designed to test the way that the UK press would represent to its readerships an international event of considerable importance in the context of very deep long term issues, on which there were very different perspectives but as yet no well established cultures of understanding. It would provide a test bed for studying how the Summit was presented, how it was integrated with established values and ways of seeing the world and how the various newspaper audiences responded to those variations of the 'truth'.

Our preparation for monitoring newspaper coverage of the Summit had been fairly thorough. We had carried out a dry run of some of the methodologies that we would use, for example on the way that the Sudan famine was reported. This was carried out in a restricted range of national newspapers and revealed substantial differentiation. However, it did not prepare us for the astonishing degree of differentiation in content, quality and quantity revealed by our study of a wider range of newspapers which reported the Earth Summit.

The results

The way in which the broadsheet newspapers interpreted their brief in covering the Summit was impressive. Most of these newspapers set up small teams of expert correspondents in Rio and in addition brought in guest writers and freelance reporters to cover particular issues. While it was possible to discern particular lines of argument, different emphases and different styles of writing, the overall impression gained from reading the entire coverage was of an impressive service of information dissemination and public debate. The professionalism of the journalists seemed to overcome editorial inhibitions, the accounts of the Summit did not seem to differentiate more markedly along political lines as the Summit approached and obtained substantial coverage. However, differences in coverage did occur and we were able to monitor a parallel difference in their readers' perceptions of the Summit, particularly on the issue of Third World Debt.

Despite this impressive achievement in covering the Summit, the broadsheet press has not maintained its interest in the subsequent conferences and developments. As the sequence of United Nations Conferences on the environment and population have proceeded, the press interest has declined spectacularly. The last conferences were hardly covered at all. The phenomena of a cycle in press interest has been enacted in a stark and abrupt manner (Worcester 1993, 1994)

The coverage of the Summit by the tabloid press contrasted in every respect. The quantity of coverage was by any measure inadequate. There simply was not enough space devoted to explain the major issues. Few of the tabloids sent reporters to the conference and those who were sent did not possess the understanding or the expertise to write about complex issues in ways that would break through the barrier of prejudice represented by the desk editors. The result was that the coverage published by the whole tabloid press amounted to fewer, shorter articles than appeared in the *Daily Telegraph*. The tabloid reporters reverted in many cases to styles of reporting that trivialised and misrepresented the purpose and achievements of the Summit.

When we examined the coverage of two of the most important concepts used to describe the central concerns of the conference organisers, 'sustainable development' and 'biodiversity', we found that no tabloid newspaper had ever used the term 'sustainable development' in its reporting of the summit and the use of the term 'biodiversity' was minimal. An analogy might be to report a Conservative Party conference without using the terms 'privatisation' or 'freedom of choice'. It is true that some of the issues represented by these terms did attract some sympathetic and supportive comment from two of the tabloids, in particular the *Today* newspaper and the *Daily Mirror*. However, by not fully explaining the purpose of the Summit, the difficulties in the way of progress and the outcomes of the Summit, in particular the commitment to a continuing process of working towards international solutions, the bulk of the tabloid press with-held information of importance to all its readers. In our terms, it made a major contribution towards cultures of ignorance.

When we turn our attention to the issues pursued by the individual tabloid newspapers, the selection and distortion of information is even more marked. The overall impact of the *Mail*'s coverage was to raise one problem, population, above all others and link it to feelings of threat, immigration and racial prejudice. In so far as the paper anticipated any optimistic outcomes to the Summit after it had poured scorn upon it, these were attributed to John Major. Blame for failure was attributed to the Third World for its greed and desire to get money from the richer Western countries and to George Bush. The longest article printed by the *Mail* and connected to the Summit was about the rape of a Portuguese teenage girl by an Amazonian Indian.

The *Sun* was even more devoid of information and more condemning than the *Daily Mail*. It poured scorn on the Summit and derided its purpose, its methods, the participants and anything else it could link with the Summit. The Sun seemed to go beyond supporting cultures of ignorance. It *celebrated* its own ignorance of the Summit and most of the issues that the Summit was set up to consider. This celebration of ignorance we can call idiocy. The *Sun* used humour to justify the removal of responsibility from its readers to understand important issues and relevant problems. All serious issues were subjected to distortion and trivialisation and ignorance was justified. The *Sun* reached about 10 million readers with its version of the Earth Summit. More than all of the quality press.

These widely contrasting treatments of the Summit provided us with the test-bed to be followed up by examining the responses of one-newspaper readers in the Mass Observation directives.

The Mass Observation directives

The analysis of the response of readership groups was deeply disquieting. Our panel of respondents represented a collection of people selected by their will-ingness to observe contemporary social and cultural events and write about them. In short they represent an alert, interested and relatively well informed collection of people with the time to respond to fairly frequent demands on their time. They did not represent the large minority, who in Zaller's analysis are ill informed and most easily and superficially influenced by press and media reports. In addition to this general characteristic it is clear that they were fairly sceptical about their newspapers, the media and politicians.

Despite these characteristics it was clear that they were influenced by the press reports that they read. In our view this influence was both superficial and deep. It is superficial in the sense that Zaller describes. When individuals are asked about events they search back in their memory for relevant information. This recall is superficial in the sense that the most recently stored is, in general, the most easily remembered. However, the information or impression left in the mind by reading a newspaper account is also affected by the presentation and how that presentation links to a deep framework of values, beliefs (concerns) and understandings held by that individual. By providing informa-tion in ways that links it to these deep frameworks the newspaper becomes influential. It can intensify feeling about a topic by linking it to feelings of fear, a sense of justice or other deeply held beliefs. On the other hand by minimis-ing, trivialising or demonstrating hopeless conflict and divisions (complication and loss of trust), a newspaper can deflect events from influencing its reader-ship in ways it would like to prevent.

In their different ways the *Sun* and the *Daily Mail* accomplished this with respect to the Earth Summit. The *Sun* has developed a culture of idiocy which it shares with its readers by posturing and pontificating in an absurd but witty manner. It gives the impression that a debunking humour is the only worth-while framework in which to consider most events that seek to face up to important issues. However, behind this humour it seeks to influence. As Zaller has made clear, if information is with-held from individuals they are more sus-ceptible to shallow contemporary influence, not less. The *Sun* has perfected this kind of journalism and by doing so has gained the admiration and respect of many, especially those who respect power and influence, irrespective of its source. Others find the *Sun* and its creator and owner a more sinister devel-opment in UK journalism. Will Hutton the editor of the *Observer*, wrote recently in a satirical piece:

There have been media tycoons before over the twentieth century, but Rupert Murdoch is the meanest, most powerful and demonic of them all. He disdains governments, is the single most important reason why British tabloid journalism has plumbed new depths, and has championed a right-wing xenophobic populism that had few roots in British culture until his ownership of British papers. He has ruthlessly cross-subsidised his operations in a satanic quest for monopoly. He is the media Mephistopheles of our times : a man who holds politicians in his devilish thrall and whose carelessness of fair play and civic responsibility – indeed of Britain – knows no bounds. (Hutton, 1996)

The sentiment is clearly expressed and represents the strength of feeling within some sections of journalism about the development of a culture of idiocy and the underlying sinister power it wields our *Sun* readers.

The recognition of this kind of development has not been confined to this side of the Atlantic. Carl Bernstein in his evidence to the Issues Committee accuses 'media moguls, such as Rupert Murdoch, owner of the Fox Network', of 'helping to bring about an idiot culture.' He points out that the day Nelson Mandela returned to Soweto after his years in the South African gulag, and the day that the allies of World War II agreed to unification of Germany, *Newsday* filled its front page with the break-up of the marriage of Donald Trump. This kind of prioritising represents in his view, the triumph of an idiot culture over the media. We hope to have contributed evidence and precision to this insight (Hardin, 1994).

Within this book we have demonstrated press influence at all levels ranging from national quota samples (MORI) through small one reader samples to individuals (MOA). The evidence we present is open to questioning and debate. Further research is of the utmost importance. Nevertheless we believe that our evidence must strike all but the most objurate opponents as substantial and the most convincing so far.

At the macro level we have shown that public concern increased as newspapers (collectively) revealed the global problems of pollution and over-exploitation beginning to affect a range of environments, global and local. Within these generally high levels of concern, those newspapers which had most coverage were associated with the highest levels of readership concern. The critical case here was the *Today* newspaper, whose readership demonstrated very high levels of concern while the paper gave priority to environment issues and which then sank back to normal tabloid levels when the paper abandoned this policy.

By making detailed comparisons between newspapers, the *Daily Mail*, the *Daily Mirror*, *Guardian* and other quality papers, we were able to demonstrate that specific issues introduced into the discussion about the Summit were picked up by readers and incorporated into their understanding of what the Summit was about. While it can be argued that *Daily Mail* readers are more susceptible to their reports about a population explosion, it remains true that without the *Mail*'s particular interpretation of the Summit it is most unlikely that their readers would have differed so markedly from the *Daily Mirror* readers over their understanding of the relevance of the population issue or in the case of the *Mirror* readers, the nuclear pollution issue. In other words, these comparisons illustrate the construction of cultures of understanding and the way in which new, major events are assimilated into them without producing obvious contradictions or the need for a radical overhaul.

The case studies of individual readers produce evidence of the way undersandings are put together by individuals. The selection of cases, in particular in the case of the *Daily Mail,* illustrated the range of readers from 'core members' of the readership to 'reluctant readers'. In the case of Mrs B.I., a reluctant reader it, is possible to trace a negative case in the development of understanding. Her basic values are out of tune with the *Daily Mail,* she believes in the need for collective action to solve problems of the environment and development and is prepared to make personal sacrifices in her standard of living. However, she is cut off from news that could encourage these ideals and make her feel part of a culture of understanding and she remains a blocked idealist. By reporting a highly selected, slanted view of the Summit a major opportunity for Mrs B.I. to understand the issues that so concern her was lost.

The problems that Walter Lippman wrote about so convincingly in the 1920s still exist. Very little has been done to avoid the worst outcomes. Despite the fact that we now possess the technical and intellectual capacity to overcome the worst excesses of selection, distortion and bias, they still continue. In fact there are grounds for fearing that things have got worse as competitive pressures, audience ratings and sales become more prominent in determining media output (Carl Bernstein, reported in Hardin, 1994). The global problems that we face have intensified and the uncertainties about the future mean that there are no obvious or easy solutions. The control of the media has become even more remote and unaccountable as media moguls have become international powers and hold national parties and national politicians in their 'thrall'. It is our hope that as the public realise the extent to which they are badly served; uninformed, misinformed and misled and thereby rendered less intelligent, they will demand a better service. It is, after all, a central tenant of the market economy that customer satisfaction is paramount. This effort must rest with individuals and organisations that are centrally concerned with the future of our environment and our development.

Research into global environmental problems still continues but it is largely unreported as news. International conferences are still held on major world issues from food and population to specific pollutants, but they generate little press interest beyond the relatively occasional article, which might oddly focus on the size of the car allowance that delegates can claim. As a result, cultures of understanding that could encapsulate major environment and development issues cannot develop. The public remains deeply worried by the problems and the future but the worries are suppressed and individualised. They have little opportunity for collective expression and the development of intelligence. A deep sense of pessimism and alienation pervaded our MOA directive responses relating to the future of the environment. This failure to respond to middle and long term problems is not simply the fault of the press. The fault is widespread, from politicians and industry to the public and NGOs. Nevertheless the press must accept an important part of the responsibility. As institutions with the power to educate they have generated cultures of understanding which have been marked by short term concerns and a frequently changing diet of sensations which is designed to increase circulation in a highly competitive market place. Editors are not moved by longer term issues and are 'careless' with the evidence and the quality of the debate. They have influence and a powerful educational function but they are unwilling to recognise it and absolutely unwilling to take any responsibility for it. The reforms that we now propose are intended to address these issues.

They must be seen for what they are. They are proposals, based on our analysis of the problems we face and our demonstration of the power of the press. They are intended to encourage/pressure individual newspapers to improve their coverage of news, to broaden the views that are expressed in their columns, to improve the quality of debate (evidence and argument) and to recognise the longer term educational function that they possess and to hold them accountable. We are not, however, experts on the organisation and structure of the press and our suggestions are not detailed at the institution level. We make general points in the hope that others will take them further.

Recommendations

The recommendations reflect the arguments and conclusions presented in this volume.

1   Newspapers should be recognised as major public assets with the acknowledged public function of informing and educating the public. The link between the quality of public debate, the intelligence of cultures of understanding and the quality and breadth of the news reported by newspapers should be taken seriously, further researched, debated and better understood.

2   The status of newspapers as organisations, free from interference by governments, powerful organisations and powerful individuals, including proprietors, should be ensured by establishing a regulatory body, an Off-press, which has the power to intervene to ensure and to improve the breadth and quality of the UK press.

3   Well established individual national newspapers should be recognised as serving the interests of large sections of the population. Proprietors should be restricted in their rights to close them down or change them in ways that effectively cuts off an established service to a large number of readers. In this respect newspapers should be regarded more like television franchises which can be offered to new proprietors, should the existing owners wish to pull out or fail to reach acceptable standards.

4   Cross subsidising of newspapers should be carefully monitored. If a media corporation cross subsidises in order to reduce the cost of a newspaper and drive some of its rivals out of the market, Off-press should be empowered to prevent it. Cross subsidies would be allowed if an ailing newspaper needed to restructure and modernise in order to provide a better service to its readers and retrieve its market position. In other words Off-press would be acting to safeguard the breadth of newspaper perspectives and yet allow changes which would improve quality.

5   The present market structure does not safeguard quality. Competitive pressures have often driven down standards in an attempt to ensure sales through promotions, competitions, give-aways, inaccurate sensational reporting and pornography. An independent research centre, supported by a compulsory levy on newspapers, should be set up to monitor the quality of reporting. These reports should be geared to informing the public about where individual newspapers had failed to keep them informed or had trivialised important events or misrepresented them. If this failed to ensure an improvement of standards the newspaper should be open to various more stringent measures. (see below)

6   Newspapers should be required to contribute to a fund which would set up a series of awards for good reporting, quality of publication etc. Similar awards already exist. They should be substantially increased to enable individuals to undertake special assignments and to enable newspapers to set up specialist units for longer term, indepth studies of major issues. This would be a direct intervention to improve the scope and dimensions of reporting and the ability of reporters to deal with complex issues. The fund should be large and the largest contributions should be made by those who do not improve the standard of debate in their newspaper. (see 5 above)

7   A wide range of devices should be used to encourage reader/community participation. These kinds of experiments have been developed in television and are capable of extension to the press. They could range from guest editors for sections within the paper, reports on community groups to open debates on specific issues and specialist reports on topics requested by readers or sometimes institutions. Every effort should be made to make readers feel that they can participate in a debate or even initiate one.

8   Efforts should be made to improve the training and professional standing of newspaper reporters. These could range from improved initial training to secondments to other institutions as well as the possibility of other professionals from education, law, medicine etc. spending time in newspapers. This professional exchange should enable newspapers to become more open and accessible and this, in turn, should act to broaden the coverage of news and to include a better explanation of the context in which news items occur.

9   The composition and constitution of a regulatory body (Off-press) would be an important issue. This is not the occasion to recommend a detailed blueprint. Clearly various sections of the industry and community would need to be represented and democratic procedures should be used wherever possible. However, the over-riding purpose of the body to improve the quality and breadth of news reporting would in itself an issue open to research and debate. If this then becomes a focus of attention and concern then Off-press would itself be open to criticism, advice, experimentation and improvement.

10 The skills of reading are taught during the early years of schooling as if reading is a simple mechanical task. Later in secondary school children are introduced to literature with the aim of enabling them to appreciate 'good literature' and to enable them to acquire more advanced skills of compre-

hension and criticism. Relatively few schools currently teach programmes that address the need to assist school-aged children to read newspapers, or help them acquire the skills to critically appraise newspaper texts. Our research points to the need for those skills within the population. We need to reappraise the adequacy of the National Curriculum and introduce those skills which will enable young adults to interrogate the media in ways that will enable them to develop their interests and intelligence throughout adult life.

We realise that there are risks involved in implementing these recommendations. Newspapers are businesses that exist in a highly competitive market place. They have a duty to their shareholders to make a profit. They would certainly argue that the implementation of these reforms would interfere with their ability to compete in the market place. However, they would have the consolation that all newspapers would be similarly constrained. In addition it is possible that an improvement in the quality of news reporting would encourage some of the 25–30 per cent of our community who do not currently read national newspapers to re-enter the market. Certainly if present trends continue and the low public regard for the tabloid press is not countered in the manner described above, circulations will continue to diminish and an important national asset will have been squandered. Nevertheless the job of making the newspaper industry recognise that they have a deeper, educational responsibility towards their readers and the broader community, will not be easy. We hope that this book will contribute towards starting that realisation.

Appendix A

Headlines of articles from tabloid newspapers (*Today*, *Daily Mail*, *Daily Mirror*, *Sun*)

Headlines from *Today* were downloaded from *FTProfile*. The *Daily Mail*, *Daily Mirror* and the *Sun* headlines were manually created. For the *Daily Mirror* there are two sets: the first is the set of headlines of articles containing references to the Earth Summit; the second is the list of headlines of articles containing references to the issue of nuclear pollution. This latter set of articles represent the special 'mini-campaign' run by the *Daily Mirror* during the Summit.

Today

1   19 May 92 Charles to join world leaders at Earth Summit; Prince Charles (575)
2   19 May 92 10 Green issues they'll discuss; Earth Summit in Rio (170)
3   30 May 92 Miners hire their own pit (63)
4   30 May 92 Smith's green pact demand; John Smith (64)
5   01 Jun 92 Earth needs cash not cant; Comment (300)
6   01 Jun 92 The Earth is sunk; Earth Summit in Rio (300)
7   02 Jun 92 Brazil floods (62)
8   02 Jun 92 We're too broke to save the world, insists Britain (416)
9   02 Jun 92 Earth Summit; Quick Retorts; Letter (44)
10 03 Jun 92 Carey's Summit warning; Earth Summit (138)
11 03 Jun 92 My daughter wanted to help the environment. I told her to tidy her room; At the heart of Today (506)
12 04 Jun 92 Britain's poor excuse will cost us the Earth; Letter (236)
13 04 Jun 92 Siebe flies green flag; City (84)
14 05 Jun 92 Rumours of the Earth's death are greatly exaggerated; Earth Summit (1027)
15 06 Jun 92 I say, I say; Comment (292)
16 08 Jun 92 Third World War warning (294)
17 09 Jun 92 Ronnie: Please welcome me home; Ronnie Biggs (182)
18 10 Jun 92 Catholic views on contraception; At the heart of Today (125)
19 10 Jun 92 A secret admirer thinks Ginny's blooming lovely; Virginia Bottomley (404)
20 10 Jun 92 Drugs greatest threat to kids; Columbia (401)
21 10 Jun 92 Major to sign Earth Treaty without Bush (258)
22 10 Jun 92 Tory hunt for mole who shopped Hogg; Douglas Hogg (256)

23 11 Jun 92 Major 'death' hits Pound; John Major rumour (269)
24 11 Jun 92 Lilley takes loyalty test; Maastricht treaty (292)
25 11 Jun 92 30 species they saved for us all; Earth Summit (542)
26 12 Jun 92 Major U-turn to stop Europe rift (458)
27 12 Jun 92 Green treaties mean nothing (227)
28 12 Jun 92 God help you, Prime Minister (148)
29 12 Jun 92 Green protesters clash at Summit; Earth Summit (130)
30 13 Jun 92 Missing: Pounds 32bn to save the planet; Earth Summit (274)
31 13 Jun 92 Major jets back to tackle EC row; John Major (222)
32 13 Jun 92 Selling our future short; Earth Summit; Comment (142)
33 13 Jun 92 Beatle's brother has skin cancer surgery; Mike McCartney (364)
34 15 Jun 92 Rio Summit flop (59)
35 16 Jun 92 Thatcher to launch attack on Euro deal (225)
36 18 Jun 92 What a waste!; Earth Summit; Rio (70)
37 25 Jun 92 M25 is to become a 14-lane monster (350)
38 30 Jun 92 Statistics that sentence the whale to extinction (878)
39 30 Jun 92 Earth Summit; Quick Retorts; Letter (44)

Daily Mail

1   30 April 1992 The Human Timebomb (headline): Population crisis threatens us all, warns UN
2   5 may 1992 TV Mail 2: March of the green warriors
3   5 May 92 Letter: Rio hopes
4   Date? Birth control and wealth creation: Birth control should be high on the agenda of the Earth Summit.
5   Date? Assignment
6   28 May 1992 page 10 Earth Summit is a Sham, says EC Chief
7   30 May 1992 Is this the way to save the world?
8   1 June 1992 page 2 Bush's £55m bid to head off greens
9   2 June 1992 Front page headline: Beware of false claims by Extremists, Rio Delegates Warned. Top Scientists Attack Greens
10 3 June 1992 The man who discovered the link between smoking and cancer explains why the Green extremists are wrong.
11 3 June 1992 Major's mission to rescue Earth Summit (headline)
12 4 June 1992 Page 8 Planet Earth Priggery 'Our children's children could be a monstrous regiment of health freaks'
13 4 June 1992 Page 10 Fight for Earth starts in silence (headline)
14 6 June 1992 Page 29 Food and Wine Feast on green cuisine (headline)
15 8 June 1992 Page 15 Bush and Major agree to differ in Rio
16 9 June 1992 Page 10 World Wide Special as political leaders converge on Rio. Japan makes U.S. green with envy
17 9 June 1992 Page 10 Chalker in birth control challenge to Vatican
18 10 June 1992 Page 10 Major to sigfn green treaty
19 11 June 1992 Page 6 Comment: Beware the perils of party faction
20 11 June 1992 Page 10 Memo to Rio
21 11 June 1992 Page 9 Eccentric
22 12 June 1992 Page 2 Bush in teargas riots drama
23 12 June 1992 Page 6 Pawhno Paiakan saved his rainforest people from the developers ... but he couldn't save himself
24 13 June 1992 Page 2 Stop the world baby boom, pleads Major

25   13 June 1992 Page 6 Comment: Rio summit's tower of Babel
26   13 June 1992 Page 54, Letter: World worry
27   13 June 1992 Page 2 (Not summit but relevant)A Planet in Trouble
     and a 'Green Hero' in Hiding
28   15 June 1992 page 8 Fearful Summitry: 'For rich and poor countires
     alike, one man's poison is another man's meat'
29   15 June 1992 Page 12 Earth Summit Protest Goes to the Top (photo)
     On a high: The Greenpeace demonstrators make their point
30   25 June 1992 page 25: Life in Society Where Men No Longer
     Dominate

Sun

 1   2 June 1992 page 2 PM want son Earth Summit
 2   2 June 1992 page 10 10 Ways Britain's being Blighted
 3   3 June 1992 page 2 PM blasts Kinnock in aid row
 4   3 June 1992 The Sun says: Doze Zone Danger at Summit
 5   3 June 1992 page 6, Picture caption: BUSH...blocking progress
 6   4 June 1992 page 2 2 minutes silence for our future
 7   4 June 1992 page 2 Escaped: train robber Ronnie Biggs
 8   9 June 1992 page 13 Body Shop Indian 'is rapist'
 9   10 June 1992 page 2 We'll sign up for Rio
10   12 June 1992 page 6 The Sun Says: Treaty trouble
11   15 June 1992 page 6 The Sun Says: Farce in Rio
12   16 June 1992 page 19 Letters Have a Go End this abuse

Daily Mirror

 1   11 may 1992 page 6 Green Gas
 2   28 May 1992 page 1 Krypton Factor
 3   28 May 1993 page 5 Comment: Two deaths too many
 4   30 May 1992 page 14 Green plea by Smith
 5   1 June 1992 page 4 What On Earth
 6   2 June 1992 page 2 Double blow to Earth Summit
 7   3 June 1992 page 5 Aid Blast at Tories
 8   3 June 1992 page 6 What on Earth Can they Do?
 9   3 June 1992 page 33 Money Mirror: Go green and clean up!
10   4 June, 1992 page 2 Costing the earth
11   9 June 1992 page 11 WIN EarthRISE
12   10 June 1992 page 2 Brits' Rio pact
13   Date? page 7 Women's Section: Why I'm on the Wilde side
14   12 June 1992 page 2 Title: Who's Kidding Who?
15   12 June 1992 page 6 Major turns a blind eye to plight of Brazilian
     youngsters
16   13 June 1992, page 2 Major Snub for Summit
17   15 June 1992, page 6 Greens in Protest
18   16 June 1992, page 4 Rio a letdown says Major
19   16 June 1992, page 13 Major's so Unpopular as trees get the axe
20   18 June 1992, page 5 Major's £17,000 Car Bill

Daily Mirror (Nuclear pollution issue)

 1   8 May 1992 Page 9 Nuclear Nightmare: Deformed children fathered
     by our N-sub sailors
 2   14 May 1992 page 4 DOOMED! Beach alert over nuke waste plant
 3   28 May 1992 Page 1 BRITAIN is poised to open another massive

nuclear plant amid fears over pollution, health and a deadly new menace - radioactive Krypton Gas.

4   28 May 1992 Page 2-3 Special Report (Gemma D'Arcy)

5   28 May 1992 page 2 Why we won't shut up Parents battle on for Gemma

6   28 May 1992 page 3 Terrible Toll for Children

7   28 May 1992 Page 4-5 By appointment ... the SECRET

8   28 May 1992 Page 5 10 Will Die of Krypton Cancer

9   1 June 1992, page 2 Rock band U2 have joined the Daily Mirror's fight against the giant new Sellafield 2 nuclear plant.

10   4 June 1992, Page 9 Public Opinion Special: To Hell and Back

11   4 June 1992, page 9 Thanks Say Parents of Tragic Gemma

12   6 June 1992, page 11 Nuclear War: Divers go into battle against ship of doom

13   11 June 1992, page 7 Nuke Row over U2

14   12 June 1992, page? U2 Nuke Pledge

15   17 June 1992, page 2 Comment: What A Cheek

16   18 June 1992, page? (2 page spread) This protest was for all our kids and that means U2

17   19 June 1992, page 9 Safety Sense at Sizewell

18   20 June 1992, page 5 U2 blast out nuke warning to fans

19   22 June 1992, page 15 Beach Invasion

20   29 June 1992, page 20 Requiem for Jessica

Appendix B

Nature, environment and development in the year of the Earth Summit

This directive asks you for your views about environment and development issues in 1992, the year of The United Nations Conference on Environment and Development, known as the Earth Summit, which took place in Rio di Janeiro during the first two weeks of June.

In the following questions the words 'environment' and 'development' referring to a wide range of ideas. Exact definitions are not important. 'Environment' is simply the place where we live, our habitat, whether it is in the sense of our own neighbourhood, town, or country, or the planet as whole. 'Environment issues' are such well-publicised matters as atmospheric pollution, conservation of flora and fauna, ocean ecology, nuclear energy and radioactive waste, the thinning of the ozone layer, transportation and its impact, the introduction of toxic chemicals into the food chain, the destruction of the rain forests, the effect of environmental changes on climate, etc.. The list is very long and interconnected.

'Development' is a broad term which generally refers to the process by which a society or country expands economically. It is often taken to mean a progressive improvement in the standard of living. Historically the term 'development' has been associated with what used to be called 'Third World' countries (with the United States axis as the First World and the USSR axis as the Second World). 'Third World' countries were typically 'pre-industrial' or in the early stages of industrialisation, and later they become known as 'developing countries'. Increasingly, however, 'development' is recognised as a process in which all societies are engaged and today the more common distinction is between the rich countries of the 'North and the poor countries of the 'South'.

The issues and problems relating to development are also well publicised. They include malnutrition and under-nutrition, poverty, famine, debt and aid, public health provision, population growth, use of energy resources etc. Again, the list is long and interconnected.

This directive has three main aims. To ask you to express your feelings about the environment and development; to ask you to describe how you find out about these issues; and to ask you what you think can or should be done about such issues, if anything.

Please complete sections 1 and 2 as it suits you but sections 3 and 4 should be completed during the period specified.

Section 1

1 What newspapers (weekday and Sunday), journals or magazines do you read?

2 What current affairs/news television programmes do you watch?

3 List any environment/development organisations of which you are a member.

Section 2

1 Nature and 'the natural'

We hear much nowadays about 'man's relationship to nature'. But what does 'nature' really mean? Should people see themselves as part of nature? Are people just another 'natural' species? Similarly, the word 'natural' is very common. Many foods (muesli, for example) are now advertised as 'natural'. Given that most 'natural' products are now produced in factories, does the word 'natural' have any useful meaning?

2 Nature and the supernatural

Many people think that nature was created by an all-powerful God or deity. Some also think that it is still controlled by supernatural forces. If we are subject to such forces it may be that the human race can do little to influence or change the non-human world. Perhaps we should surrender to fate. Does the idea of nature carry any particular religious significance for you? If so, do you think it worth changing our behaviour in order to protect resources and other species?

3 Identifying issues and problems

What in your opinion are the three most important environmental problems facing the world today? What are the three most important development problems?

Do you think future generations will face the same issues or will there be others that are more important for them?

Do you feel any of these problems pose a threat to you personally or to our way of life in the UK?

Or are they only relevant to remote areas of the world?

Do you feel that these problems are given too much or too little emphasis in what you read in the press or watch on television? Why do you think this is so?

Do you think that there is enough choice about sources of information? Do you feel that you know enough about what sources of information are available? How do you choose your sources?

4 What can we do about environment and development problems?

What do you think that people can do about these problems?

What sort of things do you do in your daily life that take environment or development issues into account.?

Do you think that individual action is the key to solving these problems or will it require co-ordinated action by government or organisations such as the United Nations?

Do you think that richer societies such as Britain, USA and Japan should take more responsibility for these problems when they occur in poorer societies?

Would you be prepared to accept a lowering of your standard of living if this contributed to the solution of these problems?

If you are a member of any environment/development organisation can you explain what led you to become involved?

5 How useful is modern science?

We are still very dependent on scientists (e.g. physicists, chemists and biologists) to tell us about the environment, our relationship with it and changes to our behaviour is we are going to protect the planet. Does modern science have an adequate understanding of our relationships to the environment? How seriously should we take the explanations, predictions and proposals offered by modern scientists?

Section 3

Please complete the following section during the week beginning 15th June

Recently the 'Earth Summit' took place in Rio di Janeiro:

1   Did you know about this event and if so what were your main sources of information?

2   Did you take a close interest in the event or would you have done so if you had known more about it?

3   What in your view were the main issues addressed by the conference?

4   Of all the sources of information available to you about the Summit which do you feel is the most reliable and trustworthy? Which is the least?

5   Do you have an opinion as to why these differences in reliability exist?

6   Do you feel that the press could have been more informative? Do you feel that television could have been more informative?

7   Do you think that there are any issues that were neglected by (a) the press and (b) television?

8   Has the coverage of the Earth Summit changed the way that you think or do things about these issues?

Section 4

Please complete the following section during the week beginning 17th August.

It is now two months since the Earth Summit conference in Rio.

1   Do you feel that it has had an effect on the way governments or powerful organisations behave.

2   Are there any issues that you feel more strongly about as a result of the conference?

3   Are any of the issues raised by the conference still in the public mind? If so, can you say what they are?

4   Do you feel that the press has provided adequate coverage of the issues since the conference took place? What issues does the press concentrate on?

5   Do you feel that television has provided adequate coverage of the issues since the conference took place? What issues does television concentrate on?

Appendix C

Major characteristics of one-newspaper sub-samples (See Table 8.1 and Table 8.2)

	% Male	% Female	% 60+	% Prof/Man	% Retired	% SE Region
GDN	30	22	36	35	24	26
IND	16	11	36	15	16	16
DTL	25	21	49	26	24	23
DML	14	18	29	9	12	16
DMR	9	11	28	3	12	12
None	7	18	23	11	12	7

Appendix D

DIRECTIVE Samples

Directives		Gdn	Ind	Tel	DMl	DMr	None
Earth Summit	1	21 78%	10 71%	16 67%	14 82%	10 91%	10 71%
United Nations/UN	2	16 59%	6 43%	11 46%	6 35%	6 55%	3 21%
agenda 21	3	2 7%					1 7%
global forum	4						
people's summit etc	5	1 4%					
rio declaration	6			1 4%			
declaration	7	1 4%		1 4%			
treaty	8	1 4%	1 7%	3 13%	3 18%		
principles	9	4 15%		1 4%			
convention	10			1 4%			
FoE etc	11	11 41%	5 36%		3 18%	3 27%	1 7%
Oxfam	12	6 22%	2 14%	5 21%	4 24%	1 9%	1 7%
greenpeace	13	12 44%	5 36%	4 17%	2 12%	6 55%	3 21%
WWF etc	14	2 7%	3 21%				1 7%
brundtland	15						
john/mr major	16	4 15%	1 7%	1 4%	1 6%	2 18%	
michael/mr howard	17	1 4%		1 4%			
david/mr maclean	18						
douglas/mr hurd	19						
neil/mr kinnock	20						
ann clwyd	21						
john/mr smith	22						
bryan/mr gould	23						
george/president bush	24	8 30%	2 14%	6 25%	1 6%	1 9%	2 14%
ripa di meana	25						
forest principles	26						
tropical forest	27						
temperate forest	28						
rainforest(s)	29				1 6%		
deforest	30	7 26%	4 29%	2 8%	3 18%		3 21%
biodiversity	31	3 11%	3 21%	5 21%	1 6%	1 9%	
species	32	19 70%	11 79%	16 67%	13 76%	7 64%	10 71%
flora/fauna	33	3 11%	2 14%	5 21%	2 12%	2 18%	1 7%
wildlife	34	6 22%	4 29%	9 38%	4 24%	2 18%	3 21%
conservation	35	9 33%	3 21%	6 25%	4 24%		3 21%
global warming	36	12 44%	9 64%	5 21%	5 29%	1 9%	3 21%
greenhouse effect	37	1 4%	2 14%	2 8%	1 6%		
climat	38	9 33%	6 43%	10 42%	5 29%	1 9%	2 14%
climate change	39	1 4%	1 7%	1 4%	1 6%		
asthma	40		1 7%	2 8%		4 36%	1 7%
emissions	41	6 22%	3 21%	9 38%	2 12%		1 7%
public transport	42	7 26%	1 7%	9 38%	6 35%	2 18%	2 14%
road build'g/construction	43	1 4%		1 4%			
traffic	44	4 15%	3 21%	6 25%	1 6%	3 27%	3 21%

word	#												
car	45	24	89%	13	93%	24	100%	16	94%	11	100%	12	86%
ozone	46	16	59%	8	57%	16	67%	10	59%	7	64%	7	50%
carbon tax	47												
carbon dioxide/co2	48	4	15%	3	21%	3	13%	1	6%	1	9%		
environment	49	26	96%	14	100%	21	88%	16	94%	11	100%	11	79%
pollut	50	19	70%	13	93%	19	79%	15	88%	9	82%	10	71%
radioactiv	51	5	19%	3	21%	1	4%	5	29%	1	9%		
nuclear	52	13	48%	6	43%	9	38%	7	41%	7	64%	5	36%
chemical	53	7	26%	4	29%	8	33%	4	24%	2	18%	3	21%
waste	54	18	67%	9	64%	16	67%	10	59%	8	73%	9	64%
BNFL	55									1	9%	1	7%
leukaemia	56	1	4%	1	7%					2	18%		
cancer	57	4	15%	1	7%	2	8%	3	18%	4	36%	3	21%
sustainable dev	58	4	15%	2	14%	1	4%						
sustain	59	9	33%	5	36%	3	13%	3	18%			1	7%
contraception	60	2	7%			2	8%	1	6%				
population	61	18	67%	9	64%	16	67%	11	65%	4	36%	8	57%
birth control	62			3	21%	5	21%	5	29%	1	9%	1	7%
aid	63	10	37%	3	21%	10	42%	4	24%	3	27%	4	29%
debt	64	9	33%	3	21%	3	13%	3	18%	1	9%	2	14%
technology transfer	65	1	4%										
fail etc	66	3	11%	4	29%	3	13%	1	6%	2	18%	1	7%
hope etc	67	16	59%	5	36%	12	50%	9	53%	7	64%	5	36%
succeed etc	68	1	4%	1	7%			1	6%	1	9%		
0.7	69			1	7%								
g77	70												
street children	71												
global	72	18	67%	9	64%	9	38%	7	41%	1	9%	5	36%
migrant	73					1	4%	1	6%				
pope	74	1	4%	1	7%			1	6%				
catholic	75	4	15%	2	14%	4	17%	3	18%				
vatican	76							1	6%				
radiation	77	3	11%	1	7%	1	4%	1	6%	2	18%	1	7%
Occurrences of key words		414		212		328		222		138		143	
Directives in sample		27		14		24		17		11		14	
Average per Directive		15.33		15.14		13.67		13.06		12.55		10.21	

NEWSPAPER Samples

Newpapers		Gdn		Ind		Tel		DMI		Tdy		DMr		Sun	
Earth Summit	1	241	89%	193	92%	154	92%	25	83%	38	97%	20	100%	8	67%
United Nations/UN	2	83	31%	59	28%	50	30%	6	20%	3	8%	2	10%	1	8%
agenda 21	3	17	6%	10	5%	12	7%	0	0%	0	0%	0	0%	0	0%
global forum	4	11	4%	11	5%	15	9%	1	3%	0	0%	0	0%	0	0%
people's summit etc	5	2	1%	0	0%	1	1%	1	3%	0	0%	0	0%	0	0%
rio declaration	6	8	3%	5	2%	6	4%	0	0%	1	3%	0	0%	0	0%
declaration	7	21	8%	17	8%	9	5%	1	3%	2	5%	0	0%	0	0%
treaty	8	40	15%	52	25%	38	23%	10	33%	12	31%	4	20%	2	17%
principles	9	16	6%	17	8%	13	8%	1	3%	0	0%	0	0%	0	0%
convention	10	49	18%	37	18%	46	28%	4	13%	4	10%	0	0%	0	0%
FoE etc	11	14	5%	16	8%	14	8%	2	7%	1	3%	0	0%	1	8%
Oxfam	12	4	1%	2	1%	2	1%	0	0%	0	0%	0	0%	0	0%
greenpeace	13	8	3%	16	8%	11	7%	1	3%	4	10%	1	5%	0	0%
WWF etc	14	7	3%	4	2%	7	4%	0	0%	2	5%	0	0%	0	0%
brundtland	15	6	2%	2	1%	6	4%	1	3%	1	3%	0	0%	0	0%
john/mr major	16	58	21%	37	18%	52	31%	9	30%	17	44%	10	50%	6	50%
michael/mr howard	17	20	7%	13	6%	24	14%	4	13%	5	13%	0	0%	0	0%
david/mr maclean	18	5	2%	2	1%	7	4%	2	7%	1	3%	1	5%	0	0%
douglas/mr hurd	19	7	3%	6	3%	4	2%	1	3%	1	3%	0	0%	0	0%
neil/mr kinnock	20	5	2%	3	1%	3	2%	0	0%	2	5%	1	5%	0	0%
ann clwyd	21	5	2%	2	1%	4	2%	0	0%	0	0%	0	0%	0	0%
john/mr smith	22	5	2%	0	0%	1	1%	0	0%	2	5%	1	5%	0	0%
bryan/mr gould	23	4	1%	3	1%	1	1%	0	0%	1	3%	0	0%	0	0%

george/president bush	24	40	15%	42	20%	31	19%	11	37%	10	26%	5	25%	2	17%
ripa di meana	25	13	5%	15	7%	9	5%	1	3%	2	5%	0	0%	0	0%
forest principles	26	7	3%	2	1%	5	3%	0	0%	0	0%	0	0%	0	0%
tropical forest	27	1	0%	2	1%	1	1%	0	0%	0	0%	0	0%	0	0%
temperate forest	28	0	0%	2	1%	0	0%	0	0%	0	0%	0	0%	0	0%
rainforest(s)	29	16	6%	22	11%	19	11%	4	13%	2	5%	2	10%	3	25%
deforest	30	7	3%	8	4%	13	8%	0	0%	1	3%	1	5%	0	0%
biodiversity	31	52	19%	45	22%	35	21%	7	23%	1	3%	0	0%	1	8%
species	32	36	13%	41	20%	40	24%	7	23%	7	18%	4	20%	2	17%
flora/fauna	33	1	0%	7	3%	0	0%	0	0%	0	0%	0	0%	0	0%
wildlife	34	11	4%	7	3%	21	13%	2	7%	7	18%	3	15%	2	17%
conservation	35	27	10%	21	10%	22	13%	2	7%	4	10%	1	5%	1	8%
global warming	36	41	15%	38	18%	24	14%	8	27%	4	10%	4	20%	2	17%
greenhouse effect	37	2	1%	8	4%	2	1%	4	13%	1	3%	1	5%	1	8%
climat	38	58	21%	36	17%	35	21%	5	17%	1	3%	2	10%	2	17%
climate change	39	38	14%	21	10%	23	14%	3	10%	0	0%	0	0%	1	8%
asthma	40	1	0%	0	0%	1	1%	0	0%	0	0%	0	0%	0	0%
emissions	41	46	17%	47	22%	20	12%	6	20%	3	8%	4	20%	0	0%
public transport	42	2	1%	2	1%	1	1%	0	0%	1	3%	0	0%	0	0%
road build'g/construction	43	1	0%	1	0%	1	1%	0	0%	0	0%	0	0%	0	0%
traffic	44	8	3%	8	4%	5	3%	0	0%	1	3%	0	0%	0	0%
car	45	113	42%	107	51%	88	53%	14	47%	17	44%	7	35%	3	25%
ozone	46	21	8%	8	4%	10	6%	3	10%	4	10%	1	5%	1	8%
carbon tax	47	8	3%	8	4%	3	2%	1	3%	0	0%	0	0%	0	0%
carbon dioxide/co2	48	32	12%	30	14%	23	14%	4	13%	2	5%	3	15%	0	0%
environment	49	129	47%	92	44%	94	56%	16	53%	13	33%	5	25%	3	25%
pollut	50	45	17%	48	23%	26	16%	9	30%	6	15%	5	25%	3	25%
radioactiv	51	3	1%	2	1%	2	1%	1	3%	0	0%	2	10%	1	8%
nuclear	52	13	5%	12	6%	5	3%	2	7%	1	3%	2	10%	2	17%
chemical	53	7	3%	5	2%	3	2%	2	7%	0	0%	0	0%	1	8%
waste	54	33	12%	15	7%	13	8%	2	7%	6	15%	3	15%	3	25%
BNFL	55	0	0%	0	0%	0	0%	0	0%	0	0%	0	0%	0	0%
leukaemia	56	0	0%	0	0%	1	1%	0	0%	1	3%	2	10%	0	0%
cancer	57	3	1%	2	1%	4	2%	2	7%	2	5%	2	10%	0	0%
sustainable dev	58	23	8%	21	10%	15	9%	0	0%	0	0%	0	0%	0	0%
sustain	59	56	21%	35	17%	29	17%	2	7%	0	0%	0	0%	0	0%
contraception	60	6	2%	11	5%	6	4%	6	20%	1	3%	0	0%	0	0%
population	61	44	16%	39	19%	30	18%	11	37%	6	15%	3	15%	1	8%
birth control	62	8	3%	9	4%	8	5%	7	23%	0	0%	0	0%	0	0%
aid	63	55	20%	56	27%	37	22%	5	17%	2	5%	4	20%	1	8%
debt	64	29	11%	19	9%	13	8%	1	3%	0	0%	0	0%	0	0%
technology transfer	65	2	1%	4	2%	2	1%	0	0%	0	0%	0	0%	0	0%
fail etc	66	7	3%	5	2%	6	4%	1	3%	4	10%	0	0%	0	0%
hope etc	67	35	13%	25	12%	20	12%	6	20%	2	5%	0	0%	0	0%
succeed etc	68	5	2%	5	2%	3	2%	1	3%	0	0%	0	0%	0	0%
0.7	69	26	10%	18	9%	16	10%	0	0%	0	0%	0	0%	0	0%
g77	70	11	4%	1	0%	1	1%	0	0%	0	0%	0	0%	0	0%
street children	71	5	2%	4	2%	6	4%	0	0%	0	0%	1	5%	0	0%
global	72	89	33%	84	40%	62	37%	10	33%	7	18%	5	25%	3	25%
migrant	73	1	0%	1	0%	1	1%	1	3%		0%		0%		0%
pope	74	7	3%	4	2%	8	5%	3	10%	1	3%		0%		0%
catholic	75	10	4%	9	4%	8	5%	5	17%	1	3%	1	5%		0%
vatican	76	10	4%	8	4%	10	6%	5	17%	1	3%		0%		0%
radiation	77	3	1%	2	1%	2	1%		0%		0%		0%	1	8%
Occurrences of key words		1883		1571		1343		249		219		113		58	
Articles in sample		272		209		167		30		39		20		12	
Average per article		6.92		7.52		8.04		8.30		5.62		5.65		4.83	

B ibliography

Abraham, J., Lacey, C. and Williams, R. (1990), *Deception, Demonstration and Debate: Toward a Critical Environment and Development Education*, WWF/Kogan Page

Adams, S. (1984), *Roche versus Adams*, Cape, London

Bailey, F.G. (1977), *Morality and Expediency*, Blackwell

Barnett, H.J. & Morse, C. (1963), *Scarcity and Growth: the economics of natural resource availability*, John Hopkins Press

Beck, U. (1992), *The Risk Society*, Sage

Beck, U. (1995), *Ecological Politics in an Age of Risk*, Polity

Beck, U., Giddens, A. & Lash, S. (1994), *Reflexive Modernization*, Polity

Becker, H.S., Geer, B. and Hughes, E. (1961), *Boys in White*, University of Chicago Press

Bennet, J. (1987), *The Hunger Machine: The Politics of Food*, Polity Press

Bower, T. (1988), *Maxwell: the Outsider*, Mandarin

Bourdieu, P. (1993), *Sociology in Question*, Sage

Brookes, (1976), 'The growth of the environment as a political issues in Britain, *British Journal of Political Science*, 245-255

Burgess, J., Harrison, C. and Maitemy, P. (1991), 'Contested meanings: the consumption of news about nature conservation', *Media, Culture and Society*, v13, 499-519

Butler, D.E. and Stokes, D.E. (1969), *Political Change in Britain*, Macmillan

Calhoun, C. (ed), 1992, *Habermas and the Public Sphere*, The MIT Press, Cambridge, Mass

Carson, R. (1962), *Silent Spring*. Boston, Houghton Mifflin

Central Statistical Office (1993), *Social Trends*, CSO

Chaffee, S.H. (1975), *Political Communications: enduring issues for research*, Sage

Chomsky, N. (1989), *Necessary Illusions: Thought Control in Democratic Societies*, Pluto Press

Cohen, S. (1955), *Delinquent Boys: the Culture of the Gang*, Free Press

Coleridge, N. (1994), *Paper Tigers; The latest greatest newspaper tycoons and how they won the world*, Mandarin

Converse, P.E. (1964), 'The Nature of Belief Systems in Mass Publics', in Apter, D.E. (ed) (1964), *Ideology and Discontent*, Free Press, 206-261

Crewe, I. And Harrop, M. (1986), *Political Communications: the general election of 1983*, Cambridge University Press

Crewe, I. and Gosschalk, B. (eds) (1995), *Political Communications: The General Election Campaign of 1992*, Cambridge University Press

Curran, J. and Seaton, J. (1991), *Power Without Responsibility: The press and broadcasting in Britain*, Routledge, London 4th ed

Curtice, J. And Semetko, H. (1994), 'Does it matter what the papers say?, in Heath, A.F., Jowell, R., and Curtice, J. (1994), *Labour's Last Chance?*, Dartmouth

De Weese III, C.L. (1976), 'Computer Context Analysis of Printed Media: a feasibility study', *Public Opinion Quarterly*, 40, 92-104

Downs, A. (1972), 'Up and Down with Ecology - the "issue attention cycle"', *Public Interest*, Summer, 38, 5

Ehrlich, P.R. (1968), *The Population Bomb*, Ballantine Books

Ehrlich, P.R., Ehrlich, A.H. (1974), *The End of Affluence: A Blueprint for your Future*, Ballantine Books

Elliott, L. (1996), "Holding the Short Straw", *Guardian* 5/8/96

Engel, M. (1996), *Tickle the Public: One Hundred Years of the Popular Press*, Victor Gollancz

Emery, E. and Emery, M. (1984), *The Press and America: An Interpretative History of the Mass Media*, Prentice-Hall, 5th ed

Eraut, M.E. (1994), *Developing Professional Knowledge and Competence*, Falmer Press

Eraut, M.E. (1997), Perspectives on defining "The Learning Society", unpublished paper

Ericson, R.V., Beranek, P.M. and Chan, J.B.L. (1987), *Visualising Deviance: A Study of News Organisations*, University of Toronto Press

Ericson, R.V., Beranek, P.M. and Chan, J.B.L. (1989), *Negotiating Control: A Study of News Sources*, University of Toronto Press

Evans, H. (1994), *Good Times, Bad Times*, Phoenix, Orion Books, London, 3rd ed

Fairclough, N. (1992), *Discourse and Social Change*, Polity Press

Fan, D.P. (1988), *Predictions of Public Opinion from the Mass Media: Computer content analysis and mathematical modelling*, Greenwood Press

Fishman, M. (1980), *Manufacturing the News*, University of Texas Press

Fowler, R. (1991), *Language in the News: Discourse and Ideology in the Press*, Routledge

Funkhauser, R. (1973), The Issue of the Sixties: An exploratory study in the dynamics of public opinion, *Public Opinion Quarterly*, 37, 62-75

Gans, H.T. (1979), *Deciding What's News*, Pantheon

Gardner, H. (1968), *Frames of Mind*, Methuen

Garnham, N. (1992), 'The Media and the Public Sphere', in Calhoun C (ed), 1992, *Habermas and the Public Sphere*, The MIT Press, 359-376

Graber, D.A. (1984), *Mass Media and American Politics*, Washington DC, Congressional Quarterly (2nd ed)

Giddens, A. (1991), *Modernity and Self-Identity*, Polity Press

Giddens, A. (1994), *Beyond Left and Right: The Future of Radical Politics*, Polity Press

Gieber, W. (1964), *News is what newspapermen make it*, in Dexter, L.A. and White, D.M. (eds) 173-182

Glover, S. (1994), *Paper Dreams: The Story of the Independent and the Independent on Sunday*, Penguin (rev. ed.)

Gould, S.J. (1981), *The Mismeasure of Man*, Norton

Greenslade, R. (1996), *Media Guardian* 12/8/96

Greenslade, R (1996), Streetwise, *Guardian* 17/5/96

Gregory, R. (1972), Conservation, Planning and Politics, *Int. Journal of Environmental Studies*, 4, 33-39

Guardian, 25/3/91, Media: 'Hello to the new *Today!*'

Guardian, 22/11/94, 'Hamilton says media hounded him out'

Guardian, 12/12/96, 'Willetts pays the price: New blow for Major as key player quits'

Hall, S., Critcher, C., Jefferson, T., Clark, J. and Roberts, B. (1978), *Policing the Crisis: Mugging, the State and Law and Order*, Macmillan

Halliday, M.A.K. (1966), 'Lexis as a linguistic level', in Bazell, C., Catford, J.C., Halliday, M.A.K. and Robins, R.H. (eds), *In Memory of J.R. Furth*, London, Longman

Hansen, A. (1990), The construction of science in the mass media, paper to the XVIIth Conference of the International Association for Mass Media Research, Yugoslavia

Hansen, A. (1991), The Media and the Social Construction of the Environment, *Media, Culture and Society*, 14, 4, October, 443-458

Hansen, A. (Ed) (1993), *The mass media and environmental issues*, Leicester University Press

Hardin, M (1994), "Idiot Culture' being formed by tabloid TV' programming, *The Daily Beacon*, 3/10/94

Harrison, C. And Burgess, J. (1994), *Social constructions of nature: a case study of conflicts over the development of Rainbow Marshes*, Trans. Inst. Br. Geog, NS19, 291-310

Herman, E.S. and Chomsky, N (1988), *Manufacturing Consent: The Political Economy of the Mass Media*, Pantheon Books

Hilgartner, S. and Bork, C.L. (1988), The rise and fall of social problems: a public arenas model, *Am. Journal of Sociology*, 94, 53-78

Hirsch, F. (1977), *The Social Limits to Growth*, RKP

Hoch, P. (1974), *The Newspaper Game: The Political Sociology of the Press; An inquiry into behind- the-scenes organization, financing and brainwashing techniques of the news media*, Calder & Boyars, London

Homans, G.C. (1951), *The Human Group*, Routledge & Kegan Paul

Hornbeck, K.E. (1974), *The Role of Age in the Environment Movement's Attentive Public* (1968-72), Doctoral Dissertation, Michigan State University

Houghton, J.T. (1995), *Climate Change 1995. The Science of Climate Change*, Cambridge University Press

Hovland, C.I. (1949), *Experiments in Mass Communication*, Princeton University Press

Hovland, C.I. (1959), 'Reconciling conflicting results derived from experimental and survey studies of attitude change', *American Psychologist*, 14, 3

Hutton, W. (1996), The Tiddler Halloween, *Observer*, 1996

IIED (International Institute for Environment and Development) (1991), *UNCED: A User's Guide*, IIED

Intergovernmental Panel of Climate Change (IPCC) (1990), *Scientific Assessment of Climate Change: Report of Working Group 1*, IPCC. June 1990

Intergovernmental Panel of Climate Change (IPCC): Meira Filho LG, Callander BA, Harris N, Kattenberg A & Maskell K (eds) (1996), *Climate Change 1995: The Science of Climate Change*, Cambridge University Press

Katz, E. and Lazarsfeld, P. (1955) *Personal Influence: The part played by people in the flow of mass communication*, The Free Press

Kellner, P. (1995), *Sunday Times*, 22/7/95

Knightley, P. (1975), *The First Casualty: The war correspondent as hero, propagandist, and myth-maker from Crimea to Vietnam*, Andre Deutsch

Kraus, S. And Davis, D. (1976), *The Effects of Mass Communication on Political Behaviour*, Pennsylvania State University Press

Lacey, C. (1984), *The Socialisation of Teachers*, Methuen

Lacey, C. and Longman, D. (1993), The Press and Public Access to the Environment and Development Debate, *Sociological Review*, 41, 2, 207-24

Lazarsfeld, P., Berelson, B. and Gaudet H. (1944), *The People's Choice*, Columbia University Press

Leggett, J. (ed) (1990), *Global Warming: The Green Peace Report*, Oxford University Press

Lippman, W. (1922), *Public Opinion*, Harcourt Brace Co

Linton, M. (1995), *Was it the Sun Wot Won it?*, 7th Guardian Lecture, Nuffield College

Little, W., Fowler, H.W. and Coulson, J. (1983), *The Shorter Oxford Dictionary on Historical Principles*, Book Club Associates

Lopez, S.P. (1953), *Freedom of Information*, Report submitted to United Nations Economic and Social Council, New York

Love, A. (1990), The Production of Environmental Meanings in the Media: A New Era, *Media Education Journal*, 10, Winter

Lowe, P. And Morrison, D. (1984), Bad News or Good News: Environmental politics and the mass media, *The Sociological Review*, 32(1), 75-90

McGuire, W.J. (1969), 'The Nature of Attitudes and Attitude Change', in Lindsey, G. And Aronson, E. (eds) (1969), *Handbook of Social Psychology*, Addison-Wesley, 136-314, (2nd ed)

McKie, D. (1995), 'Fact is Free but Comment is Sacred: or Was it the Sun Wot Won It?', in Crewe, I. and Gosschalk, B. (eds) (1995), 121-136

MacLure, M. And Pettigrew, M. (1995), *The Press, Public Knowledge and Education*, ESRC Report, ESRC Ref: R000235314

Marr, A., *Independent* 7/10/96, 'Ten years on'

Merton, R.K. et al (1957), *The Student Physician*, Harvard University Press

Miller, W. (1991), *Media and Voters*, Clarendon Press

Minton, D. And Brody, L. (1970), *American Public Opinion and Environmental Pollution*, Ohio State University, Behavioural Science Laboratory, Dept of Political Science

Moore, C., *Guardian* 13/5/96, 'A military operation - Sometimes I feel like my uncle, who was an officer in the war'

Mughan, A. (1995), *Partisan bias and leader effects in the national tabloid press*, Paper to EPOP Conference, September 1995

Newton, K. (1991), *Do people read everything they believe in newspapers?*. British Parties and Elections Yearbook, Wheatsheaf

Nicholson, E. (1996), *Secret Society : Inside and Outside the Conservative Party*, Indigo

Noelle-Neuman, E. (1984), *The Spiral of Silence: Public opinion - our social skin*, University of Chicago Press

Neumann, W.R. (1987), Parallel content analysis: Old paradigms and new proposals, in Comstock, G. (Ed) (1987), *Public Communications and Behaviour*, Academic Press

O'Kane, M. (1995), Bloodless words bloody war, *Guardian* (16/12/95)
Observer (4/2/96)
Pateman, C. (1970), *Participation and Democratic Theory*, Cambridge University Press
Page, B.I. and Shapiro, R.Y. (1992), *The Rational Public: Fifty Years of Trends in America's Policy Preferences*, University of Chicago Press
Page, B.I. and Shapiro. R.Y. (1989), 'Educating and Manipulating the Public', in Margolis, M. And Mauser, A. (Eds) (1989), *Manipulating Public Opinion: Essays on Public Opinion and as a Dependent Variable*, Pacific Grove
Page, B.I. and Shapiro. R.Y. (1984), 'Presidents as Opinion Leaders: Some New Evidence', *Policy Studies Journal* 12, 649-661
Page, B.I., Shapiro, R.Y. and Dempsey, G.R. (1987), 'What Moves Public Opinion?', *American Political Science Review*, 81, 23-43
Petty, R.T. and Cacioppo, J.E. (1986), *Communication and Persuasion*, Springer-Verlag
Philo, G. And Lamb, R. (1990), *Television and the Ethiopian Famine*, in Abraham et al (1990), 43-62
Radford, T. (1994), "The Profits of Doom", *Guardian* 14/7/94
Redclfit, M. (1987), *Learning from the Environmental Crisis in the South*, in Lacey, C. and Williams, R. (Eds) (1987), *Education, Ecology and Development*, Kogan Page, 21-38
Redclift, M. and Benton, T. (eds) (1994), *Social Theory and the Global Environment*, Routledge
Reporters San Frontières, (1993), *1993 Report: Freedom of the Press throughout the World*, John Libbey, London
Richardson, J.J. (1977), *The Environment Issue and the Public, in Decision Making in Britain: Pollution and the Environment*, Open University
Robertson, G. (1983), *People Against the Press: An Enquiry into the Press Council*, Quartet Books, London
Sandbach, F. (1980), *Environment, Ideology and Policy*, Blackwell
Semetko, H., Scammell, M. And Nossitas, T. (1994), 'The media's coverage of the campaign', in Heath, A.F., Jowell, R., and Curtice, J. (1994), *Labour's Last Chance?*, Dartmouth
Seymour-Ure, C. (1968), *The Press, Politics and the Public*, Methuen
Shaw, M. (1996), *Civil Society and Media in Global Crisis: Representing Distant Violence*, Pinter
Shawcross, W. (1992), *Rupert Murdoch : Ringmaster of the Information Circus*, Chatto & Windus
Siebert, F.S. (1952), Freedom of the Press in England (1476-1776): *The Rise and Decline of Government Controls*, University of Illinois
Siebert, F.S., Peterson, T. and Schramm, W. (1956), *Four Theories of the Press: The Authoritarian, Libertarian, Social Responsibility and Soviet Communist Concepts of What the Press Should Be and Do*, University of Illinois Press
Silverstone, R. (1994), *Television and Everyday Life*, Routledge
Simon, J. (1981), *The Ultimate Resource*, Princeton University Press
Simon, J. and Kahn, H (eds) (1984), *The Resourceful Earth: a response to Global 2000*, Blackwell
Solesbury, (1976), *The Environmental Agenda: An illustration of how situations may become political issues*, Public Administration, 54, Winter, 379-39?
Sunday Telegraph, 12/4/92
Tiernay, J. (1990), "Betting the Planet", *Guardian* 28/12/90
Tunstall, J. (1996), *Newspaper Power: The New National Press in Britain*, Clarendon Press
Wallace, M. (1993), *Discourse of Derision: the role of the mass media within the education policy process*, Education Policy, v8, 4, 321-337
White, D.M. (1964), *The 'Gatekeeper': A case study in the selection of news*, in Dexter, L.A. and White, D.M. (eds) 160-172
Worcester, R. (1993), 'Are Newsrooms Bored with Greenery?', *British Journalism Review*, 4, 3
Worcester, R. (1994), *'The Sustainable Society: What we know about what people think and do'*, Values for a Sustainable Future, World Environment Day Symposium, 2, June 1994
Worcester, R. (1995), 'The use of panel studies in British general elections', in Crewe, I. and Gosschalk, B. (eds) (1995), 192-212
World Commission on Environment and Development (WCED) (1987), *Our Common Future*, Oxford University Press
Zaller. J.R. (1992), *The Nature and Origins of Mass Opinion*, Cambridge University Press

Index